THE END OF
THE LINE

THE END OF THE LINE

A Memoir

RICHARD COBB

JOHN MURRAY
Albemarle Street, London

First published in 1997
by John Murray (Publishers) Ltd,
50 Albemarle Street, London W1X 4BD

A catalogue record for this book is available from the British Library

ISBN 0-7195-5460-8

Typeset in 11/13pt Monotype Sabon by
Servis Filmsetting Ltd, Manchester

Printed and bound in Great Britain by
The University Press, Cambridge

For
Roger Butler,
friend and sometime pupil

Contents

Editorial Note

Richard Cobb (1917–1996) wrote and saw published in his lifetime three books that were specifically autobiographical, *Still Life*, *A Classical Education*, and *Something To Hold Onto*; there were also longer or shorter memoirs in the introductions, preambles, or prefaces to several of his other books, and personal reminiscence informs much of his writing and, particularly, his collection of broadcast talks, *Promenades*.

This new book contains chapters that were written in the late 1980s, but its final sections were composed very shortly before his death. It has been put together by Professor Cobb's widow and with the help of three or four friends, but inevitably without its author's own arrangement or final revision.

Since Richard Cobb wrote no single or consecutive account of his life, and since this book begins when he was a thirteen-year-old schoolboy and ends when he was seventy-eight, and over eleven years after retirement from his Chair, the reader may be helped by a brief biographical framework. After The Beacon School at Crowborough, not far from his parental home in Tunbridge Wells – though he was a boarder – he was at Shrewsbury School between the ages of fourteen and seventeen; he won a Postmastership (scholarship) to Merton College, Oxford, where he went up to read History – after his first visit to France and to Vienna – in the Michaelmas Term, 1935. He came down in 1938, and there followed his long period of historical research on the French Revolution and its effects and

implications in diverse parts of France. This was early on interrupted by wartime service in the Army (some of it recounted in
this book) in England and Wales, France, and Belgium; but his
researches were resumed in full after his demobilization in 1946,
when he lived mostly in Paris until 1955. In the early 1950s, his
first works of French history were published, in French. In 1951,
he married a Frenchwoman; but after a time they were divorced.

Richard Cobb's strictly academic career – if that adverb is
applicable – began in 1955 with his appointment as Lecturer in
History at the University College of Wales, Aberystwyth. In
1960–2 he was Senior Simon Research Fellow at the University
of Manchester, and for a year Lecturer in History at the
University of Leeds, where (soon after his 'Balkan experience')
he met Margaret Tennant, whom he married in 1963. From 1962
to 1972, he was a Fellow of Balliol College, Oxford, and Tutor
in History and Dean of Degrees there; he was made Reader in
French Revolutionary History in 1969, and, in 1973, moved to
Worcester College as Professor of Modern History in the
University of Oxford. He was elected a Fellow of the British
Academy in 1967, and his acclaimed and influential teaching and
writing of French history brought him Honorary Doctorates of
the Universities of Essex, Leeds, and Cambridge, and the award
of the CBE, in this country; in France he was made an Officier
de l'Ordre National du Mérite in 1977 and in 1985 accorded the
proudly worn *ruban rouge* of a Chevalier de la Légion
d'Honneur.

His fifteen books in English, of history, literary criticism, and
autobiography, have been published during the past thirty years;
and he and Margaret Cobb have had four children. He and his
wife retired eventually to Abingdon – where he had stayed in a
hotel so agreeably on his own as a studious undergraduate (see
pp. 65–7) – and he died in their home there, early last year, in her
arms, two days after writing the last pages of *The End of the
Line*.

Richard Brain

I

The Offshore Continent

SOMETIME in 1930 – I think it must have been in the early summer, for I was experiencing well in advance the nagging dread of the cricket field – an old boy of my preparatory school, with the impressive name of de Courcy Ireland (he was too grand to run to the intimacy of a Christian name) came on a surprise visit to The Beacon School, Crowborough. His visit caused a sensation, as no doubt it was meant to, for he came furnished with a double pass-port to fame and glory, the one at once visible, the other more secre-tive and later to be passed round, to be admired furtively by each of us. I remember him standing by the Headmaster's chair, at the head of the right-hand table, at the beginning of lunch, with a large parrot in brilliant green and yellow perched on his shoulder and squawking loudly in what the Headmaster's wife told us was Spanish. It seemed that the parrot and its owner had, more or less, just disembarked from the nearest port to Crowborough; the two of them had come with the speed of light so as to appear before us on our Beacon at a moment when the whole school would be gathered together in the big dining-room. He was a very tall man with fair hair and very blue eyes, the washed-out blue of a traveller over the Ocean; and he carried with him all the mystery of the traveller just returned. I suppose there had been some sort of vehicle just outside, at the front of the house, by the private entrance used by the Headmaster and his family: no doubt a red open sports car, low slung, and with silver pipes curling out of its sides, for he and his colourful and repetitive companion, having presumably just crossed the immensity of the Atlantic, could hardly have come on the branch line from Lewes, via Barton Mills and Uckfield, getting off at Crowborough Station. Anyhow, I decided on the red sports car as the appropriate form of transport to be adopted by someone on what appeared to be a mission of some urgency, as if he had been carrying Government Dispatches or Diplomatic Bags. Later that day I discussed the matter with my friend Arthur Cooper, who had a brother in the Foreign Office and who knew Russian, and Arthur stated authoritatively that it would indeed have been a very red sports car, with an extra powerful engine; nothing else would have done – though he could perhaps have landed by plane on the sports field.

The parrot spoke for itself, loudly, emphatically, and, as we were told (and Arthur later confirmed this), in Spanish. It did not need any further introduction, and constituted the dramatic proof that its tall owner had only just arrived from the banks of the Orinoco or from the delta of the Amazon. This would have been sensational enough; but there was more to come, an extra bit that had been cunningly held back while we took in the exotic reality of the South American link. There had been a further limb to the travels of the intrepid Old Beacon boy, though it was not clear whether his exotic companion had been on his shoulder in the course of this northern and presumably frigid Baltic loop in the direction of the north-east. A score of coins, some of them round, others square, which all looked as if they were silver and were of various sizes, were passed down the table from boy to boy; Arthur, having given them only a summary scrutiny, handed them on to me, as if he had been in a hurry to get rid of them, explaining casually, while doing so, that they were Latvian – though this was not quite the word engraved on the coins, it was something slightly different, but he went on to say it was what 'Latvia' was in Latvian, an item of information he had come by from the brother who seemed to have thrown in three or four of the Baltic languages as small change in the process of acquiring Russian. Arthur went on to tell me that Latvia was the middle one of the three Baltic States, between Lithuania to the south and Estonia to the north. All three were quite young states, not even as old as *we* were. I found it hard to imagine *any* state being younger than our thirteen years. Latvia, he went on, had started off as a democracy, with several parties and a parliament with an upper and a lower house, but for some years now it had been a dictatorship. The dictator was not quite as bad as the dictator to the south. There was a dictator to the north as well, but he was the least brutal of the three, so that it seemed indeed that Lativa occupied a middle position in the moral sense, as well as geographically. Though all three were dictators who had promoted themselves Generals in their respective armies, they did not get on well together. One of the reasons why Latvia and Estonia were a bit better than Lithuania was that they were preponderantly Lutheran, whereas the southern member of the trio, very much the odd man out, was Catholic; and I did not need Arthur to tell me that that was the Mark of the Beast. Only that term I had started reading Motley's *Rise of the Dutch Republic*, a book that had satisfactorily confirmed for me the rightness of the Protestant Cause and the heroism of the Dutch; and I had been told by my mother, who had worked with Dutch teachers at the Eunice High School, Bloemfontein, in the early years of the century, that, of all Europeans, the Dutch were the most like ourselves, indeed, they were *almost* English.

As far as I can recall, they were handsome coins and they had on them engravings of ships and fish, which seemed appropriate to a coastal Republic (it was still nominally a Republic), even if the sea froze up for about half the year; the fish, at least, would be able to cope. But they also had on them horses, trees, and farm animals. I don't think that they had on them the profile of the dictator, perhaps he had not been there long enough to get his effigy minted on a coin. I passed on the coins, as if I had been long familiar with them and had myself spent some time in each of the Baltic States (why had de Courcy Ireland not taken in all *three*, while he was about it?) to my small neighbour to the right. But in fact I had been very impressed: I had never heard of any of the three states, by at least two years my juniors. (There was a problem there, too. What would the boys and girls of our own age from those countries have been *before* their creation, that is in the two years before being Latvians – or one of the other two – and what, for that matter, would their *parents* have been? After all, they were grown-ups, so they must have been *something*; everyone had to be, you had to have to have a nationality, everyone I knew had one. There had been an Argentinian boy at my previous prep school, and he had been Argentinian because his father was, though his mother was English. I asked Arthur about this, but he had no satisfactory answer, side-stepping the problem with the lazy, and – for him, always so knowledgeable – uncharacteristic explanation: 'Well, silly, they would have been something *else*, don't you see?' But I didn't, I wanted to know *what*. And in a rare moment of doubt I even entertained the disloyal thought that Arthur did not *know*.) And it was only later on, that exciting day, that I looked up the three of them in the last section of my *Everyman Historical Atlas* (my Motley had been in Everyman, too) and learnt that their capitals, starting from the very bad, through the not quite so bad, to the marginally better, were respectively Kaunas (but it was also Kovno, it did seem to be rather a confusing part of the world), Riga, and Tallinn.

This was to be my only direct contact with Latvia, if actually handling the currency of a state amounted to something as positive as that (de Courcy Ireland had not produced any banknotes, presumably because he thought that our grubby hands might have destroyed their pristine lustre and crispness). Still, I could now reasonably feel that I had something in common with the Latvians, even if I was two years older than *any* of them. And de Courcy Ireland's momentous visit set off a brisk trade at The Beacon in Latvian stamps; indeed there was such a run on them that it was soon impossible to find anyone willing to do a swap. Putting ideological principles aside, I even started a couple of pages of Lithuanian issues.

De Courcy Ireland's sudden descent on the school was not quite my last encounter, albeit an indirect one, with Latvia. The small country was to surface once more, in an even more marginalized manner, in one of the early Simenons, *Pietr-le-Letton*, published in 1931, which I was to read shortly after my wartime arrival in France in July, 1944. It must be said that Latvia itself was assigned little more than a walking-on part in that novel, and as an adjective rather than a sovereign state, most of the action taking place in Paris, where Pietr, or rather his identical twin, had arrived by train, after murdering his brother and dressing up in his clothes, between the Belgian frontier and the Gare du Nord. Most of the action was to take place in Paris, moving on from there to Fécamp. Still, it was a tribute of sorts, indicating at least a vague awareness on the part of the Belgian Master of what the French used to call 'La Lettonie' (Simenon also refers to it in the narrative as 'La Latvie', and he gives the impression that the twins could have been either Latvian or Estonian, that they had come from Reval, the earlier name for Tallinn, and that the victim had once been a student at the University of Tartu – also called Dorpat): it is all a bit confusing, like the interchangeable twins themselves, and one can sympathize with Maigret, when, in bewilderment, he was to comment that he got mixed up with all three of the small Republics. It seems clear that Pietr's creator had himself never visited any of them; he would no doubt have acquired, early on, as a schoolboy and an adolescent, some knowledge of the existence of the three of them from some of his mother's lodgers, many of them Jewish from those border areas, in her small house Quartier Outre-Meuse in Liège, in the 1920s, who had come there to study science or engineering at the university.

One or two French scholars seem to have shown an early interest in the place, perhaps as a potential base for anti-Soviet activities in the years just after the Russian Civil War. While still in his twenties and a *caiman* at the École Normale Supérieure, Rue d'Ulm, my friend the historian Jean Meuvret had made the trip to Riga, travelling by train, and had the same year brought out a small book called *La Lettonie*, an up-to-date account of the history and the particularities of the country. I don't know how he had come by most of his information, for he certainly did not possess a single word of the language, nor what had prompted this unusually venturesome excursion to a Baltic Republic in the fifth year of its existence (that is, I think, before the advent of the dictator) on the part of a French scholar who was to consecrate the rest of his long life to the Paris region in the reign of Louis XIV. It might have been merely curiosity; but I think he had been given indirect encouragement by the Quai d'Orsay. Even at the age of twenty-four, Meuvret, as a *normalien*, had friends in high places. But it was curious how, at various stages of my own life, Latvia had thus acquired the habit of casually calling in on me, uninvited but not unwelcome, as if only to remind me that it was still there.

There are many ways of skipping the discomforts and uncertainies of physical travel. Seven years after the Opening Up of the Window on to the Baltic at the top of the Beacon (the school was almost at the highest point of that fog-bound eminence, visible, on clear days, from Calverley Park, Tunbridge Wells), I spent several days at the Paris *Expo 37*, travelling on foot, and in easy stages, from country to country: I took in the Soviet Union, buying there a pocket edition of the Constitution of 1936: Freedom of the Press, Freedom from Arrest, Trial by Jury, and all that, a handsome little volume bound in red (one could also get it in blue) simili-leather, its pages gilt-edged. I visited Rumania, had a meal there, avoided Germany and Italy on ideological grounds, gave France a miss as I was already there, left out Belgium and Holland because I had by then actually *been* to both, paid my respects to the unfinished Spanish Republic, more as a duty than to satisfy my curiosity (I thought Picasso's *Guernica* was quite hideous). At the Polish Pavilion, I bought six packets of cigarettes, blue with a white seagull, the brand was called Mewa, thus establishing a physical link with the Colonels' Republic by smoking Polish for the next week or so. But I never even looked for the three Baltic Republics, though they must have been there somewhere, not necessarily side by side.

I expect that, in due course, after he had left school and had perfected his Swedish and his Icelandic, Arthur took on all three languages; he always went for the most difficult and the most obscure ones, so Estonian would have been a very high priority. Many years later, in the second half of the 1940s, a friend of mine who had been in my house at Shrewsbury School married a Latvian, their two children growing up bilingual and the father communicating with his mother-in-law in German, their only common language. But by that time Latvia and the other two no longer existed.

In my time at The Beacon School, at least, there was never anything so sensational and so memorable as de Courcy Ireland's sudden appearance in the public glare of the dining-room at lunchtime, almost as if he had just been spirited there by some magical form of transport. What then *was* it about him? Was it merely that he had travelled in two such contrasting directions, first south-westerly across an ocean, then north-easterly across an enclosed sea, or the other way round? Or could there have been some secret connection between his presence in South America, and his visit, previous or subsequent, long or short, to Latvia? South America could easily be explained away, at least to our satisfaction: he had gone there for the parrot. But Latvia did pose a bit of a conundrum. Would he have gone to Riga just to get some Latvian currency to show us in order to prove to us that he *had* gone to Riga? But he could have picked that up in any Bureau de Change (I knew there was one, in a funny-looking semicircular building all on its own, just outside Charing Cross Station, no doubt a straggler from the distant time when Charing Cross had been the Gateway to Europe, as well as to the Royal Borough of Tunbridge Wells) without even having to go to the place itself – rather in the manner in which I was to take in Poland, in thirty minutes or so, at the 1937 *Expo*. Or was he 'in wood'? (I knew about that, too, one could see the Baltic Sawmills, next to the Agricultural Show ground, every time one took the train from Tunbridge Wells West.)

Arthur was convinced that there was something fishy about the whole business; de Courcy Ireland was too conventionally good-looking in the English upper-class manner, tall, fair hair, very blue eyes, too much like a character out of John Buchan, to have been quite what he appeared to be. Arthur even went so far as to suggest that de Courcy Ireland was an alias, it was not the sort of name that one could have been born with, such as his own modest, unassuming Cooper, or my own even more unassuming Cobb. So the too conventionally handsome traveller was Sailing under False Colours. Why should he have done so? Arthur, who never accepted a simple explanation of anything, had plenty of suggestions as to this need of disguise: de Courcy Ireland was a Secret Agent. And was not Latvia close to the Soviet Union? (Look at the map, he would add, with emphasis, and Arthur was very keen on maps and on reading into them; he had even got me to draw the official large-scale map of the island Empire of Khraan.) I could not altogether accept that line of argument, because *Estonia* was even closer, so would de Courcy Ireland not have gone there? Arthur was, of course, ready for that one: Estonia would have been too *obvious*. My friend seemed already much at home in these murky waters, and, much later in life, twenty years or so on, he was to be sent to Australia, in the wake of the Petrov Affair, in order to advise the Canberra authorities on the reorganization of their Security Services. But, much as I deferred to his superior wisdom in all matters foreign and overseas (the Anglo-Egyptian Sudan excepted), I still could not see how the parrot fitted in with these mysterious Baltic activities. I went on to argue that the Headmaster and 'Mrs Sir' must have met de Courcy Ireland's parents and would thus have been able to check up on the boy's surname; Arthur made short work of that: the parents had probably been impostors, too, and 'Mrs Sir', who was a snob, would have fallen for the imposing family name and would have had no difficulty in turning round her unsuspecting husband.

Certainly neither of us, having mulled over the business for weeks, would have gone for an obvious explanation: namely that de Courcy Ireland, holder of a British passport in that name, and who presumably had lots of money behind him (there had never been any suggestion that he had had to *work* after leaving school, or that he had anything as banal as a *job*), liked going to out-of-the-way places; and, in 1930, few Englishmen, apart from those in shipping, in marine stores, or in the wood trade – and perhaps a handful of academics interested in learning obscure languages – all of whom had reason to work in Riga, would have thought of going to Latvia merely to *see* the place, and just out of idle curiosity. Or perhaps de Courcy (Ireland could have been dropped for such authorial purposes) was engaged in writing a travel book about Latvia: *On Foot through the Latvian Forest*, or some such alluring title, hinting of cold and extreme discomfort, or of humid heat and swarms of outsize mosquitoes, each designed to be read about in comfort, in the cool of a summer garden, or in front of a blazing fire, very much in the literary mode of that time, a period already favourable to 'Balkan snatching' and that sort of thing: in fact, just the kind of book that my mother would have put down on her list, waiting to snap it up at Boots' Circulating Library, next to the Chalybeate

Spring at the entry to the Pantiles. It is true that he didn't look much like *my* idea of a writer, someone who would have been more in the style of Arthur's Clever Brother, with heavy glasses and a slight stoop. But *travel* writers would be in a slightly different category, owing to all the physical exertions to which they would be subjected, if they were to be able to hack their way through all sorts of difficult terrain; they might indeed look more athletic, more rugged, more bronzed; and de Courcy Ireland had long legs, as if he had been habituated to difficult mounts such as mules or the low-slung horses of the steppe. Or, come to that, there might have been a Latvian, or a Baltic German, or a White Russian – there would have been plenty of them hanging about in Riga in the late 1920s, some of them even with temporary Latvian passports – girl friend (or boy friend). But neither of us would have thought of that. Despite our deep and intimate knowledge of European Intrigue, we were both still rather innocent in those respects.

One result of the Visit was that, in my gradually unfolding perceptions of the complexity and of the exciting diversity of Europe in the early 1930s, I had managed to get the alphabetical order of precedence somewhat out of the straight, with the result that the Baltic had temporarily taken a lead of the Balkans. The Balkans would indeed come later: my first brief, but sharp, intimation of some of the specialities of that area was provided by a photograph that appeared in a number of the *Illustrated London News* sometime in the winter of 1933. The photograph depicted a score of severed heads, laid out in a neat row – a bit like vegetables, cauliflowers or giant lettuces, at a horticultural show – and each head had a long drooping moustache and a shock of tousled black hair. There was no sign of the bodies; perhaps they had not seemed worthy of display, as inferior parts, or lacking in any personal identity (although, to my rather horrified eyes, all the heads themselves looked remarkably alike, as if they had come off rather a large family of brothers). But a little to the rear of the heads, one could just pick out an equally neat row of uniformed legs in long, shiny, well-polished leather boots. The upper areas of their owners, or at least of those standing in them, were likewise missing, so that one could not see the no doubt jovial faces, long drooping moustaches

9

and shocks of tousled black hair of the men who had thoughtfully laid on the display for the camera. Beneath the photograph there was a brief note which explained that the former owners of the heads had allegedly (I savoured the prudence of that adverb, the *ILN* was taking no chances) been members of IMRO, a Macedonian terrorist group formed to promote, no doubt through similar methods, the cause of a Greater Macedonia. It was demonstrably clear that this particular lot had *lost*.

I was reading that illustrated weekly during an early-evening period of private study in the long classroom at the top of the School Buildings, the windows of which faced down on to the big bend of the River Severn, the Boathouse, the little ferry on its wire, the suspension bridge and the town, silhouetted, as in an eighteenth-century print, beyond the Quarry Park and its delicate green bandstand. Shrewsbury, with the spires of St Mary's, proudly affirmative in its steep ascent, and St Alkmund's, more modest, as if to concede its secondary role as the close companion and retainer of its soaringly ambitious partner, the tower of St Julian's, the phallic object emerging from the grey rotunda of St Chad's, the jumble of the very red Ear, Nose and Throat Hospital and of the very red Girls High School, the ugly Victorian clock-tower of the Market Hall, the canopied tower of a Jacobean house with a gold weather-vane at its summit, the Column, with its little figure on top of it, and the outline of Haughmond Hill vaguely discerned in the middle distance as a gentle, luxuriantly green and yellowish hump, which on some very clear days, would seem to come much closer: the whole, in all its rich variety, a familiar and reassuring presence from the top of Kingsland, and an object of lovingly minute scrutiny, with its promise of limitless freedom and of the discovery of scores of secret passages down steep steps between high buildings, by bored and dreamy schoolboys encased in hard collars, several times a day, from the classrooms facing on to the river. No wonder that one wanted to be taught on *that* side of the School Buildings and to avoid the classrooms that faced inwards, away from the steep bank.

The town, stretched out so invitingly, offered an entirely peaceful prospect that did not seem even remotely connected with severed heads. It was not that I was *unused* to severed heads: from the age of nine or ten I had rather eagerly sought them out in the apparently innocent pages of the *National Geographic* and in books about naked tribes of the Amazon, or of Africa, or of Papua and New Guinea; but those had been the heads of *savages*, even of child savages – head-hunting had seemed to start at an early age – and those who were holding them up by the hair, like trophies, while grinning at the camera, had not known any better and had not realized that what they were doing was wrong. It did not occur to me that evening (I am pretty sure that I can still pinpoint it down to the *day*, for that morning I had handed in a Divinity essay for the Headmaster and had dated it at the top in red ink: '3.3.33') that there had been several very eminent and powerful heads, and other bits too, displayed at the old Market Cross over in the very centre of the town of Shrewsbury, on the site occupied in 1933 by the red Castle Hotel, following the outcome of the Battle of 1405. In any case, we were a very long way from the sanguinary fifteenth century. But the photograph was only a brief and superficial, if rather brutal, introduction to a very complicated subject. The Balkans, in much greater depth, and in a less surgical form, would come to my more direct awareness a great deal later, nearly thirty years after my Divinity essay and my private-reading period of 3.3.33. Or, more accurately, it would come in the simpler form of a *single* Balkan. Unlike Latvia and its two unfraternal companions, *my* Balkan would also remain on the map, even if to a considerably shrunken extent; still, better than being off it altogether.

* * *

Murray Senior, a very recent graduate of Christ Church, Oxford, took over the History Side in the middle of a term in 1932, in my second year at Shrewsbury. His arrival, which was totally unexpected – he was all at once just *there*, not easily to be missed, thanks to his commanding presence, seated very straight at the wheel of a large and very noisy open car that had brought him up from somewhere on the far side of the town – was the first of a number of happy accidents that, without any effort on my part, have altered for the better the languid, rather sluggish course of my life, causing it to take a sudden swerve in what would invariably turn out in the end to have been the right direction.

The master whom Mr Senior had so suddenly replaced, in a temporary capacity, was to become an internationally renowned expert on late medieval bookbindings; he had been an ardent – if such an active adjective could have been applied to someone who, in the running of his form, had been quite outstandingly slothful – protagonist of the Stuart Cause. Under his supine direction, the History Side had vegetated in a semi-dormant torpor for a number of years. Mr Senior soon changed all that: now the small classroom, from which the Stuart engravings had been summarily expelled, became a hive of enthusiastic activity. Although the window of the room faced the wrong way, not commanding the much-sought-after view of the town, nor indeed that of the undesirable other side – it looked out on to a low roof to the far end of the main building – this was no disadvantage. Under Mr Senior's relentless guidance there was no longer any temptation for our eyes to wander in the direction of the external scene, glued as they were to our exercise-books and to our busy fountain-pens, as he took us, at breakneck speed, on what amounted to marathon tutorials, some of them covering two whole school periods.

The new master was, from the start, very keen that all the aspiring historians should know something about what was then just being called Current Affairs. I rather think that Current Affairs had reached us originally from across the Atlantic, but Mr Senior, who did not much like Americans (as we were soon to discover), would certainly not have admitted to such a provenance. In those years – I reached the History Side in the Michaelmas Term 1933 – Current Affairs, whether actively aided, or unaided and uninvited, by the new History master, had a nasty, pushy way of getting nearer and nearer, as if they had been actually moving in on us *personally* and with a sort of nudging insistence, wanting to come and sit with us in the small classroom that had no exciting view. We were, for instance, easily convinced of the innocence of poor demented van der Lubbe in the business of the Reichstag Fire, and the courageous and humorous Dimitrov, with his shock of curly black hair, seemed to be an almost physical presence at the back of the room, taking up the whole space of a double desk, as if he had been an addition of two to the small and (as we liked to think it) rather select form of eight. What particularly delighted us about the irrepressible and cheeky Bulgarian was the way in which he succeeded in ragging an increasingly apoplectic Goering. We were ready to recognize a superior performer in one of our own favourite pastimes on the days on which we were confronted with the unfortunate master who was supposed to teach us a smattering of Ancient History; we did not want to *know* any Ancient History, it seemed – and we were quite wrong – too far removed from Current Affairs.

From the time of my arrival on Kingsland, late in 1931, there seems to have been an increasing awareness of contemporary issues at least among the more enlightened members of the school. As reported in the *Salopian* of 19 December that year, the 1918 Society had been addressed on 22 November (a Sunday to boot!) on the subject of 'Soviet Russia', by a Mr Cemlyn-Jones, an old boy. His talk had been introduced by the Headmaster, Canon Sawyer, who had explained that Mr Jones 'had undertaken his tour of inspection as the impartial delegate of the three political parties . . .'. The speaker had not come out with anything very startling: 'The prevalent impression left in the mind about it all was, how little really *new*! God had been jeered out of public life, but Lenin had been canonised . . . a splash of vermilion turns the icon into the "red corner" . . . . The new industrial Kharkov is, architecturally at least, no more than an imitation of any recent German "industrial settlement" . . . . ' And more of the balancing act: continuity, nothing much actually changed, a bit of painting over, new gods for old, endemic inefficiency, and so on. Perhaps I am exaggerating the degree of awareness and interest provoked by the subject, because the report ends, rather lamely, with a reference to 'the half-filled Hall' (and its appalling acoustics). Still, most of the boys would have had other things to do on a Sunday evening. I *wanted* to think well of the Soviet Union, and was prepared to listen to anyone who had something positive to say about its achievements.

In March 1933, I had attended a talk given to the Modern Languages Society in the Sixth Form Library by Mr Paul Rotha on the state of the European film industry and on the problems of production and distribution. I think that he was himself a film producer in some small way, and that he was of Hungarian origin (he referred several times to Alexander Korda). Anyhow, I found his talk very stimulating, as he introduced me to the works of Pabst and Jean Vigo, and to a whole range of European avant-garde films, including *The Testament of Dr Mabuse* and *Zéro de conduite*. The talk represented an important step forward in my own *éducation européenne* (though I would not have called it that at the time), revealing to me what had been going on in Weimar Berlin and in Paris in the 1920s, and taking me far beyond the familiar bounds of popular British comedy films.

Later in the same year, an anonymous and rather pompous editorial in the *Salopian*, dated 21 October, ranged around much of Europe, starting with Germany leaving the League, taking in the Reichstag Fire trial in Leipzig, then glancing at the recently concluded Metro-Vickers trials in the Soviet Union ('all its mysterious contradictions and its wild affirmations . . .'), pausing at the spectacle, not especially frightening to the author of the editorial, offered by the Italian blackshirts, then going on to refer to Dollfuss's 'stormtroopers' active in a starving Vienna (but with waltzes still going on), and ending on a rather sour note when it concludes its lightning tour with Paris, a city which is described, uncharitably, as living under 'the Dictatorship of Fear'. In the autumn of 1933, the Parisians had everything to be fearful about, though that would not have occurred to me at the time, living as I was high above the upper reaches of the Severn. Additions to the School Library in that term include, dutifully, *The League of Nations Year Book, 1933*, and, boldly, *Lenin* by James Maxton. The school magazine of 13 December, the last number of the term, carries a pretty atrocious poem entitled, in Gothic letters, 'Germany', and opening, crashingly: 'Germany, Germany!! Battle and confusion! / Swastika, Swastika! / Awful disillusion!' But, on the subject of Hitler himself, referred to later in the poem as 'Adolphus', as if he had been a character in one of Hilaire Belloc's *Cautionary Rhymes*, it goes on to express, albeit as clumsily, sentiments that seem entirely healthy: 'I cannot, will not praise his name

/ He persecutes the helpless Jews . . . .' The poem is signed 'Ion'. However poor a poet 'Ion' (who I suspect was a member of the History side), he seems to have had the right ideas about Hitler.

* * *

I had escaped from the Classical Vth and reached the much-desired goal of the History Remove in the autumn of 1933. At that time, there were eight members of that form and of the much grander History VIth, who together constituted the History Side and who all sat in the same small room – though the members of the VIth to the back of it, as further removed from too close a scrutiny by the unfortunate Ancient History master; it was also easier to conduct a campaign of that kind from the rear. A year later, when I had moved up to the History VIth and the numbers had gone up to nine, I also moved, along with other members of the form, to the back.

In the Michaelmas Term of 1933, all eight members of the Side were at once assigned by Mr Senior various parts of Europe. The United States was excluded from our inquiries, as no doubt being peripheral and unworthy of our attention, with the result that it was not till two years later, when I went up to Merton in the autumn of 1935, that, thanks to friendly contacts with the American Rhodes Scholars then in the College, I became at all aware of the American dimension in world affairs and was introduced, for the first time, to the hopes and wonders of the New Deal, and that I first heard of 'FDR' in terms of extreme adulation or of extreme execration (both groups were represented in the small College, the Southern and Midwest contingents tending to execration, the East Coast and California, to adulation). Though Roosevelt's America was thus permanently excluded from our Salopian orbit, Canada, or rather a smallish part of that vast country, *Alberta*, all on its own, just managed to scrape in, being offered, rather grudgingly perhaps, a narrow folding-seat in Mr Senior's carefully vetted club.

Once, in a sort of unconscious preview of the Vienna Award, the History master had dispatched us to our various countries, we had to write about each in relation to contemporary political or social issues, *coups d'état*, abdications, depositions, assassinations, riots, landslides, earthquakes and other natural disasters, or mere elections. It was a bit as if each of the eight of us had then been, say, the Third Secretary or Commercial Attaché to an embassy not of his own choice, some of them prestigious, others obscure, uncomfortable and even dangerous. We were each given a fortnight to read up our designated topic, on which we were then expected to produce a detailed verbal report, and a general discussion would finally follow. We were further encouraged to enliven our reports with pictorial material: photographs cut out of the dailies and the weeklies and then stuck into our exercise-books, beside the text of our notes – House copies of the *Illustrated London News*, or even of the *Tatler* or the *Bystander*, were liable to emerge, after these discreetly conducted operations, sadly mutilated, resulting, in one particularly unfortunate instance, in the engagement photograph of the youngest daughter of a local double-barrelled Shropshire gentleman (who was also a Governor of the School) losing the lower half of her somewhat bovine face at the level of the jaw (the picture of a recently murdered Croat politician had been on the other side of the page). Such brutal and inconsiderate resort to scissors, generally after evening Prayers, undoubtedly served to increase the suspicions felt by most of the Housemasters, great enemies of change, about what they regarded as the dangerous innovations being introduced so cavalierly by the intrepid and enthusiastic young History master. It was really just a case of differing priorities: the Housemasters opted for engagement photographs of girls wearing strings of pearls round their shapely necks, whereas *we* on the History Side tried to look beyond the rather parochial boundaries of the County of Salop so as to take in a wider vision comprising the whole of Europe. I suppose we would have put it something like that, had we been asked; but we hadn't: what we *had* been asked was to replace the mutilated copy of the *Tatler*.

Our master also urged us to make use of cartoons and election posters as further illustrative aids. Many of these were subsequently pinned up on the classroom partitions in the blank spaces where the Stuart engravings had previously hung under the recently terminated regime. I was able to get a very colourful set of Spanish ones, representing *all* the political parties involved in what was to turn out a fairly violent campaign, merely by writing to their London Embassy, an initiative that Mr Senior encouraged the other members of the form to emulate, the Soviet Embassy in particular proving most responsive, though the posters that *they* sent seemed a bit repetitive, as they only represented *one* party.

One of my friends found himself saddled with the latest ministerial crisis in Paris; in this instance, his brief was overtaken by the rapidity of events. He had no sooner mugged up the composition of the newly formed Government than there had been an extensive re-deal, a *remaniement*, obliging him to start all over again. Another was packed off to the latest civil war in Greece that had either just broken out, or had just stopped, or that – after a brief respite to give both sides a breathing-space – had broken out again. Someone else was sent away to take a long look at the apparently indestructible Dr Colijn and his Anti-Revolutionary Party in The Hague, Queen Wilhelmina's favourite politician, and chosen, I suppose, as a study of immobility and as a reminder that Current Affairs were not necessarily always about things *happening*; yet, desite Dr Colijn's tall, elaborate wing-collars, there *were* actually quite serious riots, sometime in 1934, in, of all places, Amsterdam. One of the eight of us was ordered off to Fascist Italy; it might have been 'The Draining of the Pontine Marshes', for, again in 1934, they were still being drained, enabling Mussolini to strip to the waist and to display his muscular torso.

Pilsudski being still alive, though only *just*, Poland did not get an envoy, as nothing much could happen there to disturb the Marshal's long afternoon nap before he joined his daughters for tea. There was always the Corridor, of course, but it was a subject that Mr Senior, who was the son and the grandson of Low Church Anglican clergymen (his younger brother was to become one, too), failed to warm to, as it did not seem, at least on the map, to raise Moral Issues; and our master liked to make moral judgments (even on the subject of foreigners, about whom I think he had only rather a theoretical or literary knowledge; I doubt whether he had ever *met* any, and I am pretty sure that, at this early stage of his life, he had never crossed the Channel. Even so, he obviously felt that, however distasteful foreigners might be personally, we should know something about them, if only to discover that some were better or at least marginally less repulsive, than others.)

Yugoslavia must have come in under some sort of umbrella – possibly that of opposition to King Alexander, a powerful and very courageous ruler who had only one more year to go – otherwise, the youngest daughter of the Governor of the School would not have lost her lower jaw and all that went with it, including the pearl necklace, to the assassinated Croat politician.

There would have been no question of including Horthy's Hungary in our Kingsland-based European Tour. In the 1920s and even in the early 30s, it had been the country most highly favoured by the Northcliffe and Rothermere press: the Magyars, it was argued, were horse-lovers just like ourselves, and they had been shamefully done down by the Treaty of Trianon. Anyhow, I am grateful to Mr Senior as much for his *exclusions* as for his positive enthusiams. He would not have gone for candle-lit processions outside West Hungarian cathedrals in Easter week, the noble-born Cardinal in red arriving at the last moment in an open carriage drawn by six black horses, his right hand raised in blessing of the kneeling multitudes. And Shrewsbury was not the sort of school that provided riding lessons. So the proud and discontented Magyars could stew in their own juice as far as we were concerned. I don't think I am speaking only for myself.

Apart from the Reichstag Fire trial and my own assignment, those topics may well have been the full extent of Mr Senior's European Deal for that year; though I think de Valera and the Fianna Fáil were introduced in the following one, 1934. Nor can I remember just who got what. Nothing particular can have been deemed to have happened in the Soviet Union, as no one was assigned East, though, at regular intervals, two or three times a term, we were all offered fast-moving, jumpy films about physical activities that appeared to be disagreeably energetic and visibly febrile, always carried out in conditions of the most extreme cold: cutting through the tundra, or piling up earth with bare hands or primitive-looking spades, in order to make a railway embankment, or to provide the course for a future canal (the water would come triumphantly churning in in a later film). Mr Senior also passed on to us, generally without comment, the fortnightly *Soviet Newsletter* sent by the Embassy as 'something we might like to take a look at'. His general attitude was that the Soviet Union should be given the benefit of the doubt, things seemed at least to be on the move there and, in due course, might be getting better, but there was still a very long way to go; and we were all happy enough to go along with that, too. Let us at least hear what they have to say.

My own assignment that year was to Madrid, to cover the election campaign that was just getting under way in Spain. The monarchy had been but recently overthrown and the deposed king, Alfonso XIII, had driven off at speed at the wheel of his own open Hispano-Suiza. The new Republic had gone to the polls in what was said to be the first free election for a great many years, so that its outcome would be an important test for the future of Spanish parliamentary democracy. I even managed to familiarize myself with the numerous initials of the many parties, and of their supporting institutions, trade unions (of which there appeared to be several), regional assemblies and that sort of thing, that were contesting the election. Of the leading candidates I can now only remember the name of Gil Robles, for whom I at once conceived a very strong dislike, and one that survived into the years long after Shrewsbury. I think his party was called something like 'Acción Popular' – in whatever language, a reliable trade mark. Mr Senior was very sound on such organizations: I remember him referring, in the following year, 1934, to 'two Frenchmen, Charles Maurras and Léon Daudet, who are outstandingly evil, and, unfortunately, brilliantly intelligent, and capable of inflicting an immense amount of harm, as apostles of hate, on that unfortunate country' (for Mr Senior, France was *always* unfortunate). It was a summary judgment that I was ready enough to accept at the time (the first word in Action Française gave the show away); but once I got to France, I became less convinced of the brilliant intelligence of the odious pair. As for the Spanish elections, I cannot remember anything at all about their outcome. Perhaps they did not produce any straightforward result. But I can recall a politician with the decidedly *un*-Hispanic surname of Leroux, or Lerroux. I think he was some sort of a Radical, though this did not seem to mean very much in the 1930s on either side of the Pyrenees. However, the operation in which I had been so diligently engaged had not been entirely useless, since I had learnt about such initials as POUM, FAI, UGT, PCE, JONS, CEDA, so that, three years later, when confronted with the complexities of the alliances and the bitter antagonisms within the Republican and Nationalist camps, once the Civil War had broken out in July 1936, I was able to guide myself through the maze of opposing allegiances, while following the course of events from the comfortable distance of Paris.

All in all, our History master had done pretty well by all eight of us (nine in 1934). He was perhaps too ready to make special allowances for the Soviet Union (I think now that he may have been an old-fashioned nineteenth-century Russophile, who had early been made aware of the futility of the Crimean War and of the fact that, momentarily, we had ended up on the wrong side, in an unnatural system of alliances, and had found ourselves briefly in very dangerous company. He was completely sound on Hitler and Mussolini, and was always ready to point out the connection between the various forms of Green Fascism, such as were then to be found in Austria and Poland, in Lithuania, Croatia, Hungary and Slovakia, and the influence of the hierarchy of the Roman Catholic Church and of the Catholic Press in this country.

I don't think there can have been any Catholics in the form at my time; we would have known, we would have spotted their absence at Sunday matins or evensong in the School Chapel, and there was a Catholic church somewhere in the town, though I did not know *where* it was; but I had spotted the Welsh *Yglys*, which gave forth cheerful waves of male-voiced harmony on Thursday market day and Sunday morning, and that lent the tight little town an agreeable international dimension within its surround of walls.

As a fervent 'Georgist', who had all of us reading *Progress and Poverty*, there was a hallowed place in Mr Senior's system of things for the Province of Alberta in the Dominion of Canada. 'Georgism' was really the only eccentricity that he allowed himself, and it rubbed off on some of us more than on others. I could never make head or tail of any form of economics, so I was more or less immune to the appeal of the Master; but some of my companions were to remain convinced 'Georgists', sometimes for years. I think many of us regarded Henry George as a bit of a joke; but schoolboys warm to mild forms of eccentricity, and our History master's touching faith in a Single Land Tax, and in greenbacks, added a very human dimension, which was further strengthened in our inquisitive eyes by the knowledge that, at that time, he was on the brink of becoming engaged to a Scottish girl from the evocative Highland locality of Rumbling Bridge (morning periods tended to begin with the apparently innocent question – we took it in turns – 'Sir, have you had a *letter* this morning?' And, if he smiled, a little uneasily, we would know that he *had*, and that his jubilant mood would last throughout the teaching day).

But Current Affairs meant above all *Europe*. It may be that he saw what was coming – it would not have been too difficult in 1933 and 1934 – and that he was seeking to prepare us for the worst. I don't think any of us were in much need of guidance in that respect; from the time I left Shrewsbury in December 1934 to when I went down from Merton in June 1938, I was only too unhappily aware that foreign affairs were, quite literally, a matter of life and death. It must have meant a considerable effort of will on the part of a man who was so profoundly and happily *English* thus to have given us a very extensive coverage of the fast-moving political map of Europe. This was not the only thing for which I felt very grateful to him. Perhaps even more important was that he had introduced us to the wonders of Namier's masterpiece, *England in the Age of the American Revolution*, with its chapter on the Shropshire gentry of the late eighteenth century, and had warned us against the seductive wiles of Arnold Toynbee and his anti-historical Cycles of 'Withdrawal and Return', and similar pretentious nonsense. We were not allowed to forget the liberties that Toynbee had taken with the narrative of events, especially in the matter of Peter the Great's sojourn in Western Europe: pushed back or forward ten years – a *mere* ten years – in order to fit its assigned place in a grander scheme of things. There were quite a number of frauds, both national and international, who were being acclaimed by a gullible public during the 1930s, and Toynbee had already acquired a reputation as a seer who made History *fit* and who was widely read on both sides of the

Atlantic. Mr Senior had the great merit of convincing us that *dates* were important and that *facts* did matter.

I am sure that there remained many areas of my concerns that stayed both quite outside Mr Senior's influence and beyond the range of his approval or disapproval. For much of the time that I was on the History Side, I was going through a decidedly mawkish Hardy phase, revelling in the ancestral gloom of the doom-ridden Dorset countryside and actually enjoying the relentlessly piled-on tribulations of poor Jude. As I was relatively happy, at least as long as I was away from my House, and as I had never had to live in the country, a prospect that would have appalled me, it was nice to read, in the comfort of the School Library (which also overlooked the town) about the stark horrors of nineteenth-century rural life, and the apparently unavoidable misfortunes of ill-used country girls who had become pregnant out of wedlock and had ended up, with distressing regularity, down the bottom of conveniently placed wells. My reading of Hardy was marked by a considerable degree of innocence. I knew vaguely that pregnancy was one of the hazards of sex as far as women were concerned, but I had no idea about how this might actually come about. Hardy was not the place to which I would have gone in order to titillate my fairly mild and timid voyeurism in that mysterious, but deeply enticing area. At about this time I had acquired a book of Bernard Shaw's illustrated by Eric Gill, *The Adventures of a Black Girl in Search of God*. The appeal of the book was not in the least theological, and I was really not concerned to know whether she did nor did not end up finding a suitable Deity. What did appeal to me was the girl's engaging nudity, so attractively innocent, and yet not quite so, and her beautifully shaped black buttocks, clear-cut and perfectly rounded, their contours silhouetted in the form of a woodcut. The book remained for a long time in the relative privacy of my desk, in the study I shared with three others, to be glanced at every now and then. The perfect curve of her assertive bottom had nothing whatever to do with Current Affairs. As for Hardy, and the more local Mary Webb, it was not till I was at Oxford that Stella Gibbons provided me with the perfect antidote to rural doom and gloom. I liked to have several horses running at once. Tess and the Black Girl did not get in the way of Mosley, Green Fascism, the Five Year Plan, the infamous Maurras and the convinced Henry George; they were just not in the same race. I had already discovered the pleasure of living at several different levels at the same time and in keeping my different interests in strictly separate compartments.

* * *

I remember one morning when, in 1935, Murray Senior and I were travelling back to London from Tunbridge Wells. (After my father's death that year, my mother had asked Mr Senior to act as my guardian, till my majority.) I was looking out of the window of the carriage on to the Gustave Doré landscape far below us, tiny houses, diminutive pubs, huge brick railway arches, grimy churches, enormous warehouses with black writing on them, when all at once my guardian broke the silence, as if he had just stumbled on some great truth, coming out with the ponderous statement: 'Of course, War' – and that was what he had been thinking about from Chislehurst, or Dunton Green, or from further back, Hildenborough or even High Brooms – his impressive lowering brows had been deeply puckered in grave thought from the very start of the journey from the Central Station, and, observing them, I had decided not to talk; or the remark might have been sparked off quite suddenly, there and then, as the train came alongside the flag manufacturer's many masts, on the far right side of the tracks, and he was sitting on that side of the carriage; it was, I remember, a windy day, and all the flags, scores of them, including, I imagine, those of the three Baltic Republics, were flapping out most vigorously, as if they had learnt their cue and were determined to show themselves off to best advantage, straight out at right angles to their masts, with the huge White Ensign in the place of honour, right in the middle and at the very top, yes, it could have been that large expanse of white with its red cross, the handsomest and cleanest of flags, Omo whiter than white, it could have been *that* which had set him off, completing his sentence – 'brings out the best and the worst in everyone.'

I did not know *what* to say to this: it was the sort of statement that seemed quite meaningless; I even felt a bit embarrassed for my guardian, but fortunately there was nobody else in the compartment (not that the presence of a stranger would have stopped him, for he was much given to *ex cathedra* pronouncements to anyone within listening range, perhaps a result of his clerical family background that no doubt induced each member of the family to think out morally aloud). My guardian's sudden pronouncement had caught me unawares, because, for once, *I* had not been thinking about war (or The War: it seemed so inevitable as to earn the definite article and a capital), but had wandered off agreeably into the remembered contemplation of the photograph of a naked girl, long-legged, and French of course, lying in some sandy dunes among tufts of rank grass, the dunes blown into caressing, corrugated white mounds so as to cradle her, that had recently been in one of the weeklies, *Men Only*, or *Lilliput*, possibly. So I kept silent, and very soon we were crossing Charing Cross Bridge. Still, it was perhaps just an occasional lapse. Even so, I preferred Mr Senior up on his dais and gowned, in the little classroom. Sharing a carriage with me, his huge frame at the same level as myself, he seemed somehow considerably reduced in majesty. Perhaps one should never meet one's masters in such circumstances.

Soon I would not need a guardian any more; and, after 1935, I rather lost touch with my former History master. I wonder whether the War brought out the best or the worst in *him*. It certainly brought out his anti-Americanism.

2

Rouen – A First Sketch

Rouen, April 1935. It was a very important experience for me, for this was the first time I had ever gone off on holiday *on my own*. You can imagine what this would have meant to a boy who had spent a matter of years at prep school and public school and had never had a moment's privacy. It was all the more exciting because this was also the first time that I had to cope, unassisted, with a stay in a French provincial town where I knew no one. There *was* some assistance: the Hôtel Louis XIII, in the Rue Beauvoisine, was recommended to me by a friend of Mme Thullier* who had a bookshop in the Rue Thiers, and it was suggested that I should take a *demi-pension*, that is breakfast and dinner, leaving me free to have lunch anywhere. I remember the hotel both for its whiteness and its quietness. Everything was very white: the walls of my room on the first floor looking out on to that narrow, ancient street that cuts the city in two on a N–S axis, from the suburbs to the Seine. The bedspread and the curtains were white, the table-cloth in the little dining-room on the ground floor was startlingly white, the table in the window of my bedroom had a flower-patterned white cloth over it and gave forth a sort of white glow when the afternoon sun fell on it. The whiteness, the luminosity, that I can still recall. And the quiet. It was a very silent, still hotel, the only sound the bell when

* With whom I had been staying, and her two sons, in the Boulevard Bonne-Nouvelle, Paris; see my Introduction to *A Second Identity: Essays on France and French history* (1969).

the outer door was opened. At the other tables there were elderly couples, their white napkins tucked up under their chins. They looked as if they were full *pensionnaires* and actually *lived* there perhaps all the year round. They had their napkin-rings in little boxes. They talked in low tones, there was no talk between the tables. The atmosphere was decorous and restrained. I felt a bit prominent at my little table alone, but there were three or four other people who also sat alone. The waitress who took the orders, a very blonde girl with pale blue eyes, dressed in black with a white-laced smock, black stockings and mauve bedroom slippers, whispered the menu as if afraid of being overheard or as if 'raie au beurre noir' had been a secret code (my love of skate dates from that Easter holiday). I generally got in early, sixish, worked on my sketching-pad till the dinner gong went; then, after dinner, walked down to the quays and had an evening *calvados* on the terrace of the big Café Victor, from which I could watch the Finnish, Norwegian, Soviet and British boats being unloaded. I put lumps of sugar in my *calvados*, then sucked them. Sometimes I had a second *calvados*. I remember the banknotes, they had on them a female Republic with rather gauzy draperies hanging off her; she was, however, quite decent, nothing much was showing. She seemed to be stretching, as if she had a stiff neck. I enormously enjoyed my observatory, the lights of the ships, the ferries, the *pont transbordeur* taking people across the broad river to the industrial Left Bank. I walked up the Rue Beauvoisine past sleepy *crémeries* and quiet little antique shops, pushed the door with its bell, picked up my key, and went to bed tennish, perhaps reading a bit of Maupassant.

Each morning I would head for the bus station near the river and take a little brown Renault bus, Les Cars Normands, to Caudebec, or Dieppedalle, the Forêt de Roumare, or the Forêt de la Bouille, carrying my sketching-pad. I liked taking this form of public transport, there would be voluminous adults with baskets, and talkative children. I would listen, finding that I could understand almost everything. For lunch I would go to a *pâtisserie* and buy some cakes and a bar of Chocolat Meunier. Once, in a village in the forest, I gave my Meunier to a small boy wearing a blue peaked cap; I had to buy another bar. Then I would get down to sketching. I sketched in the main square of Caudebec: a Decorated church, half-timbered houses, an old car, farm carts; I was closely watched by a small group of children in black smocks. I have lost the sketch – a pity, for Caudebec was bombed in 1944, it nearly all went. On the other bank of the Seine, near la Bouille, I remember going to a café with a terrace overlooking the huge bend of the river; the café was black-, brown-and-white timbered, *faux manoir normand*. The waitress, in black and white, had wonderful, caressing black eyes. The café was next to a very modern brick École Communale that looked as if it had just been built. I had some conversation with black-eyes and felt myself blushing purple, and she laughed at me, not mockingly, but I suppose encouragingly, to put me at my ease, but she didn't. I hated myself for my shyness, but could not do anything about it. Later, perhaps another day, I lost my temper with a taxi driver who had overcharged me, and I realized that I could speak French.

In a fortnight, I did about twenty sketches, some of which I did not complete in pen-and-ink, leaving them in pencil outline. I remember one of a Finnish ship unloading wood, the *Suomen Poika*, which a member of the crew who spoke English told me meant '*Son of Finland*'. He was, too, and looked it, a very tall man with a sandy moustache and very pale blue eyes. I enjoyed each outing to the full, going to a different place each day, sometimes just staying in Rouen *and sketching ships*. Once, I climbed up the steep hill of Bonsecours and did a panoramic sketch of the whole of Rouen, l'Île-Lacroix in the middle of the river, the big bridge, the *pont transbordeur* and the iron spire of the Cathedral. Panoramic sketches were not my thing, I was much better on small detail, a half-timbered house, pear and apple trees, a line of washing; especially a line of washing, there was something invitingly domestic about it, it seemed to be taking me in, telling me not very exciting secrets. Mostly I went through the day without speaking to anyone, save to ask for my bus ticket. But then I did have the long conversation with the red-faced docker, who was a Communist. I went back once to la Bouille, the café there, hoping to have another glimpse of black-eyes, but she was not there, just a rather surly waiter with acne.

With my meals in Louis XIII, I always took a *quart* of white wine

(I think it was included), I generally opted for a sweet Graves or a sweet Entre-Deux-Mers. If I had had a very good day sketching or walking or both, I would boldly order a second *quart*. Tastes change completely over the years. Then, and later, as an undergraduate, I went for sweet white wines, Tokays, and that sort of thing. I can't remember when I switched to *red*.

What might have been the high spot of my Rouen stay was attendance at Pontifical High Mass on Easter Sunday in that fantastic cathedral. I remember a very old Archbishop, Mgr de Villerabel, all bent up, lines of white-robed monks from Saint-Wandrille, choirs, etc etc, the organ growling, in fact *the works*. I was fascinated and repelled; it was a bit like being in the enemy camp: there were young women with faces of extreme devoutness, one of them, quite close to me – I had got myself a chair on the aisle – suddenly went down on her knees, in the middle of the aisle, and kissed the Archbishop's large reddish ring, she kissed it *gluttonously*, almost as if she were going to eat the whole hand off as well. But the Mass was not like going to the cinema or sitting on the terrace of the Café Victor, for it did *not* give me the impression of *belonging*; quite the contrary, I felt alien, an interloper, I was even afraid that I might be caught out, exposed, as a fraud and a spy, by doing the wrong thing, crossing myself the wrong way round – or with my left hand (which would have seemed correct, it was, is, my *important* hand). Throughout the service I had been a bit apprehensive, it seemed so likely that I'd put a foot wrong, be kneeling down when everyone was standing up, or the contrary. Here was an aspect of France that made me feel very much of a foreigner, even very English. The Cathedral, however, is very beautiful. A Governor of Normandy, a Plantagenet, the Regent for Henry VI, is buried under the high altar (but I didn't know that in 1935; he was discovered after the Cathedral had caught fire in the summer of 1944).

I had come to Rouen from Paris, by bus via Pontoise and Magny-en-Vexin (the frontier), and I went back the same way. It was very hot and dusty on both journeys. I enjoyed both: *la route haute*, the old coach road, between Normandy and the Île-de-France, and the two Vexins. I had been quietly happy pretty well all the time. I thought that I should have more holidays on my own, the formula seemed to work, left me free to do what I wanted, to observe and listen; it would not have been nearly as much fun with a companion, then there would have been disagreements and arguments. It was wonderful to think that really no one knew where I was, though I did send my mother daily postcards; I still have them, the postmark 'Rouen RD' is accompanied by a circle with dates, and a box containing 'VISITEZ ROUEN VILLE MUSÉE' – it was that, too, but a great more as well. Once or twice in the evenings I had gone to the Public Library; I liked the large frescos depicting nineteenth-century textile factories and the raw cotton at the quayside. I also liked the company, which was varied and unassuming. The Public Library did give me the feeling that I belonged.

I am still very fond of Rouen, though the Hôtel Louis XIII and the quays have gone. I suppose it is the abiding memory of having been so young, so enquiring, so excited, so much enjoying my own company, exploring the place on my own, seeking out things to sketch, and having no fixed plans, apart from returning to the white bedroom, the white dining-room, the pale walls of the hotel, 'HÔTEL LOUIS XIII' in gold letters on a black marble background shaped like a palette, and something like 'EAU CHAUDE DANS TOUTES LES CHAMBRES', though in smaller letters than the pious monarch's.

3

The Wrong Europe

THE IDEAL country, I had decided for myself, in 1935, was Czechoslovakia, a true democracy and infinitely mysterious, and with a language apparently in a consonantal code. Later, when I was in Paris, one of my poses – and I had a great many of these when I was just under eighteen – was to buy a Prague newspaper (I think it was the *Listy Noviny*, it sounds right), from the kiosk on the Boulevard Bonne-Nouvelle; I would take it into a café and unfold it rather ostentatiously, though, of course, I could not understand a word of it. The paper and the newsprint gave off a rich odour, a hint of cigar smoke accompanied by very strong coffee which I rather liked and which I imagined to be the very smell of Central Europe. I was convinced that Karel Čapek must be a great European figure, though I had not read anything of his even in translation; anyone with a surname beginning with a funny Č had to be very talented, and anyhow he was a Czech, and there were all sorts of exciting things going on in that country (which also supplied me with a full range, from HH to BB, of drawing-pencils). My admiration for Czechoslovakia was quite unreasoning, the sense of mystery had something to do with it, but I also knew that the place was a democracy, and that the Czechs at least were Protestants of some sort, or were nothing. There is something rather ironical that I should have been arrested under my borrowed trappings of 'Student von Prag'. I was rather pleased about it at the time. Actually, right from 1935 to 1938, I used to make a habit of buying (and not reading) Prague newspapers. Later, in the war, when I was attached to No 24 Liaison, that with the Czechoslovak Independent Brigade Group, I had found the Czechs rather stolid, a bit dull, and the Slovaks much livelier. But that came later.

Many of these attitudes were strengthened once I was in Paris, reading every day *L'Oeuvre*, every Wednesday *Le Canard enchainé*. I was pretentious and posturing, I liked to walk with an appearance of urgency, as if I had just come out of an important meeting and was walking towards the waiting news cameras. Almost as soon as I got to Paris, I purchased, for 75 fr, an important-looking leather dispatch-case, which I would carry round with me everywhere, even in the evening; I felt it added to the visible seriousness of my public purpose. Later, a black trilby was added to the kit, and even in the heat of July Vienna I wore a three-piece blue suit: no concessions to the sun. There was often a *Listy Noviny* in the dispatch-case. I seem to remember that, every now and then, I'd vary the menu of my non-reads by buying a Bucharest newspaper, *Curuntul*, or something like that, certainly ending in *-ul*. Then again, in 1936, at the beginning of the Civil War, I would sometimes stack up with a very badly printed Madrid newspaper on yellowed paper. I was self-satisfied and firmly fixed in my opinions and I had a Scoring List of the main European countries. I was a show-off. From 1935 on, I wore only French ties, done with a very large knot, I had a brownish French pullover that had a collar that would go over the collar of my jacket, and I often wore, indoors, a black and silver scarf, as I imagined in the French manner, hanging on the outside of my jacket, or, if I had my jacket off, round my neck and down my back. Nearly all the time I was acting a part.

But for that I had to have an audience. Later, in 1936 and 1937, I would bombard my Merton friends, Meredith, Coddington, Wastie-Green, Biggs, with long, descriptive letters, and sometimes with sketches of the view as seen from the long windows of my room, Rue Saint-André-des-Arts. It wasn't just a matter of wanting to be in Paris, of enjoying it there for its own sake – and my enjoyment was perfectly genuine and unaffected – it was also a matter of wanting my contemporaries to *know* I was there; and, indeed, I must have been prepared to give up quite a lot of time, sitting at the table in my dark room on the third floor, to make sure that they *did*.

There was certainly a large element of posturing in this, too, playing the Continental, the experienced European traveller, the man who knew his way round France, Belgium, and the Dutch border. Hence all those picture postcards posted from railway stations like Liège, Antwerp, Breda, Bergen-op-Zoom, Rouen, Nogent-le-Rotrou, La Ferté-Bernard, Chartres, just to show that I had been there. Some of the trips by bus to Tongres, to Lille, to Rosendaël had no other purpose than to impress my contemporaries with yet another postmark. Already, by 1936, I was living at two levels at the same time: being in Paris, and writing long letters *about* being in Paris. I needed to display my wares.

Once back in England at the beginning of my time at Oxford, I would have *L'Oeuvre* sent to me every day, not so much to read, as to be seen reading it or having read it, piled-up copies of it, their wrappers removed, would be casually strewn about my table and my armchairs in my sitting-room at Merton. And, of course, I smoked, or rather puffed at, Celtiques, and I had a bottle of Cointreau on a side-table (actually, I liked Cointreau). My bookshelves full of pink-covered collections of Verlaine, Rimbaud, and Baudelaire, Éditions de Cluny, were supposed to call attention to themselves as reminders of the extent of their owner's impregnation in French culture. And I liked to be able to show off my French, not just at college, but also at university level, becoming, in my second year, Treasurer of Oxford University French Society (the posters had a bright red cockerel on them, it was my job to put them up in college porter's lodges). In my third year at Merton, 1938, I got to know two very attractive French girls, both of them from Paris: Anne-Marie Lévy and Sophie Lindheimer, friends of the numerous and affluent Alden family, printers and stationers who lived in a big house a little way up the Banbury Road at Oxford. Both of them were Jewish, though I did not identify them as such at the time. I liked having them around, giving them tea (cucumber and smoked salmon sandwiches provided by the chef), showing them the Grove, the Wall, the seventeenth-century Gazebo, the Tsar Alexander I huge font in Odessa marble, the Old Library and its chained books, in short *les honneurs de la maison*, as much as anything an opportunity to display my spoken French.

In 1938, I liked to be *seen* entertaining two pretty Parisiennes. There had been no flirtation, I was still very frightened of girls; but Anne-Marie and Sophie also provided me with intelligent company; they were very well-read and liked making fun of my evident shyness and gaucherie. Whether I fooled anyone other than myself by all this play-acting it would be hard to say. I suppose I was not much sillier than most young men of eighteen or nineteen. One must remember, too, that, in the 1930s, 'going abroad' was not as commonplace as now, there was quite an element of excitement and exploration about it and it still retained something of a rarity value. It was also very much a class thing. Nothing would have induced working-class people to cross the Channel in those inter-war years. Anyhow, once back in Merton, Term would serve a purpose: that of displaying my skills as a well-qualified Parisian who 'knew his way about'. I must have been slightly convincing, for, before the end of my time in Oxford, I had managed to persuade some of my closest friends, John Biggs (the poet Christopher Lee) and James Wastie-Green, to follow me across the Channel. There was no per-suading the incurably insular Meredith, but, the war over, even Coddington would be induced to cross to the Continent and to come with me as far as Lyon.

Perhaps, looking back, I may have taken too severe a view of what I have described as mere posturing and undergraduate showman-ship. I think that there was a good deal more to it than the desire to impress some of my contemporaries (those whom I thought could be impressed). I did not just take *L'Oeuvre* for it to be seen, I liked to be able to keep up with day-to-day events in Paris, if only to pre-serve the link and to keep the place within easy reach while on the wrong side of the Channel. I found the paper interestingly varied and read it regularly over breakfast and lunch, following in partic-ular the salacious details of the long-drawn-out Stavisky Trial (something of a misnomer, for the principal personage, M. Serge-Alexandre Stavisky, was already long since dead and beyond the reach of Justice; the trial was that of his alleged accomplices and dupes, a very mixed and often picturesque bag). One of the reasons I had opted for *L'Oeuvre*, apart from its anti-clericalism and its inventive irreverence, had been the paper's *chroniqueuse judiciaire*, who, in the late 1930s, had been the wonderfully talented and amusing Madeleine Jacob (whom I had the joy of rediscovering, after my definitive return to Paris in the autumn of 1946, when she was occupying a similar position with *Libération*). I was also a fervent admirer of Geneviève Tabouis, whose perception of the current European scene seemed to me altogether sound, at least in its prejudices, even if in her writing she tended to rely rather too heavily on the French conditional. Sometime in 1937 I was able to persuade her to come and give a talk to the French Society. The subject of her talk was Czechoslovakia and its powerful and well-equipped army.

Similarly, the pretty pink-covered books of Les Éditions de Cluny were not merely there for display (though they were placed in such a way on the top shelf of the bookcase facing the door to my room from the staircase, that they could not be missed, they would be the first thing that any visitor would see). I had indeed read them, developing in the process an enthusiasm for some of the more obscure of Rimbaud's poems and language, as well as for the language and rhythm of Villon, the sad poems of Charles d'Orléans, and being much impressed by the sheer sensuality of *Le Spleen de Paris*. Already, in Paris, I had become aware of the discreet elegance of the letters, black on white background, *nrf* (never in roman capitals) and had taken them as a sure guarantee of the high quality of the contents.

In Vienna, I was desperately lonely. In Paris, pretty well from the start of my first six months' stay, I was *not* lonely; I had quite a wide cast of friends and acquaintances – even people I disliked; but I disliked them with *names*, they too had names, surnames at least. I could ring the chimes on quite a wide social range: the Thullier family, affluent, the two boys wonderfully anarchical, and their young cousins – a boy and a girl, both still at school – whom they encouraged (quite successfully) to behave badly at table when having lunch or dinner with their aunt; Maurice Chauvirey, an unemployed hairdresser and make-up man from the Épinay film studios; Gaston and René Renault, self-taught and on the pacifist fringes of the Left, and their truly dreadful mother, yellow-faced, exuding rancid hate – one could *smell* the hate coming out of her –

and always dressed in a greasy black. Then there were the peasants, wealthy farmers, village artisans from Saint-Germain-de-la-Coudre, in the Perche, that birthplace of René and Gaston (their father had been Maire for many years), so that my horizon was not strictly Parisian. I went off to the Orne quite often, taking the bus with Mme Thullier from La Ferté-Bernard to Saint-Germain and staying either with Mariel Veau, the local electrician, a cousin of René and Gaston, or in a farm up the dusty road to Marcilly, in which I was given the main bedroom, crucifix and bridal coverings over the huge bed.

I often went with the Thulliers to their countryside home on the river-bank at Samois, near the Pont des Valvins. So I really did have quite a big cast to fall back on, to suit my mood, within a month of my arrival in Paris. And, also within a month, I had established a set of regular itineraries, mostly on foot, and had started to notice things: trailing wisps of fog in the straight avenues of the Luxembourg, the changing colours of the Seine as seen from Sèvres, bank messengers wearing *tricornes* bearing a tricolour favour, the little light-blue PTT postal vans (French Fiats, I think, or perhaps Simcas – I was never very hot on cars, even then). I began to recognize people, in the street, in shops, in cafés and among the dusty, crumpled regulars of the Bibliothèque Mazarine, presided over by a faded, blond man in slightly tinted glasses and wearing a shiny black suit. In the Mazarine I would read, anarchically and voraciously. And I began going to the cinema and the theatre (including Dullin's L'Atelier). I suppose *the* breakthrough came that March, when all at once I found myself thinking in French, found myself enjoying Maupassant's marvellously cut-down prose, laughing at the jokes in Le Canard, immensely flattered to have understood the oblique hints and the knowing illusions. In short, I was *part* of it all; and all included already quite a varied topography: in Paris, the Xme, the XIVme, the VIIIme, the IXme, then the village (bringing back from there home-made marc or calvados), the Valley of the Seine, both below and above Paris.

I was supposed to be having German lessons twice a week, in a flat near Saint-Augustin. But I did not really warm to the language, I did not like the pile-up of all those past participles at the end of a sentence, the language seemed somehow rther ridiculous (now I would call it a Lego-language). I quite liked my teacher, Mlle Goetz, but I spent more of my time talking to a Greek lady, Mlle Cara, she shared the flat with. Mlle Cara, who had been a pupil of Gieseking, and gave piano lessons, was much more amusing than the rather ponderous Mlle Goetz. By July, I had hardly made *any* progress in German; my teacher became worried, feeling that my mother was wasting her money (as indeed she was). I had, however, met *one* person who said he knew about Vienna (I think in fact he was a Czech or a Slovak; I never found out, for having installed him in Mme Thullier's bedroom for one night, he had already gone by the time I had got up in the morning. I searched the room, but nothing seemed to have been missing – there were 5,000-franc notes among Mme Thullier's stockings). So he never told me about Vienna.

Even in Vienna, I was to have *L'Oeuvre* posted to me, it would reach me, two or three consecutive numbers at a time. This attempt to maintain even a frail link turned out to have been a mistake, because it accentuated my nostalgia and my feeling of loneliness. Even a largely *empty* July–August Paris would seem so much more desirable, especially from all that distance to the east, than a crowded Vienna. Of course, I should have called the whole thing off; it had been pretty clear from the start, when the move had first been mooted, that I was not going to give it much of a chance.

* * *

As a traveller especially by rail, the approach to a great city has always been important to me; it is also much the best way to get a first flavour of a city – the allotments, the first peripheral tram or bus stops, the washing-lines, the transition from shacks to villas, from villas to blocks of flats, gasworks, more and more sidings, and it is always exciting and always different. The approach to Turin–PN (*Torino–Porta Nova*) is one of my favourites, though I have not tried it for well over twenty years. How I would like to do Berlin in that way! Anyhow, I think, in my first approach to Vienna, I was unlucky from the start. I reckon I must have left Paris – Gare de l'Est it would have been, for the Bucharest train – on a Saturday morning. I woke up in Switzerland, which was rather beautiful. But as soon as we crossed the border into Austria things started to take an ugly turn. It was now Sunday morning and, at each stop, more and more people in disguise started crowding into our (SNCF – I did at least take that bit of France away with me) third-class compartment. It looked as if the recently arrived passengers had been taking part in some ghastly revival of *The White Horse Inn*: women in embroidered smocks and bodices, silk flower designs, crude colours, men in funny hats with feathers in them, velvet or furry hats with wide brims, *leather shorts*, long socks with things in them holding them up. Even the old people and the children were in disguise. I should add that I had been quite used to French peasants, or at least to Lower Norman ones from the Perche, but when *they* travelled the men wore black suits, white collars, black boots and black hats; one knew that they were peasants, because, when they travelled to Paris, or to Chartres, they put on their Sunday best, or what they wore at funerals and weddings, there was nothing folkloric about it. Normal peasant women simply wore black cotton or serge when travelling, there was nothing ostentatious about them (for that matter, all the time I was in Strasbourg, I never saw an Alsatian dressed up, save for some military do at a war memorial). And all through Switzerland, I had not noticed any dressing-up, merely an up-and-down accent.

Even the men's jackets were alien: green or greyish, with edible buttons like nuts, funny frogs, buttoned pockets, and those velvet things on the lapels; some of the men had hats with long pheasant feathers. Every time the train stopped, more and more members of the *White Horse Inn* cast got off, to be replaced by others who began eating nasty-looking sausages with clasp-knives. The whole scene was hideously, irremediably rural. Now I cowered in my corner in my blue suit; the Hungarian with whom I had struck up an acquaintance earlier on in the corridor, while still in Switzerland, was also normally dressed – in a black suit, he had a black trilby on the rack above him. Everyone else was decked out in folklore gala. I thought that at any moment accordions and mouth-organs might come out; but at least we were spared that.

It was not just the bizarre, aggressively rural, tribal clothes –

which could probably have told me a great deal more about their wearers than the mere fact that they were all Austrians, that they were from this province or that; and the food they were eating, so messily, on their folklore-covered knees, was probably rural too: home-made sausage and squashy, smelly cheese – it was also their *appearance*: the men all seemed uniformly dark, with little, clipped black moustaches (these must have been an affirmation of something or other), the women were vast, many with blue eyes like china dolls', the children seemed podgy and ugly, and there was a lot of noisy talk, funny-looking squiggly pipes with porcelain bowls, and they seemed to be covered in leather, even the shaggy tobacco- – no doubt home-grown, among the tall sunflowers of rural gardens – pouches were made of leather. Everybody seemed to have very white teeth, the black moustaches accentuated the whiteness, making the men look like beasts of prey. The French had not struck me as alien, the first time I had seen them *en masse* earlier that year; a lot of them had red faces and very pale blue eyes.

Folklore travelled with us the entire length of the red-and-white Republic; there were even some in long white socks on the open balconies of some of the carriages that had been added on after Switzerland. I walked down the train; in one second-class compartment there was a group of priests and young seminarists with pale, pinched faces and currant eyes; they too were eating sausages with clasp-knives – one of the priests had spread out over his cassock-covered knees a huge handkerchief in red-and-white check.

I really felt that the whole train had been set up to put me off. On a weekday, it might not have been so bad, but here were whole families, perhaps whole villages, travelling with earthenware jugs and things rolled up in huge coloured cottons. And much of the rural element persisted right up to the outskirts of the big city: a small dusty square, the grass a dirty brown, cobbles, a single red tram, people drinking out of jugs at tables under the blowsy trees; a little further, an orchestra playing on another square. Utterly, utterly alien, like the great big ugly monastery of Melk, a huge baroque brilliantly white house of death.

When the train stopped, I looked out for Frau Salten; she would be holding up a copy of the *Wiener Journal*. I saw her all right, waiting level with the middle of the train; I remember looking with envy at the dark Rumanians who were going on to Bucharest (in SNCF carriages). Frau Salten took me by both my hands and started shouting for a porter (whatever the word was). It was a bad start. I think my reactions were healthy, for folklore, embroidery, ribbons, feathers, funny hats, leather shorts are generally the outward trappings of some form or other of Green Fascism. Anyhow my arrival had not suggested a good start. Perhaps it served me right for having travelled on a Sunday. The folklore was a premonition of worse to come: a red eiderdown, with the sheet attached to it, apricots with meat, potatoes, and dumplings, rusting wells with roses growing over trellises and with ornamental wheels at the top, baroque churches, too much statuary (including dolphins, water beasts, mermaids, on fountains and façades, in this inland city), coffee topped by whipped cream, crocodiles of little boys led by sallow-faced priests straight out of the Counter-Reformation, the stupid *Wheel* in the Volksprater; it was all there really in the *approach*, there had been *nothing* reassuring, even what was painted on walls – not the good old French wall advertisements, 'Cadoricin', 'Vichy 400km' – I did not know what these ones said, and what they said was in Gothic script; even the clothes-lines failed to reassure, to convey a message of domestic familiarity and ordinariness, for they carried vast quilts, red eiderdowns, a battalion of long white socks, flowered bodices, and ample black skirts with red flowers on them, shirts in bright checks, blackish leather shorts, funny braces. It was all a bit like the cartoons by Hansi of Germans in Alsace before 1914. I noticed from the train that the cafés or beer-places were indicated by branches of fir, or some other tree: anyhow more rural folklore.

I think I have made my point. It all came back to me, my first year in Merton, at the old Scala, when, before the Marx Brothers, one had to sit through awful creamy Austrian films with Paula Wessely (liable to break out into song at any moment) drooling over a rose-covered well with an iron wheel at the top, having her hand kissed by some idiot in a white uniform; the Ch Ch bloodies would soon be in full cry, blowing hunting-horns, yodelling or simply shouting 'Well! Well! Well!' The Bullingdon out *en force*. So much for the creamy Viennese kitsch. Like most of the audience, I was glad of the wonderfully noisy presence of the Bloodies. We had not come for the *well*. Why this ghastly unasked-for hors-d'oeuvre? Then, of course, with the appearance of Groucho and his necessary foil, Margaret Dumont, the start of the serious business of the evening, no hunting hounds needed, but the welcome release of *real* laughter, wave after wave of it: 'Hail Freedonia!', the cabin scene, the opera, and so on, all drawn together by Groucho's long-faced gait and his marvellous responses. We were all positive disciples, and this is what 'a night at the Scala' was all about. If, indeed, there had been any dissidents, they kept quiet; they would not have been heard in any case over the smoke-filled din of laughter (as long as Groucho was in command and in control): the very spirit of the late 1930s.

* * *

I got off to a wrong start with Frau Salten, my hostess. Initially, it had certainly been my fault. She had met me at the station, greeting me, as I have said, with embarrassing exuberance, she had talked incessantly in the taxi in her appalling French, and she had tried to *mother* me, keeping on using what sounded like diminutives. The next day, she had insisted on showing me the sights; I remember wincing with embarrassment in the tram that was taking us around the massive Ringstrasse as she designated each outsize building in her unlovely rendering of French – she pronounced 'Louvre' like 'Louvah'. I suppose it was well-meant, but I resented it deeply, I wanted to discover the city on my own. I must have made my feelings so apparent that she did not persist, writing me off as *mal élevé* and *ingrat* (pronounced 'mallellerfay' and 'ankratt'). I hardly saw her after that; there was *one* dinner-party, attended by Herr Felix Salten and some of his friends from the *Wiener Journal*, in the big dining-room. The food was frightful, the most horrible mixtures – for instance, apricots with meat and normal entrée vegetables. I suppose this was meant to be a foretaste of the realities of Central Europe. An even clearer indication of Central Europe was provided by my *bed*; it did not have a tucked-in upper sheet, it was covered with a huge and stifling red silk eiderdown to the bottom of which the sheet was attached. The red horror always fell off in the course of the night, leaving me cold in the early hours, my feet protruding from the end of the bed. In my bedroom, which was on the ground floor, next to the dining-room, there was a lingering, stale, goulash sort of smell. My bedroom, leading straight from the impressive (but lonely) dining-room, formed a small unit with its own wash-basin and lavatory. The bathroom was down in the basement, where the young maid lived. Thinking back now, I would guess that, perhaps in Habsburg times, the room had been assigned to some sort of superior servant, possibly a butler or a head cook – either would have gone with the Saltens' former *train de vie* in a pre-1914 or 1920 Cottagegasse – but I may be reading too much into the rather odd disposition of my 'family' enclave and its lingering hint of peppery food. The *real* frontier between the two Europes is that between beds tucked in, and beds topped with unattached red things.

I had been told about the Saltens while in Paris. An Austrian friend of the Thulliers, with one of those rather awful Christian names like Heidi or Rudi – anyhow, a girl – had recommended them warmly; it would be just like living in a family, I would learn German over meals, and that sort of thing. Herr Salten, it appeared, was a well-known literary figure, with a wide circle of friends in Viennese society. Later, when I met her at her parents' flat, off the Fleischmarkt, I told her how it had worked out (or, rather, had *not* worked out), that there did not seem to *be* any family, or, if there had been, it had been hidden away upstairs; I did not even know how many children there were, I had just heard vaguely of the son, who was away. Heidi (?) had not seemed surprised. Her family asked me out once to some cousins of theirs who lived in the country near Melk. There had been no mention of the Saltens then. I suppose Felix Salten was quite famous already, *Bambi* had apparently been a great success as a children's book. I don't know whether he made a living as a writer of children's books. The young maid, a pretty seventeen-year-old country girl with very dark eyes which were always smiling, who brought me my supper in solitary splendour in the big dining-room, indicated that he ate upstairs so as not to be disturbed. Perhaps he spent most of his time up there, writing. She also told me, by expressive gestures, that Frau Salten spent most of *her* time in bed, with a little smelly dog on it. I had seen the little dog coming down the stairs, the only emissary from 'up there'. Each time, it sniffed disagreeably around my feet, and went up again. I suppose I could have been a bit nicer to Frau Salten at the beginning; but she was overpowering, and her French was so awful.

I never saw Herr Salten again, after the famous dinner, with the revolving inner circle of the round dining-room table in active motion. The only evidence of his continued presence somewhere upstairs in the fuggy house was a weekly paper addressed to him, *Le Journal de Bulgarie*, which used to arrive once a week, and would lie, rejected and disconsolate, in its wrapper, on a brass tray in the hall. He never took it out of its wrapper; I was the only one who looked at it – at least it was something I could read in this alien neighbourhood, it was a reminder of a still lingering French cultural influence in even the most remote areas of the Balkans. Perhaps Herr Salten had been attached to the Bulgarian Forces in some liaison capacity during the First World War. He might even have known Bulgarian. Certainly, the only time that I met him his French had seemed as rudimentary and as grating as that of his over-zealous wife. I used to read *Le Journal de Bulgarie* whenever it made its timid appearance in the gloomy hall. After 'La Chronique de la Cour et de la Ville' – receptions at the Royal Palace, State Banquets, Government announcements, trade treaties, a brief social column – there was not very much in it, other than articles about the Tsar, Boris, driving trains.

According to the little maid, who seemed to take pity on my evident isolation, there had at one time been a third inmate of the big gloomy house, a son; but he was away now, undergoing treatment. I suppose living in Freud's city, especially in the Cottagegasse, and growing up among the little baby deer of the nearby Wienerwald, would have driven anyone pretty mad. I never saw the son. Frau Salten, however, I was destined to see again, in most unpleasant circumstances. Come to think of it, it must have been Heidi, or whatever her name was, who had given me the name and address of Mme Kallay, a Hungarian lady, as a good German teacher. I was rather relieved *not* to have to talk German over my supper; I ate alone and in silence, save for the 'Grüss Gott!' that the young maid uttered, like an incantation, followed by the removal of my plate, after each course. After I had eaten, I would go to my room next door to read *Les Confessions*. Very soon I lost any motivation for learning German, though I must have had some vague aspirations, for I bought some little books (which I still have) and which I have never read; four of them are dated, rather pretentiously I find: 'Wien, 5 August, 1935', the fifth, 'Offenburg, 15 August, 1935': there are two Grimms, a Ranke, the Book of Ruth, the Book of Judith, and a Goethe. They look nice, are in Gothic script, are prettily bound in decorative covers in flower motifs, and were published in Leipzig. They seem to have been a modest monument to some intention never realized, like some of the books I have in Flemish and in Dutch. Perhaps I was living a bit in a fantasy world, I certainly had very little contact with the real one. What contact did I have with Vienna and with whatever it had to offer? Absolutely nothing, merely the evidence of my eyes, as if I had been deaf and dumb. With Mme Kallay I talked and argued in English; I remember even defending the dreadful Béla Kun, to get a rise out of her (which I did). She greatly admired Schuschnigg and had been alarmed when it had been reported that he had been involved in a car accident. I quite liked Mme Kallay, I think we both enjoyed our disagreements about politics. She also said that I was wasting my mother's money, we were not even making a pretence of conversing in German. She used to laugh when I told her about Frau Salten.

I expect it would have been possible to find out a great deal more about Felix Salten, a public figure no doubt of some repute, as well as about his wife and family. I know that some of them at least ended up in California sometime before or after the Anschluss. But there did not seem any point; Herr Salten was a mysterious recluse, only seen once, who lived upstairs and, as far as I could make out, never went out (an array of hats, one with a feather in its brim, another furry like a beaver, of overcoats, one black with a velvet collar, several belted macs, sticks, umbrellas, alpenstocks, remained undisturbed, unused, in the dark hall). His wife, after the preliminary outing for my benefit, never seemed to go out either. She

44

at least did have some reality. Felix Salten has remained for me the name, in small letters, at the beginning of the Disney film. I seem to remember there was a deer's head, also some antlers, in the musty hall: quite an oldish, experienced deer, not something in Bambi's wide-eyed, milky, pseudo-innocent age-group. Bambi seemed almost to rhyme with Heidi. It was always with a feeling of release that I walked through the sad hall to open the front door on to the street, even on to the 'artistic' Cottagegasse, which one reached down a flight of steps, with its dusty lime trees and its pseudo-rustic chalet-type houses with long wooden eaves, plaster beams disguised as wood, steps up to the front door, basements for the servants, North Oxford Tyrolese. The Cottagegasse had a fake-rural awfulness all of its own. I was ever in a hurry to get out of the 18ster-Bezirk. In the end, I did not even bother to go back home for lunch, I took lunch at sausage stores out in the open, one ate standing up. It was better than the empty dining-room with the round table and the revolving centre, the heavy red velvet curtains, the huge, jug-like stick-stand in the entry. Coming back into the house, through the silent hall, I felt myself enveloped in a sort of airless sadness.

* * *

It was typical of my time in Vienna that summer, as well as my immaturity and my mounting self-pity, that I should have read, with a strong sense of self-identification, Rousseau's *Confessions* (bought, in a rather handsome edition, just before leaving Paris). Apart from this lachrymose companion, I spent a great deal of time walking down immensely long and wide boulevards, exercises in perspective, stretching out for miles between peeling, yellowish blocks of flats with long, unseeing windows, on each window-sill a sort of greyish bolster, what the French call an 'accoudoir', and, on each bolster, at *every* window, pairs of elbows, sleeves rolled up, surmounted by pale, hopeless, male faces, looking out on to the desolate emptiness of those pitilessly straight avenues, constructed, I suppose, to bring in armies of Croat peasants, to keep the workers down. Certainly, in 1935, it did not look difficult to keep the inhabitants of Ottakring and Grinzing (there was even something despairing about the very *sound* of the places) down: they were beaten, unemployed, and hopeless.

One of the things that I retain the most vividly from Vienna in 1935 is the all-pervading sadness. It had a sort of dusty, yellowish, midsummer, run-down feeling about it, an undramatic hopelessness, as if it too had given up. This was most marked in one of the northern areas through which I would sometimes walk to the centre, rather than taking the tram from the corner of Cottagegasse to its terminus at the Michaelerplatz. I would walk a mile or two, then take the overhead, the Gürtel. First of all, a lingering, frayed nostalgia for Better Days seemed to hang over the dreary streets like a yellow cloud: all those seedy little shops – bakeries, laundries, butchers' – using the word 'Habsburg' on their fronts, thus 'Habsburg Wäscherei' (perhaps the Archdukes had indeed been very clean, changing their pants every day). The family name was varied with Christian ones – Rudolf, Otto, Elisabeth, Franz-Josef, Josef, Ferdinand – in a rather pathetic effort to give some sort of lost sparkle to these sad little enterprises. The evocation of the past confronted one from every other shop-sign, this less than twenty years after the death of the ancient Emperor. I recall a 'Radetsky Bücherei', a little shop, bookshop-cum-*Tabaktrafik* with two or three dusty books, all published in Germany, most uninviting and badly printed, in the dirty window, *Volk ohne Raum*, a great favourite in these confined spaces, as if it had been making a point, Kästner's *Emil und die Detektive*, in a cheap, shoddy edition, mixed up with toothpaste, shaving-brushes, cigars, and cheap shag tobacco. There was a shoe shop, with cheap shoes (Bata) and sandals (Bata), that had the word 'Trieste' in its sign. I could have walked the whole way in from the Cottagegasse to the Michaelerplatz following the Habsburg evocations of the generally fading signs, some of the letters askew, producing bizarre, stuttering words: 'FER INAN ', and things like that.

I went once only to Schönbrunn, on a very hot day when there were hardly any visitors to that immense palace, quite as sad as Versailles, but of a sadness much more recent, and so more potent. I remember a small, rather intimate dining-room, under a green dome, the rounded walls in cream-and-gold plaster, the table laid, place-cards beside each plate, one for the ancient Franz-Josef, typed out as 'SMK und K', then a Lobkowits, and other eminent names I cannot remember; it seemed suspended in time, in 1916 or so. There would never be another meal served there, the diners had all gone, or, maybe, had never come, had never been invited for that date. (Perhaps the place-cards, the beautifully starched cloth, the napkins *en éventail*, the magnificent tableware, the shining silver, the candle-sticks with their unused candles, and the meticulously printed menus had all been laid out posthumously, at a time when the huge palace had become a museum? Perhaps it had been based on an old invitation list, dragged up from an archive? Perhaps the whole thing was a charade thought out by a curator, under the Republic?) There was something immensely sad about the ghostly table, the empty glasses, the empty plates, the empty chairs, the menu that would never be tasted, the air of expectancy – and one that would never be realized, the host and his guests were never going to turn up – the names, on *bristols*, of a vanished ruling class. There was a sadness everywhere, there was no escape from it: the gigantism of the Ring, of the University, of the immense Ministries, of the huge neo-Gothic Rathaus, of the vast ornate hotels: everything outsize, much of it, as in the Heldenplatz, proclaiming itself in Latin.

I remember seeing a fire-eater warming up somewhere on the long road to Schönbrunn, thinking that Parisian ones were much better: they took their time, did not rush it, had their children pass round the saucers; but of course I could not understand this one's preliminary sales talk, it might have been equally good: he certainly made people laugh. I recall lots of rather ragged-looking soldiers in greenish uniforms, sitting outside on the steps of a baroque church, playing cards, the cards looked greasy, the soldiers seemed bored and defeated. There were a great many soldiers about, in a variety of uniforms, in the central area of the city; I think some belonged to semi-private armies – Mme Kallay had told me that there was one run by Prince Starhemberg. There were churches everywhere in the centre, most of them baroque and ugly; next to each one there was a church soup-kitchen, handing out ecclesiastical charity in bowls of thin soup to listless queues of dispirited young men with black hair and pale faces, wearing dark trousers and frayed striped shirts without collars and well-worn greenish jackets. There were long queues at any time of the day. Among the crowds in the Volksprater on weekdays, there were always large numbers of young men walking up and down aimlessly, as if killing time.

As if to assert the power of the Church, shortly after my arrival in Vienna, I had been woken up early in the morning by the insistent sound of tolling bells, coming, it seemed, from every tower in the older part of the city. The continuous, solemn jangling of hundreds of bells – churches, monasteries, convents, seminaries – carried quite clearly up to the heights of the Cottagegasse, as if amplified by the huge bowl in which the lower city was situated. My room seemed to hum with the noise. Bringing in my breakfast, the little maid had indicated to me that it was the first anniversary of the murder of Dollfuss.

Very early on in the course of my stay and of my succession of rudderless days, walking to no particular purpose, save just to fill the time, going in this direction or that, I had been drawn to the periphery: beyond the gasworks and the low-lying, smokeless factories, one of which had manufactured cars at some remote time (the Archduke's car that had not arrived in time, at Sarajevo, had been of that make), the big river port on the dirty, greyish Danube, with white river boats going to Bratislava, Budapest, and, on one landing-stage, marvellously exotic and also with mysterious Cyrillic lettering, 'BEOGRAD', with words that must have been in Serbo-Croat. I spent quite a lot of time hanging about that area, watching the passengers embark with their bags, and trying to guess their nationality, for their clothes did not give anything much away; they were not got up in folklore, but, for July, they all seemed heavily clad, as if they had been carrying their entire wardrobes on their backs. I noticed that one woman, as she climed up the steep gangway to what I took to be the Belgrade boat, was wearing four skirts. I suppose I gravitated towards the river port, as, later, I did towards a railway terminus, because it offered the concrete evidence of the possibility of escape from this inland city. Railway stations, the quaysides of ports, are the natural haunts of lonely people.

In a misguided moment, one day I even took a boat that was going upstream (I did not enquire *how far* upstream; the price of a return ticket, which was very reasonable, only a few schilling, suggested just a quick turn-about). It was an appalling experience: on the lower deck, a noisy, apparently yodelling bar, with people swilling down beer out of china jugs, tables set for lunch (surely there would not be enough time for a *meal?*), a string orchestra on a raised platform playing vigorously, with a sort of awful gaiety, without a pause. The top deck turned out to be even worse: another orchestra, tirelessly churning out Strauss waltzes, young couples dancing in close embrace and in apparent blissful union. I felt myself conspicuous as about the only person who was unaccompanied, though I suppose that in fact no one would have noticed me (save, of course, for my heavy winter attire). The trip filled the best part of an entire day; shortly after we had at last turned round, about at the level, I think, of Melk, to head downstream, the lights were turned on on both decks, with clusters of coloured ones on the top deck, and we now had Strauss by moonlight, as the young couples, tireless, whirled around. I stood gloomily leaning over the rail at the stern, watching the white trail left by the boat in the inky water, longing to get clear of the damned river and my feet once more on land. I don't think in fact anyone noticed me, they were all enjoying themselves much too much. I got back to the Cottagegasse too late for my supper. I apologized to the little maid, who was clearing up in the kitchen. She said she hoped that I had had a good outing, Vienna got so hot in July – I could make out most of this – and that she would fix me up with some cold meat and gherkins and a carafe of white wine, which she did. At least I was on dry land again; the gloomy dining-room seemed pleasantly quiet.

The experience should have been enough to have put me off day or half-day trips out of the city. But I thought it might be all right provided I avoided the river. Once I took a sort of tram train to Wiener-Neustadt. The journey was quite agreeable, this was not a pleasure outing, my fellow passengers were silent, reading their papers, or were talking in low voices. I have always enjoyed trams, and this one was a long affair, with three carriages. But, on arrival, I went to an open-air café to have some lunch. A rather surly waiter directed me to a table at which there was only one chair, while at the same time eyeing my clothing with evident disapproval. Everywhere there were couples or family parties. My table was very small, there was just room for a plate of salami, a hunk of bread, and a large carafe of red wine (which was quite good). I sat reading *L'Oeuvre*. There was an orchestra, of course.

Another time, instead of heading downhill towards the Habsburg shops and the Gürtel, I turned left at the end of the Cottagegasse and walked up in the direction of the Wienerwald, in the hope that it might be a bit fresher up there. It turned out to be an uphill climb through several different layers of kitsch. That, relatively restrained, of the massive pseudo-chalets of the Cottagegasse soon gave way to a more and more varied extravaganza of garden gnomery: terracotta rabbits, cats, and dogs, little red forts with painted bricks, moated and guarded by fierce little scarlet guns on wheels, herons in white stone bending over rock pools with concrete bottoms, large concrete toadstools sheltering sugary girls dressed in blue and pink pinafores, and an architecture of an altogether more human proportion than the heavily professional arrogance of the Cottagegasse. Here, many of the houses were entirely of wood, some looked as if they had been put together from a variety of odd bits and pieces: window frames that were slightly askew, shutters of different sizes and contrasting colours, planks of wood forming outside walls in differing grain and texture, even letter-boxes that seemed to have been made out of something else – by their owners. There was something appealing and humble about these life-size, multicoloured, ill-constructed dolls' houses, with odd bits and pieces added on to them, as if in afterthought, or in recognition of some fairly modest material promotion. From what period had these ramshackle dwellings, superior garden sheds with trimmings, dated? Had they been mute witnesses of the breakup of the old Empire? Had they been *safe*, because out-of-the-way, havens from the violent politics of the Vienna of the 1920s and 30s? Anyhow, it looked as if the inhabitants of these little places – there were house names burnt in in black, Gothic script (I expect they were unassuming ones, the German equivalents of 'Sarmesoufy', and that sort of statement of limited intent) on dark-brown wooden pallets – would have been living at a level that was beyond the reach of Freud and his kind (I felt that the Cottagegasse, and perhaps the flats overlooking the Ringstrasse, would have provided their ideal terrain) and safely above the embattled ideologies of the dreadful, collective Karl-Marx-Hof, now roofless, shot through with cannon holes, and uninhabited.

I passed men in shirt-sleeves working in their miniature gardens, among the towering sunflowers. Some of them waved to me, as I clambered, sweating profusely, past, calling out what must have been greetings. I wished I could have responded. They must have thought me an odd figure, in my black hat and winter overcoat, and clutching my leather dispatch-case (which went along on all such trips – it had even been with me on the Danube – and which in fact only contained the latest number of *L'Oeuvre*, my current and always lachrymose Jean-Jacques, and possibly a volume of Villon). The further up I climbed, the more and more nervous I became of being thus exposed to more friendly greetings, more verbal signals that called for recognition, some sort of response, the expected exchange, if only of banalities. I felt myself very conspicuous (I certainly was) and wished that I could have found a path further away from the close, but apparently friendly, scrutiny of the tiny front gardens.

The straggling line of the little brightly coloured wooden houses gave out at the edge of the forest, at the same time as the dusty, unmade road. This was *walkers'* country, rather consciously so, as if designed for people who made a sort of profession of walking. The point seemed to be emphasized by the well-laid-out paths, clearly bordered by neat lines of bricks, and by the wooden seats that were placed at carefully selected points that gave recommended views, whether of the city, or of the distant hills beyond. Just in case any walker should find himself losing his way, little wooden signposts were attached to the bark of every tenth fir-tree. Clearly, I was unsuitably dressed, but it was all the same to me: walking beneath the high, double, yellowish wall of barrack-like flats, in Ottakring or Grinzing, or walking on the pine needles along the carefully indicated, authorized paths. At least it was cool under the trees, and there was a slight, rustling breeze. I was overtaken by several couples, as well as by large groups of *real* walkers, properly dressed and properly shod, and carrying rucksacks and long sticks, slightly bent forward, giving a sense of purpose to their outings. Some of the groups were singing, presumably they were walking-songs. Eventually, I found – I could hardly have avoided doing so, it had been indicated a dozen times on signposts with pointed arrows – an open-air café, in a large clearing of the woods. The setting was pleasant, and could have been restful. But there was an orchestra playing, and it looked as if it were not going to go away.

In the early evenings, I often used to walk to the nearby Türkenschanzpark, only ten minutes from the Cottagegasse. It was a small, very formal park, perched on a steep mound, and it offered a print-like general view of the city, spread out in the plain below, with all its towers and spires and bulbous domes, the long skyline dominated by the twin towers of the Stefanskirche. I was sitting on a green-painted seat, waiting for my supper-time. An old man came up and, with slow deliberation, letting himself down slowly, sat down beside me, smiling and saying something that might have been a question or a greeting, or merely an observation on the subject of the weather (it had been yet another scorching day). All I could manage in reply was that I was English and that I did not understand very much German. The old man turned away, disappointed, spat copiously on the concrete path, and, pulling deeply on his squiggly pipe, said: 'Ach so.' It seemed to be the final comment both on my stay and on my total inability to communicate. *Ach so*.

* * *

It was of Lamartine, I think, that it had been said: 'Il était devenu révolutionnaire pour se désennuyer.' In my own case, it can only have been a combination of loneliness and boredom: a potent and dangerous concoction. If I had been fully occupied, had learnt a bit of German, and had acquired even a working level of sociability, I would no doubt have found a more profitable way of spending my time. I have never been one for Causes, have always steered clear of collective actions, have never been involved in Protest, have never joined an organization, and have always refused to sign petitions. This was the *one* exception, and it was caused by boredom. My, mercifully brief, Vienna period was the only time I have ever been bored in my life. You might say that the terse, ill-produced messages may have been timid efforts to escape from loneliness, smudged signals, on dirty bits of paper, to communicate with other nameless human beings. Or perhaps I am making too much of it. I think I was just silly, thoughtless, and a bit arrogant. And, after all, I was a British Subject by Birth, I had Sir John Simon, together with his spidery signature and our country's elaborate coat of arms, to protect me. Alas, when he *could* have protected me, I left him at home in the Cottagegasse and had my pockets, *all* my pockets (jacket, trousers, overcoat) full of all those bits of paper that did *not* protect me, making me into an alien acting suspiciously.

On one of several visits to the flat belonging to 'Heidi's' parents, high up overlooking the Fleischmarkt, near the fashionable Graben and the wealthy Kärntnerstrasse, I had spotted the plate of the Quaker Office. In those days, I greatly approved of the Quakers: they seemed everywhere to support the right side. Anyhow, one afternoon, I went in, and was eventually introduced to the head of the Quaker Mission in Austria, an American lady with rimless spectacles, very cool, despite the sweltering heat, brisk, businesslike, and welcoming, Miss Cadbury, of an American branch of the chocolate family. Could there be any part-time work for me? *Indeed*, there could, room was made for me at a table facing on to a backyard, and I started there and then. I was to put into grammatical English a series of reports that had been prepared by Austrian volunteer helpers and sympathizers; the reports were to go to the Quaker Headquarters in the United States. They concerned health and hygiene conditions in the various camps that had been set up, well away from Vienna, in rural areas such as Carinthia and the Steiermark, for the wives and families who had lost all their possessions in the bombardment of the Karl-Marx-Hof the previous year, and whose husbands, brothers, and sons were either living in exile in Prague, or had been killed in the fighting, or were in prison awaiting trial. There were also reports on individual families who were still living at home, but were deemed to be in urgent need of relief. As can be imagined, the Schuschnigg Government did not look on the *Freunden* with very much sympathy.

53

I took to working there four afternoons a week, as much as anything else for something to do. I found the work tedious: a lot
about digging drainage trenches and latrines, water supply, injec-
tions, condensed milk for the infants, basic rations, bandages,
medical supplies, the issue of tents and blankets, the distribution
of warm clothing at the approach of autumn, regular inspections
by teams of American doctors. But the circular, and the cyclostyled
or stencilled pamphlets, that were given to me by sympathizers
were less so: references to 'in Gefängnis', and that sort of thing –
men held in prison, with their names, messages of support and
encouragement from Otto Bauer and Karl Seitz. I was just over
eighteen, priggish, self-righteous, fixed in my opinions, and drift-
ing in an alien limbo. At each of my visits to the Office, I acquired
more papers; some of them I would leave under my empty glass,
after calling, 'Herr Ober', and paying for my beer or glass of wine.
(*Herr Ober* was generally a splendid pre-1914 figure, in black
jacket, white shirt, black tie, and long white overall: hardly potential revolutionary material.) I wasn't particularly zealous about my
distribution of these little bits of paper protest, but I did get rid of
quite a few, leaving them on the seats of trams, on those of the
Gürtel, or on those of municipal parks (the Türkenschanzpark was
well served in this respect). Later, for I kept getting fresh supplies,
I think I even left personal messages in metal letter-boxes. Others,
with glued backs, I stuck up on lampposts at eye level. It all seemed
rather fun.

I am not sure whether Miss Cadbury was aware of this aspect of
my unpaid 'part-time work', but she must have known that some of
the literature came off the typewriters and stencils in use in the
office. The Consul told me later on, when he visited me, that there
had been a search of the Quaker place. I don't suppose that, after
that, Miss Cadbury can have had very Quakerish feelings about me.
Or she may have told the authorities that as I was a volunteer helper,
her organization could not be held responsible for my 'out of
school' activities. For that matter, the authorities may have taken
the line that my modest essays at sedition had been harmless
enough and had not been worth any serious consideration. It is
equally possible that Miss Cadbury may have been sent somewhere

else; there was always plenty of work for the Quakers in the second half of the 1930s.

* * *

Did I stumble on the strange place only that once? Or did I make several visits? That I cannot remember. But I do well remember the excitement of discovering the place: a once handsome, even grand, city terminus, in a heavy classical style, a pale yellow like so much in that yellowy city, a station that had gone dead at some distant point in time, 1918 or 1919, just as the Emperor's little round dining-room had gone dead sometime in 1916. I never went to the War Museum, which I think was in the Belvedere Palace, so I never saw the blood-bespattered light-blue uniform of Franz-Ferdinand and the beautiful dress worn by Sophie Chotek, with the white bird as a head-dress, nor the borrowed car that had turned the wrong way by the bridge, giving Princip his second chance. I don't know why I missed this.

But the Ostbahnhof was *not* a museum, there was nothing self-conscious or arranged about it, I don't think it was even meant to be seen at all; indeed, as I recall, I had to get through some rotting wooden fencing to get into the place. The glass had fallen out of the cover over the forecourt: the *pavé*, on which, at some remote time, taxis, cabs, and private carriages had pulled up, was overgrown with thick purple weeds; all the glass had gone from the huge roof over the dozen or so platforms. Most extraordinary of all, there were eight or nine complete trains standing idle at the platforms. Some had the engine facing inwards, towards the buffers; others had the engine at the far end, as if they had been about to leave. The engines had tall stacks and huge wheels. The carriages had open platforms, like little balconies, at each end. They looked as if they dated back to the First World War; I had seen photographs of the mobilization of the Austro-Hungarian armies – men on their knees being blessed by priests – and these carriages were similar. Now I cannot remember what colour they were (the paint in any case was flaking); they might have been a dark red. There were some mouldering postal vans wide open, with black eagles on their sides. The first-class compartments had beige upholstery with yellowish and greenish damp marks, the stuffing coming out. Most were passenger trains, but there was at least one goods train at the far end.

The locomotives, the carriages, the goods trucks, the postal vans were all covered in ivy; reddish creeper, prickly-looking weeds had settled firmly in between the lines. I was at once fascinated by the place, by the decay, the stillness, the immobility, as if time had suddenly stopped on a given day. Had the trains facing inwards actually brought their passengers to their destinations? Had the people in the trains facing outwards had to get out? Had all this happened in one go? Or had the station gradually slipped into immobility and silence in a sort of creeping paralysis? On this last time – assuming that I had been there before, and I think I had, I seem to remember asking Miss Cadbury about the Ostbahnhof, and she told me she thought that it had been pulled down, at a time when the frontier with the newly formed Czechoslovakia had been closed – I spent three-quarters of an hour in wonderment, taking it all in, even climbing on to some of the open carriage platforms which, under the cascading ivy and creeper, could have formed a beer garden. Everything was covered with pigeon droppings. Most of the window glass had gone, some of the windows were down, with mouldering leather straps hanging inside, the first-class compartments had light green curtains.

I had been so absorbed that I had not noticed the shambling figure of a middle-aged man with white hair, who was in semi-uniform: he was wearing a green military tunic and civilian trousers. He said something to me, it sounded angry, and like a question; then he took me firmly by the right arm, walking me towards a glass door that had been painted over. He opened the door with a key, went inside, saying something like 'Wait for me here.' I should have made a bolt for it, I had noticed that the man had a limp. But I waited outside the door, letting things take their course. I think I was curious to know what would happen next. He led me out of the ruined station, saying something about it being military property (it didn't look to me as if I had inadvertently stumbled on the secrets of Austrian post-war rearmament, but rather as if I had walked back into 1914 or 1917), and, getting out another key – my middle-aged companion seemed to have been the sole guardian of the ghostly terminus – opening a gate in a part of the fencing that was still intact.

We went down a long, straight, desolate avenue, the pale faces were at their usual posts, looking out, their elbows resting on the greyish window-sill bolsters. We must have made an odd pair: the limping semi-soldier, his rifle held unmilitarily parallel with the ground by its long green strap, and myself in a blue suit, dark over-coat, but for once without the dispatch-case, my fair hair sticking up in a tuft at the crown. I had to slow up so as to keep pace with my captor, who had now lit a cigarette of blackish tobacco. The pavements were empty, but several red trams, three carriages each, went clanking by. I wasn't particularly worried, I could not see that I had committed any grave offence: trespassing, perhaps, but that was all.

After about ten minutes, we came to a police station. There were three men in uniform, their collars unbuttoned, their belts hanging on the backs of their chairs. Playing-cards were scattered on the table. The man in the middle, fat and bald, was smoking a squiggly pipe. One of the three, younger than the other two, made me take off my overcoat and my jacket, going through the pockets. This was a very bad moment and I was suddenly really frightened. For the last three or four days I had been carrying around the little bits of paper bearing the stencilled slogans. I had not been doing any deliveries for nearly a week, and the papers had accumulated in all my pockets (soon it was the turn of my trousers to have the pockets turned inside out). The man in the middle went through the papers, small squares and rectangles, with the skill of a card-player, as if he had been shuffling the pack (would indeed it had been a pack!), exclaiming every now and then in amazement and apparent anger. He started shouting questions at me; I said I did not understand German very well, so the younger man kicked me in the stomach, and I was sick on his green uniform trousers. My captor was sent away, my tie, my braces and shoe-laces were removed. The pamphlets, papers, and the contents of my pockets, including some schilling notes and my fountain-pen, were put in a bag.

Two of the policemen took me out into the street and made me walk between them in the middle of the road; I kept stumbling on the tramlines. The pale faces at the windows started shouting (perhaps they were shouting words of encouragement), the policemen made me walk faster and faster, they were shouting, too, at me: 'Schneller, schneller.' We stopped at a second police station. This time I had my face slapped very hard; luckily, I was not wearing my glasses (they were in the bag). I was told that I was a Czech. There was a third stop, paperwork, a long form that I tried to read upside-down, I thought it must be a warrant. A very long walk, this time, still between my two companions, but now we kept to the pavement, walking at a normal pace; there were more people about, shops, quite a lot of traffic. It was a part of Vienna I had never been to, very run-down, but noisy, with a lot of cafés, the people at the tables looking at me briefly, then taking up their newspapers. It was clear that I was not an object of any great interest. I had no watch, quite a lot of time must have gone by since my 'arrest' at the former terminus, for people seemed to be coming out of work, lights were going on; for many perhaps the best part of the day was beginning. I was not at all certain how the best part of the day was going to end for me. Fortunately, I was not hungry. I had pains in my stomach and still felt a bit sick. It was a relief to reach the big, dark prison building. I was checked in on a huge, black-covered prison register, my name written down in elegant copperplate by an ancient scribe, who took his time over it: 'Kob, Student, von Prag.' Then I was taken to a cell on my own, and locked in, after my shoes had been taken away.

Early next morning I was unlocked and taken to the wash-room and the lavatory. There were lots of tough-looking men with tattoos on their arms and their chests, one had a mermaid in three colours (I have been thinking about him, while writing this up: he must have been a sailor; perhaps he had been in Horthy's navy in the First World War? – though he did not seem *that* old).

My fellow prisoners seemed friendly, though I could not understand what they were saying. Later I was given a mug of weak coffee. Then the doctor came, examined me briefly, and spoke the single word: 'Gut.' The prison must have been pretty central, from the cell I could hear the sound of trams, their bells ringing insistently, the shouts of market salesmen. The cell was cool and rather dark. It did not seem like July. I had been arrested on a Monday so it must be Tuesday.

I had given my Cottagegasse address when I had first been admitted to prison and they had written my (Czech) name down in the huge register. But they had been in no hurry to follow it up and it was about a week before two detectives had called up there, causing, so I gathered after my release, the Saltens something of a panic. They had searched my room and found my passport. This had at least established both my identity and the fact that not only was I not from Prague, but that I had never been there. This was the first passport issued to me (in the name of Sir John Simon) and there had been no Czech visa in it. When I was arrested, I had not been carrying my identity papers; I had never carried any in Paris. The British Consul had been informed of my arrest. A day or two after they had been to the Cottagegasse, I was interviewed in the prison office by a member of the State Security. He was not in uniform, but had green velvet frogs on the lapels of his collar. He was a mild-looking man, middle-class in appearance, and rather academic. He asked me one or two questions, wanted to know how I had obtained the seditious material; I said that I had been approached by someone in the street. He did not press me on this, and went on to say that I had been very foolish, but that I was very young, that it had been unwise to play with the politics of a foreign country, and that I had to realize that the current political situation in Austria was very fluid and insecure, and that the future was very uncertain. Austria was not England. He spoke rather like a schoolmaster, extended his hand after he had finished, and left, saying that I would be released very shortly, but that I would be hearing from the State Police Headquarters.

The Consul came to see me on the same day; he was a jolly, hearty man, with a rugged face: 'You seem to have got yourself into quite a mess, old man' was his opening remark. He said that of course I had been very unwise to have gone around with all those incriminating bits of paper in my pockets – after all, it had been none of my business (he was perfectly right); but, he went on, it would have been even worse if I had been caught trying to distribute any of them, then I would have been in very serious trouble. He even apologized for not having come sooner, but he had not been informed of my arrest when it had taken place. Let this be a lesson always to carry my passport, or some form of identification, around with me at all times. I took his advice in this respect. Before leaving, he told me that 'my landlady', as he described Frau Salten, had been very rude to him and had said that she had known from the start that I was a trouble-maker; he ended up by calling her 'an old trout'. He was the first British Consul I had ever met. Those I were to meet much later in life were not nearly so nice, nor so effective.

When I was released from prison, I still had not discovered its name: it was almost certainly a very prestigious one, they nearly always are. And I still had not found out in what part of the city it was situated. Clutching the little bag containing my belongings, I took the first taxi I saw in the street outside – there was quite a line of them waiting there, I don't know whether this had any political significance – and had myself driven to the Cottagegasse. My room was in a terrible mess, with papers, books, clothes, and bedding scattered all over the place, drawers open. It was clear that it had been thoroughly searched. The house was as silent as usual, no one had heard me come in – which was just as well, I was not relishing the prospect of coming face to face with 'my landlady'. There was a bathroom (that was used by the little maid) beyond the kitchen, in the basement. I had been sleeping in my underclothes for well over a week. I went to have a bath, and changed into clean clothes. I was not exactly glad to be back in the Cottagegasse, which could not have even been described as a base, but rather as a point of departure; but it was nice to be free again. I decided to take a walk to the Türkenschanzpark, and, on the way back, I treated myself to a couple of beers in a grubby little café frequented by men in long off-white coats – they seemed to have been from the nearby *Apotheke*. Their coats brought out the redness of their faces. They were talking very loud and seemed to be sharing some huge joke. For once, I felt genuinely sorry that I could not share it with them. I decided to stay on a bit longer, had a third beer, and ate a cooked sausage in a rich sauce. I felt almost happy. It was an unusual experience. I even felt a little sad that I would soon be leaving Vienna, only a matter of days. I walked home, and went to bed, without reading *Émile*, or whatever other self-pitying Jean-Jacques I had been falling back on, before my arrest and imprisonment.

* * *

Each state provides its own sinister colour for its own peremptory and threatening mail. With us, it is beige and OHMS. In France, it is pale blue: tax demands for immediate payment, urgent summonses to the Prefecture of Police, a *service de refoulement*, as if a normally innocuous Cambridge blue had been transformed into the colour of urgency and dire threat. I imagine mobilization orders would likewise have come in blue. In Austria, at least in 1935, this alarming and unwelcome type of mail came in pale yellow. Perhaps it represented a hangover from the background of the old black double-headed eagle of *K und K* days, black on yellow, the Habsburg ancestral colours. The *Klagen* that would be waved at me, like a vengeful flag, by Frau Salten a few days later, would also be yellow. Anyhow, the morning after my drinks at the café with the red-faced men from the *Apotheke*, a yellow envelope was awaiting me at my place on the round dining-room table. It was a summons to report on the following day at the Main Police Headquarters, *Ausländer*-something-something.

I went there on time the next day, an official with green velvet frogs on his lapels explained to me that I had the choice between being expelled within twenty-four hours, or being allowed to stay for a further month, and reporting to the Central State Police each morning at nine o'clock. Of course I opted for expulsion, though, I suppose, reporting each day at nine might have provided some sort of structure to what had been up till then my rather chaotic and aimless days (the afternoons at the Quaker place had merely offered me two or three people to talk to and to listen to in their halting English). I just wanted to get *out*. If I had found an alternative to the Cottagegasse, it might have been different. But, before I left, I was once more confronted by Frau Salten. She served me a yellow *Klagen* – the letters of that sinister-sounding word (it had a sort of knell about it) were in very black, Gothic script, as if in an effort to add an extra sting of sheer venom to the threat; there was plenty of venom, too, in her voice, as, in her dreadful French, she explained what the yellow paper was all about, for the month that had been cut off my stay as the result of my expulsion; I think my mother had to telegraph the money before 'my landlady' would release my trunk. (I remember thinking that my mother might have been fully justified in serving a similar summons on Frau Salten over the 'family atmosphere' and 'the German at meals' with which I had not been provided.) It gave me some slight satisfaction to reflect that Frau Salten would not be quite rid of me even then; for the next month, *L'Oeuvre* would continue to arrive daily at the Cottagegasse, a mute reminder of the former inhabitant of the ground-floor bedroom next to the dining-room. Perhaps each copy would go straight into the rubbish, or, maybe, like the unwanted *Journal de Bulgarie*, it would accumulate, in its wrapper, in the stuffy hall.

My two fellow-travellers, both of whom wore green velvet frogs in their lapels, left the first-class compartment of the train at the Swiss frontier. It was a suitable farewell to Austria. I was convinced that I would never return either to Austria or to its sad capital. It was a relief to be back in Switzerland. I walked down the train to a third-class compartment and asked the ticket-collector to write me out a single ticket from the Swiss frontier to Strasbourg. I shall always remember my sense of home-coming at seeing the first French *douaniers*, the broad red stripe down the sides of their blue trousers, at the international station of Basle.

I think my trunk followed me, after a few days, sent on to my Strasbourg address, Pension Évangélique, 7 Quai Finkmatt, on the far side of the canal, in a strictly Protestant quarter, separated by water from the Old Town, *la Petite France*, and the cathedral area. The *pension* was a spotlessly clean establishment – there was something medical about the cleanliness – with very sparse, shining white rooms, run by Lutherans. There was a Bible Martin on the bedside-table next to my black metal bed. I was in good hands. No alcohol was allowed to be served on the premises, but there were several quiet, cool cafés on the quayside of the canal, just round the corner. At the *pension*, over breakfast (yoghurt) I got to know a very friendly Lebanese student of my age who had been sent by his family to work at the University medical school and who spoke beautiful, slightly old-fashioned French. He told me that Beyrouth, where he lived, was both very French and very elegant, describing it as 'the Paris of the Middle East'. We used to have drinks together, sitting by the canal. He always ordered a *menthe verte*; I drank a local beer.

Strasbourg had been my own choice: it represented some residual intention, on my part, of applying myself to learning German. In fact, in the course of my stay there, I only spoke French. At the big Berger-Levrault bookshop, I bought an anthology of Soviet litera-ture of the 1920s and early 30s in French translation, and published by *nrf*. It represented part of the cure after Vienna. I read *L'Oeuvre* every morning, *Le Canard enchaîné* every Wednesday. During the day, I spent most of my time at the University library, reading Jean Jaurès and other historians of the French Revolution. In the early evening, I liked walking in the very formal gardens of L'Orangerie. Strasbourg was full of soldiers, some of them still in *bleu horizon*, others in khaki. It was just about the time of the switch over from the former to the latter. I felt myself in the know, as if I had long been familiar with such military matters. All in all, I was very happy in Strasbourg.

4

Into and Out of the War

SOMETIME IN 1937, it would have been early in January, or it might have been at Easter – all I can remember is that it was very cold – I took a room in a quiet hotel in Abingdon for the week before the beginning of Term. I wanted to be completely on my own, in a place where I knew no one, in order to catch up on my reading. I had spotted the hotel on one of my walks, and had been attracted by its rather airless stillness and its air of satisfied neglect. The place seemed to have been left behind or had just quietly given up competing. Perhaps no one, apart from a few commercial travellers, ever had reason to stay in Abingdon, at least at that time of the year (the summer might have brought parents of boys at Radley at weekends). I had taken a good look round, and had selected, as a suitable retreat for what I hoped would be a studious week, the writing-room off the landing on the first floor, the long eighteenth-century window of which looked out on to the market square. The room was decorated with an autumnal wallpaper of dark and paler browns, and on the walls there were about twenty cartoons, marked with damp at the edges, of Edwardian worthies by 'Spy'. The function of the room was emphasized by the massive presence, against two of the walls and in the recess of the window that faced on to the courtyard, of half a dozen desks covered in green baize, large glass inkpots with brass tops inserted in holes at the top right-hand side of each desk (the room had not been designed for the use of left-handers like myself). In the middle of the room, on a faded but still handsome carpet, there stood a large rosewood round table with scalloped edges. It did not seem to serve any specific function connected either with writing or with cards, but it provided the base for an enormous green and white vase with leaf designs that held long, dusty sprigs of pampas grass. The room, which had the words WRITING ROOM, in large black letters on a dark brown background, over the lintel of the door that led off the landing, did not look as if it had been used, even for its gloomily advertised purpose, for a good many months.

During the day I sat at the desk that faced the window on to the long narrow courtyard, reading up on twelfth-, thirteenth-, and fourteenth-century English history, observed superciliously from the chocolate-and-beige wall, by 'Spy's' bewigged judges, monocled clubmen, sportsmen with double-barrelled shot-guns and wearing long yellow leggings, and characters wearing top hats and spats. Throughout the week that I worked there, no one came into the room; the fire had been lit early in the morning and I kept it going by putting on more slow-burning logs.

After a day's reading, broken by an afternoon walk by the river, I took a novel down to read in the dining-room during dinner. There was an elderly couple at a table some distance from mine. They talked in whispers as if they had been in church. I think they must have been permanent fixtures, like the heavy furniture and the dusty candelabra hanging from the ceiling; perhaps they were residents, for they addressed the elderly waitress by her Christian name, 'Hilda'. Apart from looking at me with some surprise, as if I had been too young to be in such a venerable place, and possibly because I was casually dressed in a sports coat and grey flannels, the first evening that I came down, they paid me no further attention, and I was able to lean my novel – a handsome green-bound edition, in thick paper and contemporary type, of *Mansfield Park* – against a silver toast-rack that had been left over from breakfast; the far side of the table always remained laid for breakfast, so that, when I came down in the morning, I had to sit in the chair opposite, it was just a matter of changing places. As each day I had managed to put in six or seven hours' work upstairs in the green, beige, and chocolate Writing Room, I allowed myself the indulgence of a bottle of red wine which the elderly waitress brought me reverently wrapped up in a large linen napkin. Later, I had coffee in the lounge, then went to the bar for a few pints of very good local beer. There were always the same four red-faced men playing shove-ha'penny, using Napoleon III *sous* worn wafer thin that sped with the slightest touch, and there were generally two or three couples sitting up at the bar, talking to the barman, who was dressed in a not very white coat. Apart from the Napoleonic *sous*, it had been an entirely English day so far; it could not have been *more* English.

But Europe – a fey and fancy one – started once I had gone up to the big, solid bedroom, wainscoted in dull white paint, and shut the heavy white door behind me. It had been a yellow-covered edition of *Pelléas et Mélisande*, a couple thus bizarrely twinned with the unassuming former Berkshire market town. I had managed to convince myself that somehow Maeterlinck must have been important, or it may have been just the appeal of his curiously exotic surname. Maeterlinck had been a bad mistake, but the real importance of my week's stay, apart from the hours of work in the Writing Room, had been the discovery of the sheer joy of being *alone*, on my own in a hotel. Much of my life at this time would be spent seeking out the comforting anonymity of country hotels, or hotels in small market towns. Part of the attraction would have been a delayed reaction to the lack of privacy of a Public School in the 1930s.

* * *

Of course, at this time, and still more, later, during the Second World War, English hotels were very good value, and often agreeably dilapidated, with old novels in the bookcases of morning-rooms or in faded-chintz drawing-rooms, offering an improbable perception of a not too distant Europe: for instance, a little book of Spanish short stories, in translation, discovered in a revolving bookcase in the rather damp, musty drawing-room of a small hotel in the Usk Valley in 1942 or 1943, one of those pleasant surprises provided by the blind chance of Army postings, an entirely unexpected bit of luck, pure bonus, that might make one's day, or even a week; a bit like picking up a copy of Supervielle's *L'Enfant de la haute mer*, in quite a handsome French edition, the discreet and prestigious white, black, and red of the *nrf*, in a sixpenny trough outside a small bookshop adjoining a pleasant pub the bay window of which faced on to a small harbour at Leigh-on-Sea, on a Saturday in the spring of 1944, at a time when I had been stationed somewhere near Tilbury (I would take the train to Upminster, I think). Supervielle had been a great traveller and had spent much of his life in Uruguay or up the Amazon, but it still had been a most agreeable surprise to see him turning up in 'All Books in This Box Sixpence Only' next door to Southend. The encounter on that occasion did indeed make my weekend *and* my week. The gentle Basque novelist and poet has belonged ever since as indissolubly and as improbably to Leigh-on-Sea, in the unpredictable jumble-room of my memory, as do Pelléas and Mélisande to a hotel in Abingdon.

How had so many of these quiet country hotels come by such disparate collections, ranging from Agatha Christie, P. G. Wodehouse, Stanley J. Weyman, Mary Webb, Ethel M. Dell, to translations of nineteenth-century Spanish novelists and short-story writers? No one can have planned such random libraries. Perhaps they represented an accumulation of books that had been left by previous residents by mistake, or because they had finished reading them, or had been bored by them and had given them up? Of course, there would have been few other ways of spending time on wet afternoons or dripping mornings between elevenses and lunch-time, apart from listening to the wireless or knitting. Most of the books would be stained with damp, their pages, browning at the edges, sticking together. But what a width of appeals and interests, making of small country hotels chaotic replicas, on a tiny scale, of Hall's Bookshop in Tunbridge Wells! Not commercial-traveller fare, but, like the faded chintzes, also stained with damp, sad little monuments to timid middle-class excursions into exoticism, or memories of travel, or accounts of difficult journeys that one would never have to make but that were nice to read about in front of even a sputtering fire in a smoky grate; or former business links, like the oldish man, a bachelor, who lived, as a permanent resident, in the small William IV Private Hotel, with greening iron balconies, facing on to the Common, next to the Tunbridge Wells and Counties

Club, who had spent a career in Portugal, before coming to rest in that quiet place, possibly spending part of his time reading books in Portuguese, if there were enough of them to keep him going, whom I went to see sometime early in 1940, when it had been particularly nice to find someone who would talk to me about Portugal, an infinitely desirable place, a *neutral* country apparently so far removed from it all. Or one might run into straggling tufts of former imperial experience: memoirs of Sudan Civil Servants, retired Governors of the White Nile, descriptions of service in Indian Railways, recollections of a District Commissioner in Nigeria.

So there would be something agreeably *un*predictable about such places: small country hotels on the Welsh Border, as unplanned as the non-matching armchairs, upright chairs with loose backs, tiny children's chairs low on the ground, squat gilt chairs with gilded clawed hooves to support them, two or three leather poufs with lozenge designs alternating in dark and pale brown and suggestive of the 1920s, as if the furniture, like the books, had gradually taken over these quiet, damp rooms, haphazard, moving in on separate formations, or just one at a time, over a long period. The pictures on the walls – dark green wallpaper – would be more predictable and more local: ruined keeps and castles, plentiful in that part of the world, ancient bridges, roofless abbeys, hunting prints of the local meet, a faded seventeenth-century county map, making the suddenly revealed presence of an old Nelson Classic in French all the more surprising.

It was not that such rooms were overcrowded, the disparate chairs, low tables, bureaux, writing-desks did not jostle one another; there was always room to move in between them to reach the long leather-padded seat, three sides of a square, on top of the fireguard in front of the generally empty grate, filled with curled-up old newspapers, probably the local weekly that appeared on Fridays. I think, too, one might include a few stuffed birds, standing against suitably reedy backgrounds, in their glass-fronted prisons, and, at Usk or Raglan, a stuffed pike smiling wickedly in a wide dental grin.

Each room would be suggestive of a faded gentility. Let us add full tea-sets and coffee-sets, sherry glasses and decanters, on shelves, also behind glass, never used but just visible. Of course, very soon, in a matter of a decade or so, in the 1960s and 70s, Trust House Forte would put an end to such agreeable and baffling diversity; but at least the war had the advantage of freezing such places in time, maybe even bringing new contributions from unexpected quarters and from people with a great deal of time on their hands, *waiting*, and so much of the war was just that.

Reading would be one way out (knitting might be another, suggested by three empty work-baskets, not matching, one in raffia, the other two in a silken material with long bone handles, left in corners or on a low shelf). And what could be further removed from the insistent preoccupations of a world war than the tribulations of a widowed Spanish professor in a small provincial university or school in some dormant town in Old Castile in the 1880s or 90s, with five daughters on his hands, growing up, affectionate, talkative, always eager to eat, and quite unmarriable? It was even more remote than Barchester. The story, told with wry, muted humour, and read in the damp room over tea, thin smoke coming from the grate, the wet wood hissing, would temporarily remove me completely from the Army, from my ill-kept uniform, worn so thin that it no longer chafed me, no longer reminded me of its professional purpose, identifying me as a long number in eight or nine digits, enabling me to snatch a few hours of semi-civilian freedom, indeed a brief plunge into more than just the appearance and the illusion of civilian life. I had come here on my bicycle, and I was living at the time in civilian digs. I was cycling through the river valleys, the Usk and the Wye, not on any Army business, but for my own enjoyment. I still carried the livery of the Army – later, I was often even able to shed *that*, at least in the evenings – but I had almost forgotten the fact, and the owners of these small country hotels generally seemed to be faded, rather hesitant, well-spoken middle-class ladies, perhaps even surprised to see a visitor.

So it was quite possible to keep the war at arm's length at least for a time, moments snatched from a devouring, insistent collectivity in which girlie magazines, *Picture Post*, *Reveille*, and other popular illustrateds were called 'books' ('lend me your *book*, mate, when you have finished with it' – this from the bunk above, in the Nissen hut with the big black stove, now red-hot, and a concrete floor). I expect there were refuges like this, frozen in time, up and down the country. The war, though belonging to the 1940s, helped to prolong the 30s, at least in terms of the contents of rooms, while making drawing-rooms, writing-rooms, coffee-rooms, smoke-rooms colder and damper, thus offering a reassuring sense of continuity from a time when the war (or just war) had seemed a fairly impersonal threat that might indeed be realized, but could equally still be avoided. After all, something of the kind had worked at Munich, so it could probably work again, there was nothing *inevitable* about war, it was not a scourge like the plague. Well, it hadn't worked after all. But in such places nothing much seemed to have changed; some things might have gone missing, others had been added: unwelcome reminders of the new state under which we were all obliged to live – the black-out curtains behind the washed-out heavy green brocaded ones – but one would have hardly noticed them, and in the daytime they would have been hidden. There might be fewer people about; more of those who were would wear old clothes and several thicknesses of knitted pullovers. There might be a few visitors in uniform, but not very many; it would seem as if the Thirties had been given a second chance in order to redeem them-selves – witnessed from such quiet, damp enclaves, it would even have appeared that the great divide between peace and war, between *pre*-war and war had been an illusion. The big cinemas still filled up in the evening, the electric organs went on playing, and there was no compulsion to see *Mrs Miniver*, even *she* could be avoided.

But I remember most the little hotel in Raglan. It was the sort of place that enabled one, briefly at least, to play at being a civilian again, even if one was not taken in by the play: precious moments of tranquillity, stillness, and unconcern snatched from the path of the juggernaut as it rolled on; alone in a room full of very old, very stale smells, their potency decreasing, just timid, discreet reminders of perhaps better things that had gone before – one even welcomed them for they were the smells of peacetime, that is, *normal* time – also the steady sound of rain outside, a Dickensian sound trans-ported from the east to the Welsh Border, the wireless, with its lyre-shaped front, turned off, or even broken; the gentle ticking of a clock, a peacetime noise too, like the rain, then the shuffling step of the apologetic lady bringing the tray of tea: 'No help, you can't get it these days, I have to do everything myself'; the butter spread thinly, still *butter*. It was like stumbling all at once on a map of neutrality, as if whole areas of the country had sensibly decided to opt out of the whole tiresome business. Perhaps, cycling from Newport, on almost empty roads, I had bumped on to a zone that had decided to go on as before. Did the *whole* country have to be at war? Somewhere on my way there I must have crossed the unmarked frontier between involvement and non-involvement, had wandered unknowingly into a topography of happy unawareness or of deliberate rejection, as if the war had ended at the level of a country lane enclosed by high overhanging hedges. One could entertain the illusion for an hour or so.

* * *

It was surprising what one *could* do, and how light one could travel (a single book might be enough), cycling along the narrow path, the long grass coming to the level of the handlebars and brushing against my feet and knees, the spring flowers my audience, the butterflies and the brilliant blue dragon-flies my outriders, accompanying me just a little way, then turning off as if they had lost interest and had no sense of urgency. The height of the vegetation on both sides of the almost invisible path – the wheels could *feel* it; I could *see* it here and there, where the stems of long grass had been crushed – accentuated the sense of speed, and the bicycle that I had just bought, almost new, from my Jewish friend in Cardiff, was itself so low on the ground that I seemed to be speeding through a double wall of blurred bright colours: a whole range of greens, tender, brilliant or pale blues, purples, reds, whites, pale yellows, the reds, blacks, and ochres of wings marked with strange eyes, as I stood on the pedals to gain more speed. Not a soul about, no one ever coming this way, why should they? For it did not lead anywhere, in peacetime it might have been a lovers' lane, or the semi-secret path of a Sunday afternoon walk. One would have to know how to find it, there would have been a frontier area, neither quite town nor quite country: oily, uneven dockland paving, hard on the feet, harder still on my little low-slung black bicycle, huge rusty iron rings, coils of rope like sinister snakes, apparently dormant but about to strike, giving way first to rank grass and a seedy topography of rejection: bottles, old tins, empty petrol cans, then the high grass concealing the timid pathway. I had been told the first time how to find it: follow the Victoria Dock from Mendalgief on its left side till the old railway lines run out, then keep on, it was only a narrow slit of land, not even qualifying for a navigational light, much less a lighthouse which might have served as a guide; now it just led to an isolated battery, ack-ack, at the very end of the long, thin peninsula, the tall grass and the spring flowers all at once giving way to a small, very secret shelving beach. It was so isolated that the four or five members of the battery had to be supplied with all their provisions, as well as with ammunition, by sea; there was no way of reaching them by land, no four-wheeled traffic could have got through, the path was much too narrow, and the anti-aircraft gun itself must have been brought in by sea, on a floating platform with a crane. The two huts had been carried there, in bits, to be assembled on arrival, the same way.

I even think the members of that battery had come to appreciate their isolation; they dressed much as they liked, in a mixture of uniform and civilian clothes: when I first met them, the corporal was wearing an old pair of tennis shoes, one of the privates had on a very dirty, greening pair of cricket trousers, another was bathing in his War Department issue pants, keeping his feet on the bottom; he said the water was pleasantly warm, but that there were long rainbow streaks of oil. It was always good, in wartime, to be well away from the centre of things and to find yourself in inaccessible places, immune from visits, which nearly always meant trouble, and at a safe distance from everything: in their case, at the very tip of a very narrow peninsula, marked no doubt on large-scale marine maps, but which no one, apart perhaps from a few butterfly enthusiasts, knew about. I don't think even an Army motorcycle could have negotiated the narrow path. The members of the battery entertained the hope – always a strong one in the Army – that somehow they had been *lost*, forgotten about by the Artillery Headquarters in Cwm Road, and that they would be left on their tip of land till someone got through and told them that the war had ended, it was all over. I enjoyed my weekly visits to the secret beach, and looked forward to the swift ride there and back, on the narrow path between the tall grass and the wild flowers. The members of the battery did not regard me as an intruder, they knew that I had not come to spy on them, but to bring them news of the always threatening outside world behind and well beyond their well-protected peninsula, as well as such things as cigarettes, or 'books', or mail, that I could carry in the black saddle-bags of my speedy little bicycle.

One of the peripheral advantages of this particular stage of the war – it might have been 1943 – was that it brought me into a number of such inaccessible and out-of-the-way places, some of them within easy distance of large industrial towns, but of the existence of which most people, even locals, would have remained ignorant. Luckily nothing ever happened to that battery – indeed I am not sure whether the gun was ever fired, it is possible that no planes came in that way; anyhow, my weekly visits went on for several months, the spring flowers changed to summer ones, then the butterflies and the dragon-flies disappeared, the narrow path became slippery with the early morning frost, and the wind seemed to come at me from both sides of the thin peninsula. The battery would see me through the best part of a whole year. There was always the same crowd at the top; and the beautifully oiled gun, pointing expectantly at an angle upwards, remained unused.

It was surprising how easy it could be to get right away from it all, at least for a matter of minutes, an hour, or half a day – better still, a *night* in a hotel room, in a country cottage, or in a Bed and Breakfast where no questions were asked. When I think back to that period, what I most recall are such moments of almost pure joy, a feeling of ease: a closed room with a door that shut, semi-secret and very private itineraries, even those on ostensible Army business, particularly when one had the luck to have to deal with a dozen or a score of small units scattered over a very wide area: the whole of Hunts, a strip of Cambridgeshire, the Soke of Peterborough, a small chunk of Northants, a parish so extensive for it to be impossible for them to keep up closely with one's movements from day to day. Or a brief stop, waiting for a train, in the bar of a small station, somewhere between Dovercourt and Manningtree, even there I was really alone with myself, facing myself over the bar, in a long mirror with embossed, old-fashioned golden letters that sprouted luxuriantly at their extremities: gins, whiskies, stout, or porter. I was smiling at myself, pleased for once with my appearance, perhaps because I was in high spirits and happy to be in this part of the world; and what could be *more* private than this unexpected excursion back to childhood, back to a topography both safe and familiar – well, at least familiar? Just something too about the little bar-room, a bit dingy, very quiet, I the only customer, a fire giving out a thick yellowish smoke, the barman dreamily washing out pint glasses and lost in his own thoughts, even the beer unusually good for wartime, and perhaps the fact that I was heading for my godmother's, the big house at Stoke-by-Nayland – the weir stream ran underneath her long drawing-room, so that one had the impression of floating high up in the chintz armchairs – a house where I was sure of getting a really good lunch, even in 1944. It was one of the rare occasions when I did not even mind seeing myself in a mirror (it was a rather dirty one, so I could not see myself very clearly); I even thought I was looking as well as I was feeling, I did not seem to notice the uniform, there were times, and this was one of them, when I could forget all about it.

Even the isolated brand-new bomber, all tied up, as if it had been a present, or just delivered from the factory – the cockpit covered over in some sort of transparent wrapping, no doubt to protect all the instruments, clocks, and dials – right at the farthest tip of the Chepstow Racecourse, seemed to spell out privacy, because the Welshman and I, and the guards at night (whom we never saw; we just emptied their bucket every afternoon), were the only people who knew that it was there, knew about it, brand-new – as it were, still wrapped up in cellophane, harmless, immobile, quite still and noiseless, it too was waiting and was trying to be as unobtrusive as possible, under the shade of a big spreading tree, its undercarriage staked to the ground, as if to prevent the whole thing from taking

75

off on its own. The tyres on its wheels were covered over with some sort of silver foil – I suppose to keep them dry. For the two of us, its big tapering wings, with their slits, were just there to give us shade from the fierce three-o'clock July sun; its very presence, in this isolated spot, was a welcome pretext for our long, completely unobserved walk steadily uphill, with occasional glimpses of the Wye, in its deep gorge far below to our right, the buildings of the Camp, the cookhouse with its long metal chimney, the urinals (our morning terrain), the huts, the horse-boxes no longer visible, and everything very quiet and still, save the buzzing of the midges hovering over the bucket, even after we had emptied it and buried its contents, and sometimes a very gentle breeze ruffling the tall ferns and undergrowth.

There were a dozen or so other planes, all bombers, though I would not have know of what breed, staked down under the trees (I suppose to make them less visible from the air), but this is the one under which we would stop, because it was the furthest away from the centre of things and because it was in the habit of playing tricks with us, as if it knew that we were coming. It would remain hidden in the long grass and among the leaves of the overhanging branches, some of which reached almost to the ground, enclosing the plane in a luminous greenish tent, on the very fringes of the Racecourse; and then we would come upon it all at once just when we were beginning to think that we had missed our way, or that it might have been moved in the course of the night. We became quite attached to it in its still innocent state; it had been painted with camouflage, but as yet it had no black numbers, no white letters on its long flanks, no official designation of its aggressive capacity, and it seemed to have been wrapped up as some sort of outsize gift, a mammoth toy, meant for the two of us and chosen by some unknown well-wisher with a sense of humour. It always gave us the impression that it had been waiting for us, the way it would suddenly appear, rearing its long, narrow back in snakelike dark greens, blacks, pale browns, and bright yellows above the tall ferns. The bomber-to-be seemed to have settled down quite contentedly among the ferns and the tall stems of grass, the butterflies would pause for a hesitant moment on its nose, by the little mica windows, and then fly off, quite unimpressed. It was there throughout our time in the Camp. We would have missed it if it had been taken away, its place would have been marked by a large area of darker-green grass, in the form of a double cross, then the grass would have become the same colour as the rest, and no one would have known that the plane had been there for all those weeks, maybe months. One could see inside through the transparent covering; it looked terribly cramped in there, very little room for legs. Anyhow, it lasted us out, giving a purpose and a destination to our long walk uphill (including Sundays), three or four miles of steady climb, our short, belted, malodorous denim tunics over one shoulder, and offering us the minor security of familiarity: a secret shared between us. One could cling on to little things like that. It had become part of routine, it was our last stop, then we would head back, one of us holding the empty bucket, our utterly convincing *passeport*. Then we would clean up, and I would head down the steep road into the town, where I could sit down and read or write in the green writing-room – a very pale washed-out sort of green this time – of the old-fashioned posting-house on the main street. No one ever came up there either; I could be sure of being quite alone, undisturbed, sitting at one of the big writing-desks, among the old almanacs, trade directories with damp marks, *A Guide to Preparatory Schools of England and Wales* for the year 1922, three sets of rather greasy playing-cards, with the arms and name of the hotel on their backs, in their frayed cases, empty blue-stained inkpots and dip-in pens with discoloured gold nibs, the inevitable glass-fronted bookcases, and the imperious bells with brass handles and round green covers that didn't work, and big, sad leather armchairs facing futilely in all directions. Here, evening after evening, going down to the bar every now and then to pick up a pint of beer, I was able to read the whole of *War and Peace*.

The bomber – *our* bomber – must have been moved in the end; I suppose it would have been done at night, the wings that had given us shade would have been dismantled and placed alongside the fuselage, the whole thing put on a long trailer, tied down with steel hawsers, covered over, rather ignominiously as if ashamed to display itself in its true colours, with a green-canvas tarpaulin, and driven off to an airfield somewhere far away to the east, where it would be given an official identity, letters and numbers, and Royal Air Force markings in tricolour rings.

* * *

Sometime in the autumn or early winter of 1943, I retain a comforting image of myself, in uniform, with my Sergeant's stripes on my upper arms, 'correctly dressed' – it was best to be on the safe side and not take any chances, one never knew whom one might meet – wearing a small forage-cap, perched on the right side of my small head, a belt, gaiters, and polished boots, pushing a small handcart on which has been tied down, rather perilously, a handsome little mahogany table with a deep drawer in the middle and folding wings, that I have just bought for a few pounds, £12 or £14, I seem to remember; anyhow, quite a bargain really, but St Ives remains still innocent in such matters, and the war itself seemed to favour the purchaser, military or civilian, prepared to take the time to have a good look round – from a small antiques shop off the wide main street of Cromwell's birthplace, in what then was still Huntingdonshire. I had spotted the little table, hidden away at the back of the shop, on a previous visit, and had been attracted by the long deep drawer and its elegant keyhole, picked out by a pretty brass surround that looked as though it would polish up very well, telling the owner, a shy man with a slight stutter, that I would come back for it the following afternoon. I start by pushing the handcart ahead of me, but I cannot control the sudden swerves it keeps on taking, and then one of the shafts, rising up in complicity with the other, knocks off my side-cap, bruising me on the cheek. So, halfway across the long, slim stone bridge over the Ouse – the pavement is too narrow – I decide to change around, finding it easier to walk between the rebellious shafts, pulling the cart behind me. Luckily, the direction I am to take is on the level the whole way, once I am down from the hump of the bridge, so that the handcart does not press into my back.

My destination is a large sprawling house in East Anglian-type white plaster, part of the roof thatched, the rest in red tiles, with two modern wings added (it looked quite recently) one at the back, the other at the side, set in a big garden, with an orchard, outhouses, and a long black wooden barn at a crossroads. The house is called The Old Cross Keys; it had at one time been a pub: an excellent location exactly half-way between the two Hemingfords, and within easy walking distance of the main road from Huntingdon to Cambridge. The cast-iron surround of the missing inn-sign, still surmounted by two black crossed keys, hangs over the lintel of the low-set white front door, which seems to be sinking into the well-kept grass of the strip of lawn also to the front. The white door is protected by a wooden flood-guard, unpainted, that goes a quarter of the way up. The tow-path along the Ouse, leading to the church and the churchyard of Hemingford Abbots, is a few yards to the south of the house, from the drawing-room of which one can see the course of the river, marked by a long line of willows, all of them bending towards the west.

In a country such as England, which had never had any long-term experience of compulsory military service, the Army, especially in wartime, would have to improvise in all manner of ways as far as accommodation for a huge influx of temporary, and no doubt mostly reluctant, soldiers was concerned. Permanent barracks would have been in rather short supply, save in county towns that housed the depots of local regiments, and in those areas of the country that possessed long-established military camps. Throughout most of my time in South Wales, I had had to make my own arrangements, living, while stationed in Newport, in civilian digs in a big house on the London Road that housed several families, including a very affable Bengali couple and their three children of school age. There, in addition to a bedroom, I had the use of the big front room, facing on to the road and that I used in the evenings and at weekends as an improvised study. On my very first visit to the Headquarters at Abergavenny, I had been put up on a folding army bed set up in the still relatively intact Banqueting Hall, which one approached by a ladder, and which had the luxury of a roof, in the ruins of the old Marcher castle built of reddish stone.

On subsequent visits to the small town, I stayed in a B & B off the main street, where we slept, soldiers and civilians, packed together, seven to a room, on mattresses laid out on the floor, with no space between each one, so that one had to step in the dark across the recumbent bodies of one's fellow-lodgers, most of them snoring loudly, all of them indistinguishable in their night attire of long beige underpants reaching below the knees, thick woollen vests, and heavy knitted socks: soldiers, airmen, commercial travellers, the occasional merchant seaman, men working in a local canning factory, a butcher's apprentice, and a boy of thirteen or fourteen who did the paper rounds before going off to school. On my first night, I found myself to be alarmingly conspicuous in my striped pyjamas, and switched thereafter to the universally accepted thick socks and underwear, though my pants were short. The seven lots of clothing that marked the great divide between civilian and military personnel (including the paper boy's blazer with a coat of arms over the pocket) hung off a couple of hooks on the door – or that was where they were supposed to be, for every time the door was opened most of them would fall in mixed heaps on the floor. Boots and shoes were perched precariously on the tips of the grey blankets that covered our feet and our bodies. There were no sheets.

I have vague recollections of a comfortable billet in an old black-and-white house in another Newport, this one in Salop. And on first reporting to No 24 Liaison, I was put up for a week, with four other fortunate soldiers, in a small country pub in a village somewhere near Kettering. We slept in large feather beds, and washed at a pump in the courtyard at the back. The landlord's wife cooked us enormous breakfasts of locally cured bacon, sausages, and freshly laid eggs. Unfortunately, this was only a temporary arrangement, and, at the end of what had been a blissful week, the Colonel explained to me that as I was to be assigned to a dozen or so of small units – Artillery, Anti-Aircraft, and Signals – of Czech soldiers scattered over a wide area, and as there were no barracks anywhere in the vicinity, I would have to make my own arrangements over accommodation, and the Army would then pay my landlady the standard billeting allowance of 30/- a week. One does not need to be told when one is on to a good thing, and one also knows when to keep quiet about it. I gave the elderly Quartermaster the name and address of the landlady that I had recently managed to find for myself, after looking around for quite a bit – it had not been *easy*, and the locals in this part of the world were a bit hostile to khaki; *blue* would have been different. He nodded feelingly in agreement, he was not very keen on the Junior Service. The *name* of the house seemed to him most promising, 'Sounds as if you have landed yourself up in a pub, Sarge', he commented, giving me a knowing look over the top of his army-issue steel spectacles, as if I had gone up two or three grades in ancient military lore, and was at last beginning to show a glimmer of promise – and I did not disillusion him. Still, it was up to me – and I felt that I had slipped back a couple of grades and had lost my initial good marks – it was entirely up to me, he added with a shrug, if I wanted to cut myself off in some primitive dump, with only the cows for company, that was my concern. I thought it best not to tell him that part of the house had a thatched roof – he would have seized on that to make his point – *nor* did I tell him that my landlady-to-be was my sister.

I had been staying at The Old Cross Keys for a bit over a month on the Saturday of my return from St Ives with the handcart and the little table. The purchase of the table fulfilled an immediate practical need, but it also represented a timid bid on the future and a tentative assertion of civilian priorities. Here was I officially billeted on my sister and my brother-in-law, my bedroom in a spacious attic, very quiet, in one of the wings of the big house. I had a good deal of writing in mind, in my spare time at weekends: evocative pieces for a Belgian monthly about the Bibliothèque Royale and the Mont des Arts, the Parc Royal and the Montagne de la Cour, articles in French for François Quillici's London-based daily, *La Marseillaise*, and perhaps one or two more short stories for Robert Herring, who had already published one in *Life & Letters Today* that had come out when I had been on the Racecourse, which I had first read in print – it was one of the first of my things to have come out in this exalted form – under one of the wings of our bomber.

In the previous two weeks, I had formed the bare bones of a short story, based on a wartime experience while teaching illiterates in South Wales, which I thought might do very well for *Punch*. It was in fact the first piece that I wrote on the newly acquired table, once

81

(with the help of my sister) I had installed it up in the attic, in the recess of a dormer window from which I had a commanding view of the narrow little road, hardly more than a track, which led on to the main road from Huntingdon to Cambridge.

The Editor of *Punch* wrote to me to say that he was accepting my story, which I think was entitled 'The Impostor'. It came out a month later. On my regular visits to Huntingdon, I liked to stop off and sit in the Public Library, a charming little eighteenth-century rococo rotunda, with a green dome and elegant balconies over-looking the circular reading-room, the whole approached by a double row of curling steps. It had originally been the meeting-place of the local Literary and Philosophical Society, the *Proceedings* of which, in handsome leather volumes, occupied three of the lower shelves. Now I would make rather a point of casually taking down the current number of *Punch* off the slanting shelves, so that I could be *seen* reading it, and *heard* laughing discreetly – a little more than a slight cough – as I turned the pages. Of course, I had my own copy of that number; it had come in the post, and I had left it prominently on the hall table of The Old Cross Keys, hoping that my sister would ask me about it. But all she had said was: 'I wonder why they sent it, I never asked for it; there must have been a mistake. I never read it, I don't find it funny.'

Writing was one important way of throwing out a thin, fragile, easily cut-off lifeline to a civilian existence and to a dark, mysteri-ous Occupied Europe, from which I had been – temporarily, I hoped – excluded, though, if I had thought about it at all, I would have realized that such hopes were contradictory, for the only way I was likely to get back as early as possible (once a fairly *deep* bridgehead had been successfully consolidated) to a longed-for Continent would in fact be to remain in the Army, preferably in a more special-ized organization ('Political Warfare' sounded just the right thing for me, and I had already been in touch with David Garnett, who had made encouraging noises about my suitability).

The Colonel in charge of No 24 Liaison (a Norwegian-speaker, as he had informed me, in order to still my own apprehensions as to my qualifications, or rather lack of them, as a non-Czech-speaker just posted to the Czechoslovak Independent Brigade

Group, to give it its full title; he had gone on to tell me, in a casual aside, as if it had been a great joke, that there *had* actually been a Czech-speaker, a Lieutenant, posted to No 24, seven months earlier, but that he had been transferred, after a week, to the Dutch) I only met once, when I reported to him at the Headquarters just outside Kettering for the first time. I saw his deputy, a Captain, once a month, who contented himself with the routine query: 'Everything ticking over all right, Sergeant, no problems?' And his tone made it clear that 'ticking over' was all he wanted to know about: this I took to include living at The Old Cross Keys; but there did not seem to be any need to go in to that. Let him think, as the old Cockney 'Q' had thought, that I had managed to land myself a billet in a country pub. 'Problems', I imagined, may have referred to the occasional difficulties that arose between small, isolated groups of Czechs and Slovaks thinly scattered over my very large parish, some of the latter having complained that they had not been getting their cigarette rations regularly and that the Czech officers at Headquarters had been denying them leave. There were a few Ruthenians, too, who seemed to have felt rather left out of things and who, in their talks to me, between lessons, expressed an even-handed dislike for both Czechs *and* Slovaks, though reserving their bitterest strictures for the latter (they had been, after all, a good deal closer, so no doubt were known better). But these were not *my* problems; they belonged by right to Intelligence, or to Political Warfare. I was not in the latter as yet, though I still entertained hopes in that direction, 'PW' having apparently so many literary associations.

When I think back to those days, I am surprised at the no doubt unconscious inventiveness of the Army, acting in its role as a vast, international estate agent, specializing in the somewhat gimcrack architecture and interior design of the 1900s, the 1910s, and the 20s. Perhaps there had been someone high up in Claims & Hirings who had been mad about domestic stained glass. In Dovercourt, or Hertford, or Newport (Salop), or the many other provincial towns, where, at one time or another, sometimes only for days or weeks, I was stationed, we had moved into empty, requisitioned family houses that, in the absence of furniture, did at least provide us with running water, electricity, gas, even light bulbs (drawn from the

Stores), but also the apparently standard issue of gently moving coloured light filtered through stained glass.

The time in Dovercourt represented a happy interlude, which I spent cycling around the Hundred of Tendring, on marvellously empty roads, paying occasional visits to my godmother in her 'floating' mill-house in Stoke-by-Nayland, or stopping off in Mistley and Manningtree, and once staying with a Signals unit that was billeted in St Leonard's House, The Hythe (the former home of my Cobb grandparents), for a couple of nights, sleeping on a folding-bed in what had been my father's bedroom when home on leave from the Sudan, and that still had the cupboard that opened up under the window-seat of the bow window facing on to Hythe Hill, which once contained my father's Army sword, wrapped up in oil rags, but was now quite empty: another, very brief, return to the more intimate 1920s of my own age-span from three years old to nine.

* * *

Sometime in the spring of 1944, March or April, I had managed to get myself transferred to 21st Army Group. This had meant leaving Acacia Avenue, the comfortable idleness of Dovercourt, and the already partially domesticated house with the stained-glass window over the front door. There would be some considerable time before I would be setting up my bed in a room to myself in middle-class houses situated in quiet residential suburbs of big towns, and that ran to stained glass. I had been sent to an enormous tented camp somewhere on the edge of the New Forest. This was back to the Army with a vengeance: bugle calls, parades, kit inspections, lack of privacy, sleeping on a groundsheet placed on top of a wooden duck-board, amidst an all-pervading, pungent smell of male feet, still covered in thick socks at night – most of my fellow soldiers, I had noted from the start (with initial surprise), were in the habit of sleeping with the WD-issue grey socks on in all seasons – queuing for food at breakfast-time and eating out of a mess tin, all this in an area of England that seemed to be positively bristling with khaki. I missed the civilian environment and the considerable freedom of Acacia Avenue. Here, even when one got out of the Camp in the evening, one was surrounded by khaki-clad companions, the pubs were crammed with them, and even the beer often ran out.

Worse still, there was a Commanding Officer, a Major, who was not only present, obsessively so, he was always turning up, making a fuss about this or that: generally some bureaucratic trifle, forms in triplicate, and that sort of thing. I had almost forgotten what an officer *looked* like. The No 24 Liaison Captain had cut down our four-weekly exchanges to a form of telegraphese, or to the original, tentative prototype of an early answering-machine. I cannot even remember what *he* looked like; one could have described him, not very helpfully, as nice, and that he was well-spoken and had the features of an officer. Well, *this* one was extremely unpleasant, he spoke with a sort of permanently aggrieved whine, and he didn't have the features of an officer. He was a mean-looking (and not just *looking*), stunted man, with eyes like those of a boiled cod that stared glaucously, blinking and seeking out trouble, from behind a pair of perfectly round steel-rimmed spectacles. He had a black moustache, with points at the ends, that looked as if it had been painted on to his sickly yellowish face, to cover his loose mouth beneath which there lurked a receding chin. He was always flicking his swagger-stick, as if he had been swatting flies. It looked as if he had spent many years in a fly-blown world. The overall impression that he gave was one of general seediness. I gathered later – and I had by then become quite fascinated by a man who seemed to combine in every aspect of his person and speech a sort of triumphalist mediocrity – that he had been a long-serving soldier in the Indian Army: indeed, I think he had been the son of a ranker, and that he had been to an Army school out there, and that this had been about all the education that he had ever had. It had certainly not amounted to very much; he was ignorant, opinionated, small-minded, ill-read, ill-informed, barely literate, utterly philistine in his tastes, and extremely obstinate; and he spoke with what I would have identified as a Berkshire whine (with the hint of an Oxfordshire one, too), overlaid, no doubt as a result of many years spent in the Subcontinent, with other more exotic borrowings and

85

echoes that, while hard to identify with any precision, were equally disagreeable to listen to: a rich orchestration of a repertoire of varied whines with curried overtones. He was at least predictable in the totality of his seedy awfulness. For instance, he displayed a watchful and petty hostility to all university graduates under his command, and a positive loathing for those who had been to Oxford or Cambridge, as if they had gone there on purpose, in some mysterious foreknowledge that they would be meeting him at some point later in life. From the start, I could not help feeling rather flattered that he should have taken such an active, vigilant dislike to myself; I thought that it did me credit, it was a sort of tribute. There is something very satisfying about being disliked by the right sort of people.

At first, I found him a constant nuisance, one that I had somehow to live with. I had been excessively lucky up to then, under officers whom I hardly ever saw, and who had shown only the most cursory interest in what were supposed to be my official duties, but whom, from the little I had seen of them, I could still respect. And I was sufficiently impressed by what I took to be the proper status of an officer, a holder of the King's Commission, entitled to wear a Sam Browne belt and webbing and to carry a revolver in a leather holster, to be dressed in a khaki tunic and trousers of smooth cloth, soft to the touch and of elegant cut, and to carry a swagger-stick (that was not supposed to be used as a fly-swatter): the whole thing, both the clothes and the wearer – but not the accompanying adjuncts, strapped on, or to be held, casually, in a leather-gloved hand (was there a *correct* one?) – giving off a discreet smell of polished leather and a faint hint of eau-de-Cologne, to *want* to respect anyone who had thus been placed, apparently by individual royal command addressed to him personally, and by name, above me and over me, and from whom I was separated, to the end of time, by the greatest of all man-made chasms.

I had never wanted to be an officer myself, I had always had enough self-knowledge to have known perfectly well that I was not, could never be, of potential officer material (the Army had rapidly come to a similar conclusion), 'calibre' seems to have been the key word, or, in my case, lack of it. I could never have pictured myself in a position, whether military or civilian, in which I would have been expected to give orders to others, make decisions, address words of encouragement (or blame), and, perhaps, to punish them if they had not carried out my clipped commands to my own satisfaction. Then there would have been the business of the *revolver*; I could not even have *imagined* a situation as a result of which I would have been expected to have taken it out of its holster, in itself quite a major operation, I would not have been able to undo the stiff button that covered its handle with a leather flap; furthermore, the holster and its potentially lethal content would have been strapped on somewhere in the neighbourhood of my right hip, perhaps a bit above it, in the general direction of my right kidney, and, as I have always been left-handed, this would have involved transferring the weapon itself across the middle part of my body, either by the front, or more stealthily at the back, to my left hand, and, in the rather unlikely event of having succeeded in this double operation, without dropping the main reason for it, then to have *used* it for the purpose for which it had originally been intended all along, I suppose by *pointing* it in a certain direction, then pulling the trigger. When I gave the whole thing careful thought, it seemed evident that, between first of all reaching over to my right, with my left hand, across the front of my body, or, alternatively, having prised open the flap of the holster with my right hand, then passed its content, across my middle, front or back, to my *aiming* hand, at least ten minutes or even a quarter of an hour would have elapsed, and any effect of *surprise* – and surprise would have seemed essential to the success of an operation of this kind – would have been lost. (For over four years, I had been carrying a Sten gun, but it had never been fired, even in practice, and it had never gone off on its own, on the many occasions that I had dropped it, even by accident; just to be on the safe side – I mean safety to my own person – I had generally taken the simple precaution of having first removed the magazine, a heavy, sinister-looking black object, which I had put away carefully in a drawer, among my socks, underclothes, khaki shirts, where I could be sure to find it again, in the unlikely event of an arms inspection, so that it could not be fired at all.) And, dressed in an officer's uniform, I would have felt that I was an impostor, a rather poor actor in obvious fancy dress, and that there would have been no way of reconciling a covering so impudently borrowed with what was inside it.

As it was, it took me a long time to adjust my own awareness of my incurably civilian attitudes in every aspect of life to the Sergeant's stripes on the upper arms of my tunic. They made me feel that I was masquerading as someone else, a total stranger, though by the time I had moved up from these (downwards, in fact, given their position on my arms) to the two 'poached eggs' (a crown surrounded by laurel leaves, quite handsome, in two shades of beige), decorating the folds of my outer sleeves, I had become sufficiently conditioned to such external symbols of rank as to raise both up, at fairly regular intervals, closer to my eyes, as if I had been looking at two wrist-watches at once, checking the one by the other, in order just to make sure that the two of them were still there and had not come unstitched (always a possibility, as I had done the stitching myself, at the time of my elevation). I had, by then, decided that the War Substantive Rank of Warrant-Officer Class Two (WO II) – peacetime rank had, of course, no appeal whatsoever to me – represented the summit of my military ambitions, and that it corresponded very exactly to my proper status and to my relative merits and demerits in an elaborate system of instantly visible ranks. Indeed, I had felt obscurely from the start that such an assured position, at the lower end of that particular subdivision, would be likely to provide me with a much greater freedom of movement and a much wider range of friendships, associations, and contacts (particularly, the French and Walloon Belgian ones) than would have been available to an officer, enclosed within the set bounds of all sorts of institutional constraints, including those of having to be served by a batman (from whom there would probably be very little escape – the servant would impose his own rules and his own strict timetable) and of being expected to attend formal meals in an Officers' Mess under the implacable scrutiny of the presiding Colonel. At my very first appearance at such an assembly, I would have been bound to have dropped my napkin, or to have upset over my neighbour the contents of a long-stemmed glass, or to have spilt soup down the front of my uniform, or to have come up with the wrong answers.

It was not only that I was not of officer material, there could have been no possible doubt on that score, it was also that I just did not belong among all the elaborate silver of even a wartime Mess dining-room (I presumed that there would always have been a lot of this laid out in order to emphasize the solemnity of such nightly rituals of collective pride). I was not a *belonger*; the sidelines, the banks of urban canals, the *estaminets* near railway stations, the *tavernes* in narrow streets of two-storeyed, brightly painted houses, and an always welcoming, warm cellar, from which one could see the feet and lower legs of passers-by, Rue du Couloir, off the busy Chaussée d'Ixelles, these were the right places for me. And, as a Warrant-Officer, I could cross back and forth over the frontiers, never very clearly defined, dividing the Army and the adjoining civilian world, especially in the favourable conditions provided by an industrial urban setting in the north-east of France or in Brussels. From all this it can be readily surmised that I was no revolutionary, no potential mutineer, and that I was perfectly prepared to accept the Army on its own terms, as long as I was able to keep my escape routes and my semi-secret hiding-places always available. I soon found any number of ways of making sure of that. And I had always wanted to look up to any officers whom I came across as entitled to my respect, whether on account of their birth (a good reason), their accent (another one), their expertise (why not?), or, yes, even their *courage*. Lacking courage myself – or, at least, I *believed* that I did, if I thought about it in the abstract; though, on several occasions, when finding myself in situations of some physical danger, both in this country, and, later, in Normandy, north-east France, or in Antwerp, I was to discover, very much to my immediate surprise, that in fact I had *not* been unduly frightened at the time; I think it may have had something to do with the presence of others, and how *they* had reacted – it was a quality that I expected of those thus placed over me. That was the price that you had to pay for the 'pips' which you wore up on shoulder straps; 'poached eggs' on outer sleeves, on the contrary, were not designed to provide an automatic passport to the mysterious and elusive Red Badge.

But, quite early on after the landings in France, once we had (literally) set up tent in a Normandy orchard, a few miles inland from Bayeux, the Major was to fail me miserably in what were my own not very demanding expectations of behaviour appropriate to an officer in the British Army, or in any other. It was an episode that was at once to convert my active dislike of the man into something more like contempt. I suppose that I might have previously put too much store by the fact that he had been a professional soldier, with years of experience, and not just a wartime officer (just as I was a wartime Warrant-Officer). In any case, the shock had been as genuine, as irredeemable, and as lasting as it had been unexpected. My Commanding Officer had all at once been revealed to me – I had been the only witness to the scene, and in the following weeks he had seemed to have been going out of his way to avoid me; no doubt on account of this, he would give my tent a wide berth, and, if we happened to meet, his fishy eyes would glaze over, and he would hurry on his way, his head slightly down, without a word, so that I was to derive some considerable fringe benefits from an incident that had shown him up in the worst possible light (it had, in fact, been rather *dark*, under the trestle-table, with the British Oliver on top of it, after he had angrily ordered me to put out the pressure lamp which I used for my work at night) – as nothing more than a blubbering coward. And blubber he had done, minutes on end, his narrow shoulders and his fat buttocks shaking convulsively, and in unison, as he had displayed to my incredulous and, it had to be said, embarrassed gaze, the sight of his heaving khaki-covered posterior, which, at one moment, when it had taken an unusually powerful lurch, I feared would bring both the table and the massive typewriter down on the top of the two of us.

I think he might have been away for the few days before this unexpected scene. He could have gone to Arromanches, or to Bayeux, on some job or other; he was often to be seen being driven away in a jeep, flicking his swagger-stick against its camouflaged sides, as if the vehicle had been a horse or an elephant (we kept a sharp lookout for all such departures because they offered the promise of a respite of a few hours, or even of half a day, from his sudden pounces on individual tents, in an effort to catch us out in some small failing). Anyhow, he seemed to have been taken completely by surprise at a sound that had become so much a part of our own

regular evening routine that we had got into the habit of checking
our watches with the long-drawn-out, high-pitched whistling noise
that, at its loudest, seemed to be passing quite low directly over our
heads. It came regularly, on the stroke of the hour, every hour, from
ten at night to five in the morning; I was well used to it, as, working
through the night, I would listen out for it screaming 'whoosh', as
it rushed like a huge, airborne express train, over the dirty-brown
tents, their flaps closed, and the sleeping black-and-white cows, on
its eight punctual and consecutive journeys from north-east to
south-west. It was as reliable as a minute-gun, and I would have
been a bit worried if any of the hourly journeys had been missed
out; like the night chimes of a church clock, each one helped me to
get through the long and rather lonely hours of darkness and to
reach the welcome terminus of full daylight and a fairly decent
breakfast. I expect that, in fact, I had got the timing wrong, as it
would have been regulated by German Time (as recorded by the
beautiful, much envied *Kriegsmarine* watches), which, I now think,
was then an hour ahead of the recently re-established French Time,
so that, from the point of departure, it would have started at eleven,
and would have packed in at six.

Very early on, when it had first started, the people from the Royal
Artillery had reassured us: we were not the target, which was miles
inland from our orchard – not nearly important enough to have
been subjected to such massive and pulverizing attention. Judging
from the changing volume of sound, the velocity, and the interval
between the beginning and the end of the scream, they had
managed to identify the origin of the noise as having been produced
by a huge German naval gun, removed from a battle-cruiser, and
fixed, so they reckoned, on a railroad flatcar, and, judging from the
trajectory of each projectile, sited somewhere in the immediate
neighbourhood of Le Havre, on the main line from Rouen, but
easily moved from one fixed location to another, as it sent gigantic
naval shells miles over our heads, in the direction of the battle area
in the Bocage, and, south of it, towards Condé-sur-Noireau and
Flers-de-l'Orne. So there had been nothing to worry about: despite
the threatening roar, we were not being shelled personally, the
Kriegsmarine people had in mind much more important targets.

After a couple of nights, most of my companions in the Headquarters unit, after listening out for the initial blast, had been able to sleep undisturbed through the seven others. So, apparently, had the cows.

I think the Major must have been off on one of his trips at the time when the shelling had first started. Certainly, as I recall it, it had been going on for two or three nights when, in one of his sudden descents on myself, in an effort to find me at fault – perhaps smoking a cigarette, while taking a breather outside, or reading a book, instead of banging away with one finger at the monumental typewriter – he had sidled into the tent stealthily, surprising me by announcing his presence to my back with a greeting that had seemed at the time dangerously friendly: 'I thought I would look in on you, Sergeant, just to see how you were getting on.' Luckily, this was just what I had been doing. This had been a few minutes before ten. I listened out for the sound of the first of the eight nightly shells and it came exactly on time, the scream rising in intensity to a piercing shriek as it seemed to be passing directly overhead. The effect on the Major was dramatic. Pulling off his cap with its stiff peak, and throwing it unceremoniously into a corner, he put on his steel helmet, adjusting the straps under his weak chin, the straps making it look even weaker, and holding his hands tightly across the back of his bulging neck, he literally threw himself, head first, on to the patch of dirty grass and mud beneath the table, which he evidently believed would offer some protection. From this prone position, his bottom almost lifting the flimsy table with its adjustable black legs, he shouted at me to get down at once and to put on my helmet. Unwisely, I tried arguing with him; after all, I knew perfectly well that there was no possible danger: 'It's all right, sir, there's nothing to worry about, it starts up every night at this time, it's only a naval gun, they fire it from Le Havre.' I suppose the 'only' had been my biggest mistake, for he had started screaming at me, in a high falsetto: 'Do as I say, Sergeant, put out that bloody lamp' (perhaps he thought that the shell would *see* it and, changing direction, and its mind, make straight for its tiny glimmer of light); 'get down, GET DOWN, I *order* you to get down', as I hastily joined his heaving company in the semi-darkness beneath the table. There was

not much room for the two of us, I was right up against him, and I
did not much appreciate the closeness of his company. I noticed that
he was sweating profusely, as well as heaving and blubbering. The
situation was so grotesque that all at once I felt like laughing, and
had some difficulty in preventing myself from doing so (laughter, I
felt sure, would not have been appreciated in these difficult circumstances). The sound receded. But I did not dare make the first move,
remaining crouched beside my Commanding Officer, and keeping
very quiet, feeling that any comment on my part would be superflu-
ous. Five or six minutes elapsed, I could see the time from the luminous hands of my watch, and I was getting cramp in my right leg
that was bent underneath me. I heard a cow cough somewhere just
outside the tent. Gradually the heaving slackened, then ceased, and
the regular moans right next to me died down. The Major took out
a large coloured handkerchief and, removing his steel helmet,
wiped his forehead. Then he got up, slowly and a bit unsteadily, his
body twitching with one or two lingering tremors: 'Phew, that *was*
a close shave, Sergeant', in a voice that was once more quite steady
and that had recovered its familiar whine, and that seemed to
include me in some exceptional experience that the two of us had
shared together. I thought it advisable to agree: 'Yes, sir, quite a
close shave!', while allowing him time to get up first, straighten his
belt, fix his helmet on his back, retrieve his hat, and pick up his
swagger-stick, which, in the course of the ten o'clock stampede, had
fallen into the WD-issue wire waste-paper basket. Once I had
picked myself up, stretched my right leg, put the scattered sheets of
notes and the wireless back on the table, and the typewriter at its
place in the middle, and turned up the pressure lamp, I had hung up
my steel helmet on a hook next to the Sten. The Major seemed
momentarily undecided as to what to do next; I had never known
him previously to have hesitated, he had generally been quick to
pounce and then to punish. But then, to my amazement, and indeed
dismay, for it was so much easier to dislike him, *because* he was so
dislikeable, he put out an ungloved hand to me, which I took (the
palm and the fingers were very sweaty); 'Well, Sergeant,' he said,
and his eyes, for once unboiled, as if a timid residue of life had
returned to their mud-coloured pupils, 'I am very tempted to ask

you back to my tent to share a noggin' (or it might have been a 'chota peg'), but the temptation had not been irresistible, for he hastily went on: 'but I know you have work to do, so I'll be leaving you to get on with it'; and he raised the flap and went out into the wonderful quiet of the orchard. I did not tell him that I had a bottle of calvados hidden among some books. I considered offering him some of it in a mug, but thought better of it – we were not supposed to do any deals with local civilians.

I never told anybody about the brief events of that evening. I had found them rather sad, even slightly indecent and vaguely demeaning. I seemed to have participated willingly in something a bit shameful. I think I could even give a date to the bizarre scene, for, earlier in the evening, before the Major's stealthy arrival, the BBC news bulletin had brought the first, rather patchy, reports of events in Berlin and East Prussia; and further reports, coming in throughout the stifling night, had filled in some of the details of the failed Generals' Plot. I had thought at the time how strangely ironical it was that great public events always seemed to have a way of coinciding with paltry, semi-private ones. History had a disconcerting habit of operating at several levels at once. There had obviously been a huge cock-up in Berlin, and, as it would turn out later, in Paris and elsewhere, while an obscure Major, who had served for years in India, had all at once been overtaken by sudden panic. The two sets of events had been totally unrelated, save that I could *date* the insignificant, and in its way slightly comical, one, from the tragic, and soon public, failure of the July Plot.

As I have said, the Major not only gave me a wide berth, he seemed to make a point, from then on, of leaving me alone. I went on with my night work, and the hourly naval shell went on reminding me of its punctuality, through much of that hot and cloudless summer, until, I think it had been sometime in August, Le Havre, or the little that had been left of it, had been captured. It seemed strange to work through the night without the familiar hourly accompaniment. But, by September, the sound had been replaced by another one, also regular as far as timing was concerned, but much more quiescent: that of trains coming and going on the reopened line from Cherbourg to Paris.

Late in the year, the Major and the rest of us moved to Roubaix, where I resumed my nocturnal routine, starting work at nine, and generally finishing about seven, before having a copious breakfast, after which I would go to bed till about three in the afternoon, in semi-civilian conditions, living in the Cercle de l'Industrie, just off the Grand-Place. It was a welcome change from the previous tented premises; the club had central heating and I could have a bath. It was still a long haul, indeed, longer than it had been in Normandy, especially from midnight to about four. Here, in this big mill town, the Major's and my paths became so completely separated that I only actually met my erstwhile persecutor a couple of times, and then only briefly, in a corridor of the well-carpeted Cercle, when he had looked at me, through his round spectacles, as if he had seen a ghost. I think by then he had almost completely forgotten me; it may have suited him to do so, and, in any case, I expect he had found one or two other Oxbridge graduates to persecute. I am sure that he did not know that I had a luxurious bedroom on the second floor of the Cercle, that I slept in a large double bed, that I had all my meals save breakfast in civilian homes, and that my work companion of the night, a Jewish Corporal who in civilian life had been an Antwerp diamond-cutter from Pelikanstraat, and who knew Russian and German, a French compositor from the *imprimerie* of *Nord-Éclair* (next door to the Cercle), and I produced the daily Army newspaper that the Major may, or may not, have read over his breakfast.

Then, without warning, the Major had disappeared. I think his sudden disappearance may have been related to the arrival at our Headquarters, a few weeks previously, of a new Second Lieutenant who had just been posted to us from England, after having been commissioned. The Lieutenant was extremely friendly, indeed his friendliness had seemed to have extended to all of us, which would have meant quite a stretch, for we were a pretty odd lot, with very little in common, and mainly concerned to keep out of one another's way (which was one of the many attractions of night work, though I got on very well with the Antwerp Corporal). The newcomer was a very plausible sort of officer, with a little bristling moustache that seemed a great deal more natural than the Major's own flimsy-looking effort. The 2nd Lieutenant's sustained jollity did sometimes seem rather forced, but it was all right if taken in small quantities. Without any questioning on my part, the very first time we met – I had just got up at about 2.30 in the afternoon – he told me that he was an Oxonian, and that he had 'gone up' to Merton to read History in 1935, and that he had 'taken Schools' in 1938. The information, so readily proffered, came as a surprise to me, for I had been at Merton from 1935 to 1938, and had read History. The College was a small one, and there had not been all that many historians, and I was pretty sure that I could have put names to all of them. It had been something of a shot in the dark, and it could not have been more ill-directed. But the Lieutenant had obviously not done his homework. While in the Army, I had already encountered several cases of academic fraud: people who had awarded themselves degrees from this or that university, and who had, in due course, been found out – it was bound to have caught up with them sooner or later – and I had been rather fascinated by this sort of thing, especially by the *modesty* of their spurious claims. Why a Third in English at Southampton, or a Second in Portuguese at London, when you might have offered yourself Firsts in Mods and Greats at Corpus? Surely boldness, rather than caution, would be called for in enterprises of this kind? I did ask my informant if he had been well taught at Merton; 'Oh yes,' he had said with enthusiasm, the History tutors had been first-rate, 'absolutely the tops'. I thought it best to leave it at that. My only fear was that, looking out my own files, which would have been somewhere in the Major's office, he might have found out about my own (genuine) educational qualifications, and that this might have created an awkward situation socially; but, fortunately, he had not bothered, and I was the only Mertonian in our group. I don't think he was interested in other people's curricula vitae; I suppose he was fully taken up with making up his own. I did wonder, though, whether he went around with a handful of them, producing a new one at each successive posting. What, for instance, had he been at Officers' Training? Had History at Merton been brought out, like a random and carelessly played card, just for HQ L of C, Roubaix?

Anyhow, I kept my information to myself; he had seemed a nice enough chap, he had *looked* like an officer, and in any case, it was no business of mine. Good luck to him, I rather hoped that he would get away with it. But he didn't. Something must have gone wrong. Whatever it was, the Major and the Lieutenant *went*, if not together, at least at the same time. My Antwerp colleague, who was always well informed about everything to do with our Headquarters, and who had a friend highly placed in the dread Provost Corps, thought that the two of them were the subject of a court of inquiry, but he did not know whether their cases were linked, or whether they were up on different charges. It did seem rather ironical that, if the two cases *had* been linked, the Major, who had always displayed such an insistent, and indeed alert, hostility to Oxbridge graduates, should possibly have owed his downfall, or at least his being moved on, to a man who had been neither from Oxford nor from Cambridge (nor, in all likelihood, from anywhere else).

The timing of the departure of the two of them, or at least that of the Major, whom no one would have been likely to have missed, had been most seasonal: they had disappeared just over Christmas 1944, an alarming season in other ways, for the Battle of the Bulge was then at its height, and we had all been hastily rearmed, a sudden military gift that had seemed both unwelcome and sinister; the Army had not normally been open-minded in presents of this kind, even if they had come wrapped up in Christmas ribbons, holly leaves, and tinsel. But that had worked out all right in the end – that is, a bit after the New Year – and our Christmas gifts had gone back, unwrapped and well greased, to wherever they had come from. We never had to carry arms again. After the Ardennes Offensive had been contained, and the considerable panic along both sides of the Franco-Belgian frontier had subsided, we had got a new Commanding Officer, a gentle, oldish Colonel, with an educated accent and a mass of white hair, who, from the start, had seemed very nice, and turned out to be not the least interfering. I suppose that his predecessor, the Major, had not been all *that* bad; at least – after the night of the failed Berlin coup – he had left me alone.

A few months afterwards, I vacated the Cercle de l'Industrie, and we all left Roubaix for the Ixelles ponds. Once in Brussels, the

Colonel promoted me to the rank of WO II. Shortly after this, meeting me by chance in the interval of an opera by Bizet in the foyer of the Théâtre de la Monnaie, he had mildly reproved me for having been 'incorrectly dressed'. In the evenings, I had been in the habit of replacing my khaki tie with a black one, as if I had been a Canadian. I had promised that it would not happen again, nor did it, at least not when I went to the Conservatoire or to a theatre. Once the war in Europe had ended, the Colonel switched me to the job of advising members of the ATS on the openings available to women members of the Armed Forces, after demobilization, in civilian employment. It turned out a most agreeable assignment, beckoning as it did civilian priorities and providing me with a wide range of pretty visitors. Soon I could talk at length about how to become a stewardess on an ocean-going liner, or on what was the training required of a future midwife. The Lieutenant ('Merton and History') had not been replaced. I had no more trouble with officers for the remainder of my time in the Army.

* * *

I could put a pretty precise date on it. It must have been sometime in August 1945. I had been to a news cinema on the Place de Brouckère, and had just seen the mushroom cloud. I am not sure *which* one, it might have been the one spreading out, early (just as the cheap, but reliable, alarm clocks were going off) on a bright, sunny, weekday morning over Hiroshima, or it could have been its successor, mushrooming over Nagasaki. Either way, the sight of it, especially from all that distance, as well as filling me with awe, gave me a great deal of pleasure and an enormous sense of relief. My release from the Army was not due till sometime in the second half of September 1946. I had to wait the full thirteen or fourteen months – no B-Release, for I had no job to go back to (interrupted research for an Oxford graduate thesis did not count) and I was unmarried and had no dependants (I really did seem to be travelling desperately light, with only myself, and no accompanying baggage, to account for), so there would be no opportunity to jump the queue till my demob number came up. And, had it not been for the mushroom clouds, I would have been due for an early posting to the Far East, in an area in which a Japanese Home Army rumoured to amount to something like 3 million men would still have been a formidable force to be reckoned with. And now the Emperor had commanded them all to pack it in, there and then. There would no longer be any point in shipping off me and my fellow bachelors and fellow pre-war unemployed all that way, now that the job had been finished, apart from the clearing up. So it looked as if we could see out the next crucial twelve months or so kicking our heels somewhere in the now more or less dormant European sector.

The Army, at least as represented in Brussels, had a run-down feeling about it, as more and more people hung about with nothing very much to occupy them, 'waiting for their number to come up'. It was the August doldrums, and my office, which faced on the Ixelles ponds, had closed early, as there had been no callers expected. A month before, I had been switched to working in partnership with the local representative of the Ministry of Labour, as an adviser on a whole range of civilian employments said to be available to members of the ATS on discharge. I had quite grown into this new job, which brought me a fairly steady stream of khaki-clad girls who were about to be released from the often agreeably close embrace of skirts, made in that elegant and smooth material of which I had already, in the course of a month or six weeks, become quite a connoisseur, from behind. They certainly had the merit of displaying the contours of feminine bottoms to maximum advantage, especially at the point at which their owners got up from the chair opposite my desk, and made for the door, loaded with information on such varied subjects as midwifery, hospital nursing, hotel management, becoming stewardesses in ocean-going liners, or qualifying as a hairdresser's apprentice. There seemed to be an almost limitless range of female jobs crying out to be filled in civilian life, though one or two of the more obvious ones did not figure in the glossy hand-outs supplied me by my Ministry of Labour colleague.

I had been to the news cinema in order to fill in time till my daily English class, from five to six, at the École (Royale, I think) de Coiffure, which, despite its adjective, was located in a narrow cul-de-sac leading off the dreary Boulevards connecting the two main-line stations, Nord and Midi. I had been told about the Hairdressing Academy by one of my Belgian friends, who had spoken of it very highly and who had given me an introduction to its Director. I had first gone there in order to inform myself about the usual terms of apprenticeship, the types of training and special-ization, and the conditions of employment, as they applied to female, as opposed to male, trainees. The Director had been both informative and welcoming. He had introduced me to his pupils, about eighty of them, male and female, and had come out with the suggestion that I come every evening at the end of the working day, to take any volunteers there might be, in elementary spoken English. It would supplement my Army pay as a WO II, which, of course, as a Belgian civilian, he knew down to the nearest three-pence three-farthings. I at once agreed. It seemed very much in line with my new military commitments. It offered me a vantage-point from which I would be able to observe every stage of training, if not actually in action, at least after it had been completed.

The École (Royale) consisted of a very long, deep, rectangular room with no windows at either end, and lit at all hours by bright neon tubes. There were four rows of twenty adjustable swivel chairs facing as many wash-basins. On my arrival, just as the working day had finished, the floor of the narrow spaces between four rows of chairs and wash-basins would be covered by several layers of male and female hair: a pale yellow, a dark brown, a lighter brown, a touch of ginger (reddish seemed to indicate a Bruxellois presence), jet black, curly or straight, even flecks of white (pensioners were drawn in, thanks to the cheap rates). The heat in the airless room was stifling, and there was an extraordinarily potent smell of hot hair – I would never have believed that hair, recently cut, could give out an odour so acrid and so cloyingly sweet – cheap scent and powerfully creamy rich brilliantine. The floor may have had a deceptively autumnal look, thanks to the prevailing browns, pale yellows, and blacks (as if in sad confirmation of poor Louis XVI's observation on the subject of the autumn leaves in the Tuileries Gardens), but the intense heat and the insistent combination of powerful smells, the lack of ventilation, the confined sweat rising lazily from about eighty (most of the trainees volunteered to stay on for my Elementary English) female and male armpits, and the fact that, somewhere outside, in a distant world well beyond this concrete-lined bunker, the long, sad Boulevard reflected the angry glare of an implacable August.

Each time I came in for my five-o'clock class, the 'Practical Problems' (if not solved, at least shorn and waved) would have swivelled their chairs so as to face me (they, too, were included in the course, if they wished to be), and the Pupils would have got out fragile little chairs, and would balance little pads on their knees. I would maange to teach my way through sweat, smell, heat, brilliant light, my Army jacket slung over one of the little chairs, my eyes so often drawn away from the neat rows of expectant faces (a plethora, this evening – that of the mushroom cloud – of *krooekops*, curly-tops, said to proliferate in the Quartier des Marolles, even more numerous than usual) to linger in the direction of the tortoiseshell-strewn floors that gave more and more the appearance of having been a vast cemetery of battalions of rather mousy butterflies (no brilliant reds, no delicate blues, only rare specks of white, a preponderance of dull browns and dusty blacks) that had bound themselves together in a collective suicide pact. But, that evening, my thoughts did not dwell on cemetery scenes and on the browns and yellows of funereal chrysanthemums. The mushroom clouds had given me a feeling of timid optimism, and they *did* seem to offer the likelihood at least that I would remain somewhere in Europe (preferably not in Greece) till my Number came up. Even at the time, on that euphoric August evening, I would not have put it any stronger than that. I knew that, as long as I was encased in khaki (even if I took it off every evening, to change into civilian clothes, in my friends' basement flat, Rue du Couloir, off the Chaussée d'Ixelles), I could never be certain about *anything*. A *new* war might break out, all at once, without warning, in some unexpected area much closer to Brussels than the Far East. And I think it may have been in the winter of that year, or sometime early in 1946, that, coming out of the big swimming-baths in Uccle, and back in uniform, after having shed the joyful anonymity provided by swimming-trunks, I caught sight of a very alarming headline in *Le*

Soir (normally a paper utterly reassuring in its entrenched pro-
vincialism) about some imminent new threat to peace, this time in
Iran. It looked as if the Soviet Union and the United States (and, of
course, *we* would be dragged in, too) were heading for an immediate show-down in that area. Despite the mushroom clouds, until my
number had actually *come up*, and, at the huge Demobilization
Centre in Guildford, I had stripped and had handed in my uniform,
and drawn my full civilian outfit, including socks, shoes, and underwear, there always remained the possibility that the Army might
clutch me back, as if it could not bear to do without me. At least,
I had already taken the precaution of applying to the War
Department to obtain permission to reside in France, knowing that
this would entail my complete demobilization, and ensure that I
was not put on Z Reserve – Z Reserve sounded especially sinister –
or in any other sort of reserve further back in the alphabet. I had
put in quite a lot of my Army time, in my office overlooking Les
Étangs and the ugly modern church of Sainte-Croix, to studying the
details concerning *male*, as well as female (my slot), demobilization, and had discovered that, once having got cleared by the French
Consulate in London and having obtained a visa, and then having
reported to the British Military Attaché in Paris, I would be pretty
safe for life from a reissue of khaki clothing: safe, that is, save in
insistent nightmares, probably due to a combination of red wine
and indigestion, that still take me (in my late seventies), in which,
to my intense distress, and indeed legitimate indignation, I find
myself not only being *re*-mobilized (generally in some anonymous
place in the middle of England: Northants or Leicestershire), but
once more khaki-clad, the khaki of a sticky yellowish tint, with
darkish brown stains at the breast and at the top of the back, and
smelling pungently of anti-gas spray.

I continued teaching English at the Hairdressing Academy for
the rest of my time in Brussels, though, after October 1945, I cut
down my five-o'clock classes to only two a week: Tuesdays and
Thursdays. My pupils changed every two months, eight weeks
being the full length of the training course, so that, in all, they may
have numbered up to 800, assuming that they all stayed on for the
extra hour laid on for their benefit (and mine) by the School. Most

of them were from Brussels or from its outer communes, and would have been bilingual in Flemish and French, or *Marollien*, or in a single mishmash of all three. Out of such a large and consistent two-monthly entry, it is at least possible that some of the 800 or so may have become *tri*-lingual, thus enabling them, from the standing position imposed by their work, to address the tops of the heads a little below them, which were the objects of the skills that they had acquired at the Academy, in some sort of English as well as in the extraordinary languages of Brussels. After my lessons, I would sometimes stay on in order to get my own hair properly cut, and would often be rewarded by quite a competent flow, coming from above, of workmanlike English, accompanied by a generous use of the spray. I left Brussels in July 1946, as a result of a posting to Iserlohn, the Headquarters of 1st Corps District in the British Occupied Zone of Germany.

* * *

In the spring of 1946, the British Council organized a 'British Fortnight' to be held in Toulouse. All the participants in the *Quinzaine*, apart from myself, were dressed as civilians; some wore wide-brimmed black Léon Blum hats, a few went around in *bérets basques* – I suppose the venue had called for these – and there was one who had a cap with a long peak like a stage apache from the Rue de Lappe. The Army had given me a railway warrant and three weeks' leave from Headquarters in Ixelles (I was grateful to the British Council for having made it a *Quinzaine*), so I decided that it would be both prudent (though there would be no redcaps within hundreds of miles of the Sud-Ouest – still, one never knew: better to play it safe) and fitting, as the only member of the Armed Forces – I was, in fact, *dis*armed – and of the former BLA (British Liberation Army, now going under another name), if I were to appear, initially at least and for all official occasions (involving the Commissaire de la République, a very intelligent *agrégé d'allemand*, the Cardinal, recently elevated, the Recteur of the University of Toulouse, the Doyen, all sorts of *Profs*) as a Warrant-Officer Class II of the Army Education Corps. I still had about six months to go before demobilization, and I was quite keen to display the 'poached eggs' on my sleeves; they would show up to advantage when I was giving one of my talks. The farthest I could go in the direction of a semi-civilian outward appearance, in the course of a day's outing to Saint-Bertrand-de-Comminges, was to exchange my belt and tunic and my forage-cap, with its light-blue favour, worn jauntily on the right side of my head, for a pre-war (heavily) alpaca jacket and for a dark-blue beret (tight-fitting, not of the floppy kind), a grotesque compromise that, despite several lower levels of invisible WD-issue thick vests, pants, and socks, left me freezing (there was still snow on the foothills of the Pyrenees). For the remaining week of the Fortnight I reverted to a full military accoutrement, including polished boots and blancoed gaiters and belt, and an Army motor-cyclist's leather jerkin that gave me some protection from the bitter evening wind coming from the south off the mountains. My Sten had gone, over a year earlier, when, after the failure of the Ardennes Offensive, we had all had, to our intense relief, to hand in our weapons.

The second week went off remarkably well; my civilian col-leagues let me into British Council gossip, drawn from a variety of prestigious or dusty capitals, once I had succeeded in convincing them that, as soon as I was out of uniform, I would be going back to historical research, and that they had no need to consider me as a future potential rival trying to move in on their chosen sectors – they had already carved up for themselves much of Europe and huge chunks of Central and South America and the titbits of South-East Asia, in a sort of sub-Yalta grab for the more desirable (or less frightful) locations – of British culturation. Having reassured them on my own account, I was even able to introduce three or four of them to the quiet, unassuming charms of a narrow-fronted café bar that had a tiny *terrasse* consisting of half a dozen cane chairs facing on to the circular Place Saint-Georges, a gem well hidden behind the Capitole, its adjoining Comédie, and the noisy streets along which the red trams clattered, that I had discovered, to my delight, on one of my first walks from the big hotel.

The *Quinzaine* ended most pleasantly for all concerned, in a flurry of official expressions of thanks both on the part of visitors and of their hosts, and I don't think these were just empty formalities. There had seemed to have been a plentiful supply of bottled-up Anglophilia waiting to be released in some sort of public display of sentiment, however inappropriate and clumsily worded, in a part of France in which there still existed a number of small Protestant pockets and a much greater number of enthusiastic *rugbymen* and their equally enthusiastic, and not quite so massive, female supporters. I had, in the course of the Fortnight, met one of these, a girl from the Pyrenees, who was not massive at all by any count, who had very pale blue eyes, and whose parents lived in an immaculate little villa, built on the eve of the war, of small pink brick and light-coloured wood, with a deep sloping roof in red tiles, all the downstairs floors of which shone with waxed polish, facing on to a sharp bend in the narrow Canal du Midi which left the little doll's house isolated at the tip of a small peninsula sparsely covered in rank grass and purple weeds. The house, a secret place, could only be reached by a single-carriaged little red tram that, starting from close to Matabiau, the main railway station of Toulouse, and having skirted a gasworks, a slaughterhouse, a junk-yard, a small walled cemetery, and a distillery, ended up, at a red sign ('*Arrêt du tram*') just beyond which the tram-lines disappeared among a confusion of weeds, sand, and tin cans, outside the high yellowish metal fence hiding the garden – a beige gravel path flanked by two rectangular flower-beds marked out with a border of sea shells and containing neatly regimented rows of begonias – from the unmade road, which, like the tram-lines, petered out at this suburban promontory.

The metal fence, at eye level, to the left of the gate and the electric bell, had on it a big enamel number, '*14bis*' (the Rue, Impasse, Avenue, Route, Chemin, or whatever it was called – certainly not a Cours or a Boulevard – further back, clearly gave up counting at this rather feeble point), a rectangle in white lettering on a dark blue background. The villa – I am sure it must have had a *name*, and one illustrated florally on a white metal plaque, in the shape of a palette, in blue-and-yellow spidery lettering (but a name I can no longer remember: Les Glaïeuls would have seemed likely, or perhaps the name of the family's village in the Pyrenees, or, on this treeless beak of land, the name of a tree?) – and its inhabitants, themselves all apparently built to scale – Marilène's parents, the father silver-haired, the mother a much self-proclaimed friend of the Doyen, Dottin (I think, *lettres*), Marilène herself, and her clever fourteen-year-old *lycéen* brother were all equally neat, scrubbed, and small – had been the more important of the two personal discoveries that I had made in the course of the *Quinzaine* and that I had kept to myself. The other one, one I could take away with me (and one that I still have) was a pretty little jug in Martre-Tolosane china which I had bought at the shop of a pale, very fair *antiquaire* (certainly no *rugbyman*) in the Rue du Taur.

Marilène and the three other residents of '*la maison du Canal*' (a minuscule version of the one that had provided me with a civilian refuge, *chez Maxence*, in Wasquehal, on the Canal de Roubaix, in the autumn and winter of 1944 and the spring of 1945*) I could not take away with me, on the train back to Paris and to Brussels, once the Fortnight was over and my leave had run out. But I could come back to them, and – once I had been demobilized, in September 1946 – did, for as long as, in my improbable role as an ex-Liberator of France, I could, on the SNCF; becoming quite an *habitué* from Austerlitz to Toulouse (Matabiau), and listening, as a welcome home-coming, to the voice in the night, or at first light: the station announcement 'Ici Montauban' – but it sounded like 'MontauBANG' – a sure reminder that I was now in the Midi, and that I would soon be in Toulouse-Matabiau, where the single-carriage red tram would be waiting, not on the Place, opposite the elaborate, 1925-style station, but at a terminus down a side-street, as if it had been anxious not to call attention to itself, to take me to the little villa at the end of the line (I always seemed to be the last passenger to get off). For nearly six months I made regular weekend trips from Paris to Toulouse and back, travelling both ways by night, and giving me the whole of Sunday on the perimeter of '*La Ville Rose*', at the point at which the Canal des Deux Mers, a narrow waterway covered in vaguely disquieting floating objects

---

* The home of the novelist Maxence Van der Meersch (1907–51); see my Introduction to *A Second Identity: Essays on France and French History* (1969), pp. 30–33.

and with hardly ever any *boats* on it, took a sudden lurch to the left, in search of the Garonne, the Gironde, and the Atlantic.

Then my free SNCF pass ran out, along with my strictly formal status as a Liberator. A Liberator no longer, I had to pay full fare from Paris to Toulouse and back. I soon gave up after that; the two successive journeys through the night had been exhausting enough, they were now becoming expensive, and, indeed, quite beyond my pathetically limited means as a *répéte* (*répétiteur d'anglais*) at the Lycée Saint-Louis. And by then, too, the villa had lost much of the glamour of recent discovery and as the focal point of my own latest cherished secret map. *La Carte du Tendre* had by then shed all its early mystery and had begun to be all too predictable, even *boring*. I remembered, of course, to put on the waiting *chaussons* over my shoes, as soon as I was let into the narrow hall, after ringing the electric bell, so as not to mark the waxed floors of the *entrée*, where there was a wicker hat-stand and coat-stand surmounted by a wicker-framed mirror. From there I coasted into the salon. I was beginning to get fed up with the latest weekly reports on the Doyen Dottin, his pronouncements on Dickens, his views on the *oeuvre* (vast, indeed!) of Thackeray, as relayed to me, no doubt in a simplified form, from canal-side, and to find the obsessive Anglophilia of Marilène, her parents, her young brother, and, apparently, all their friends, as stifling as the gleaming ground-floor rooms of the miniature villa. Their Anglophilia was both unquestioning and ill-informed.

That was not all; Marilène was not even her real name, which was Marie-Hélène. The diminutive seemed a further obeisance to the prevailing small scale of everyone (including a tiny tabby kitten) and of everything. Pale blue eyes – *mountain* eyes from the Pyrenees – were very appealing in themselves; I had fallen for them in the course of the long trip to Saint-Bertrand-de-Comminges – but they lost much of their primitive allure when what was gradually, but inexorably, revealed as coming from behind the azure purity of their rather fixed, quite untroubled, yet receptive gaze, was a total lack of even the slightest glimmer of a sense of humour. Marilène's loyal literalness, displayed like a coat of arms (still much worn even post-Pétain, at that time, on pockets of feminine jackets and pullovers), or like a flag fluttering straight out in a permanent wind, was both overpowering and undeviating. In fact, I was doing a sort of Maigret to gain access.

Littleness was not a virtue in itself, and, of course, it had been a mistake to have surrendered, from the start, to the rather marzipan-ish appeal of its consciously, even ostentatiously, limited scale: *little* red tram, *little* canal (but carrying, sluggishly, on its even surface, some rather big objects), *little* red-and-light-brown villa, *little* chairs, *little* side-tables, *little* (*terribly little*) glasses, *little* people (I never *saw* the Doyen Dottin, but I feel sure that he too must have conformed to the accepted measurements). The next step that way would have been towards garden gnomes, *little* china windmills, *little* moated castles, and *little* cannons, Dickens via Dottin, and, for it could only end up there, Seven Dwarfs (at least, once they had shoved off the whining Snow-White).

But no blame to the *Quinzaine* for any of this. It had offered me an entirely new dimension to my own personal *Hexagone*, and one quite unrelated to pale blue, washed-out Pyrenean eyes, but con-sisting of dusty, yellowing, damp-stained records, tied up with rotting string, Place du Salin. My second book in French came out in the autumn of 1955*; it was published under the unsuitable, indeed, misleading, imprint of L'Association Marc Bloch de Toulouse. I had never had anything to do with that exclusive *con-frérerie*; it looked as if I had been slipped in through some half-observed back door, far down in the Sud-Ouest, where orthodoxy (quite properly, on the very borders of the heretical Albigeois) had become much more diluted, and where even the *Nous* of the proud 'Nous des Annales' had been extended so as to include unwashed and unbelonging *historiens événementiels* such as myself. It was not *much* of a book: the text was all right and contained a lot of new information, based on local research; but as soon as you opened the *little* red covers, all the pages inside fell out.

A very long time after this, on returning to Oxford in the autumn for the Michaelmas Term, I found a note that had been left for me in my pigeon-hole in the lodge of Worcester College. It was from

* *Les Armées révolutionnaires du Midi.*

Marilène (she had retained the familiar diminutive, for my benefit at least). She and her husband, who was a dentist from Tarbes (she was as informative as ever), had spent part of the summer on a tour of England, clearly inspired, even after all these years, by the Doyen Dottin, for I could detect his hand in this: they had taken in, up till then, Portsmouth, Rochester, Chatham, Strood, London, and had made a special trip to Oxford in the hope of seeing me. She said in the note that she had described me to her husband as being 'typiquement oxfordien'. It looked as if, without realizing what I had been undergoing, I had turned into some sort of public monument, well worth a visit to be taken in along with the other sights, even if it meant an extra walk a bit away from the centre. I could picture the two of them unfolding their green Michelin map, Marilène's small index finger taking charge of the operation, pointing out Beaumont Street: 'He'll be down at the bottom end, it should be quite easy to find, in any case it's on the way to the Station' (as an Honorary Public Monument, I felt myself to be entitled to both 'he' and 'it'). I also assumed that they would have come by train. Oxford would not have been on any Dottin itinerary. They had got my address, she explained in the note, from the Doyen Godechot, and they had seen my name, painted in white letters on a black background (Marilène had lost none of her literalness in the course of the twenty-five years since I had seen her last), along with three others, at the bottom of the steep wooden staircase (like myself, *typiquement oxfordien*). They had climbed up to the level of the first floor, but the double door beneath my name (in white on black) had been locked. But there it was, as it were *en toutes lettres*: PROFESSOR R. C. COBB. No doubt the dentist had been impressed (he had better have been, I thought). Here was I revealed, in bold lettering, in almost the same league as the much-invoked Doyen (I don't know how Godechot stood). It had been a disappointment (I suppose a bit like making a special trip to Hampton Court and finding that it had just been burnt down); but they had admired the Benedictine cottages and had had an enjoyable walk around the lake. 'Bernard' (his Christian name was introduced at this point in the long note, written, Marilène went on to tell me, on a seat in the shade of the trees in the garden) had been so sorry not to have met me, he had heard so much about me (I felt pretty sure that he *had*). But they had also done most of the central Colleges and had even taken a punt on the Cherwell. They had still to take in Winchester, Salisbury, Bath, and, possibly, Haworth. She gave me no news of her parents, nor of the little villa, but told me that her brother, an *agrégé d'anglais*, now taught at the new University of Toulouse–Mirail, and that her two children were currently at the Lycée of Tarbes. The note was concluded: 'affectueusement'. The handwriting, small and neat, had not changed.

5

Something to Say for Teaching English

MY FIRST teaching post, once I had been demobilized (in Guildford) and had returned to Paris at last as a civilian, was as *répétiteur d'anglais* at the Lycée Saint-Louis in Paris, Boulevard Saint-Michel, from October 1946 till July 1947. Saint-Louis was an unusual educational establishment, in that it had no section *Lettres*, and so no aspiring *normaliens* with their sights on the Rue d'Ulm, and prepared candidates only for the three Grandes Écoles: Saint-Cyr (still so named, though the military school had actually moved to Brittany), Navale (*La Borda*, the incredibly tough naval school in Brest), and the proud '*X*' (Polytechnique, in Paris). Almost all those who regularly attended my conversation classes in the course of the school year were hoping to enter the French Army as infantry or artillery cadets, or the Navy (*la Royale*), as *aspirants de marine*. Indeed, their ambitions for an immediate future that lay beyond the sad and dreary Boulevard were displayed ostentatiously, and, given the angle at which they were worn, cheekily, by the military forage-caps, in various colours, or by the naval headgear – the ribbon, 'Marine Nationale' in gold letters on a dark blue background, the little *pompon rouge* at the top – that they wore constantly, not only during breaks in the bleak stone courtyard, but even into class, though all the way from the face downwards they would be dressed as civilians, which gave them, as I thought, a curiously *unfinished* appearance: neither quite one thing, nor another, a reminder, to me, of the half-clothed soldiers at the Gare de l'Est in August and September 1938.

Saint-Louis was much the most militaristic of any of the Paris *lycées*: the discipline was severe, the *censeur*, a huge man who always wore, even in June, a long black overcoat, and a black bowler stuck down over his ears, as if it had been a helmet, and his acolytes, saw to that; and the beginning and the end of each period were still announced by the roll of a drum. I was told much later that it was the last school to have employed such a method. On my first appearance in the place, I had supposed that the drummer would have been dressed as such: with perhaps a huge leopard-skin or something of the kind; and I had felt sadly let down when I saw that the drummer was in fact the concierge, wearing, as he always did, a checked cap and bedroom slippers.

The Lycée also admitted, as *pensionnaires payants*, a small number of Egyptian pupils, most of them the sons of well-to-do Wafdist politicians. They spoke rather elegant, old-fashioned French, and I felt sure that their fathers would have been daily readers of *Le Journal du Caire*. They did not seem to have any strong military motivations, but they were out to make the most of Paris, especially on Thursday afternoons; and they were quite eager to improve their spoken English. Although they must have been much the same age as the French boys, they looked older; many of them had big drooping moustaches and some of them were already quite fat.

The Head of English, Monsieur Louis Carpentier, was, like all of the best *anglicistes*, from the Nord (I think he was a Tourcennois), and his French left little doubt as to his origins. To say that he spoke perfect English would be to underestimate his linguistic talents: what he spoke was faultless North Essex. The first time I met him, in the Salle des Professeurs, I thought there must have been a ghastly mistake, some terrible administrative mess-up, that the Office des Écoles (Boulevard Raspail) had appointed two *répétes* at the same *lycée*, and that I was about to be told that I would not be needed. For he could *not* have been French: his English was unmistakably Colchester Native. He had in fact been a *lecteur de français* at my father's old school, the Royal Grammar, up the Lexden Road in that town. Even after about twenty years, his Essex twang was much better than mine (I had left the County of the Three Daggers at the age of four and a half).

M. Carpentier told me (in French) that I would have the three *classes préparatoires* for their last year. He added that I might find the *cyrards* a bit thick, but very willing, 'X' very pleased with themselves, and thinking that they knew it all already, and rather inattentive, and Navale – well, he smiled, as if letting me into a secret, he wished me luck with *them*; the emphasis seemed vaguely ominous. He went on to point out that I was the first English *répéte* to have been assigned to Saint-Louis since the Liberation. It looked indeed as if I were about to move into uncharted waters still thick with minefields – though the possible naval allusion only occurred to me later, following my very first exposure to that particular third of my volunteers for conversation classes. My predecessor had departed hurriedly, just ahead of the official end of the academic year, early in June 1940; and, save for an Irishman, a graduate of University College Dublin or of Trinity College Dublin, who had doubled up with a *lectorat* at Normale, in the school year 1942–3, Saint-Louis had managed to limp on in the absence of an English teacher *d'origine*. In any case, the *classes préparatoires* for the two military schools had presumably been abandoned by that stage of the Occupation, and by then there would no longer have been any French Fleet to prepare *for*. Or maybe there had just been a lonely *répétiteur d'allemand*. Anyhow, M. Carpentier concluded cheerfully, this time in his broadest Colchester, it was up to *me*; and I was indeed all on my own. I would have no German (not even a Saarlander) colleague; young Spaniards, or those in my age-group (I was then heading for thirty), were not on offer, the frontier was still officially closed; and my Italian colleague, a very charming forty-year-old from somewhere south of Naples, did not turn up till after the New Year of 1947. So it did look very much as if I would be left holding the flag, or indeed several flags.

M. Carpentier had been right about the *cyrards*. I had in my conversation classes the whole of the two *corniches*: Mangin (whom I later met in stone) and Leclerc (who was then still alive). They were all absolutely charming, even deferential (they knew that I had been in the Army, they probably did not know that I had only been a warrant-officer), they all came from military families, and they were certainly a bit thick. Nearly all of them, as I learnt much later from the newsletters put out annually by the Amicale des Anciens Élèves du Lycée Saint-Louis, were killed, as *sous-lieutenants* or as *lieutenants*, in Indochina (as would be my *cyrards* from Hoche, in Versailles, where I went as a *répéte* in 1950). They seemed to regard me as some sort of elderly *grognard* or *demi-solde* (though I was not yet quite thirty), and they used to take me out for drinks on Thursday afternoons at the Boule d'Or, Place Saint-Michel.

The candidates for '*X*' were supercilious, inattentive, and irregular in attendance. They seemed to be more interested in Higher Maths than in English; and no doubt they were right. I never got to know any of them individually. The reception given me on my first appearance before Navale was altogether more *positive*. As soon as I got into the room, I was greeted with derisive chants of 'Mers-el-Kébir', both as regular background noise – a sort of prolonged *monôme*, but one not out on the Boulevard, as it sloped downwards towards the river, but from within the classroom – as well as in the form of an accusatory question ('Monsieur Cobb' – hands raised in unison above the level of the red pompons – 'Mers-el-Kébir, qu'est-ce que vous en dites?') to which they knew the answer. So why ask it? I tried to put that to them, pointing out at the same time that I had not been in the Senior Service, and so could not be held in any way responsible for a decision that had resulted in the death of some 1,200 officers and sailors of the French Navy. In order to convince them of my bona-fide credentials, the next time I faced the blue-and-red flower-bed, I went in wearing my khaki jacket and medal ribbons (I was only taking my cue from them, in *their* un-finished appearance; only the tops of their heads were naval, whereas almost half of me was military). They left me alone after that, 'Mers-el-Kébir' was dropped. A few even became quite friendly in the course of the year, and twice I was asked out, for *le gouter*, on successive Thursday afternoons, to meet their fathers. One of these, a Vice-Amiral (*révoqué*), who had a spacious flat in the Rue de l'Abbaye, had been a Préfet of a Département well away from the coast – the Indre, or the Nièvre, I think – under Darlan, and had been subsequently replaced by Laval; he seemed a pleasant old chap, with a bristling white beard, and he spoke quite good

English, though with a terrible accent, explaining to me, at great length, how he had 'tried to keep the show on the road' in the land-locked territory that the Admiral of the Fleet had assigned to him. The other, a *capitaine de vaisseau* (also *révoqué*) had been a Sous-Préfet in a southern Département, also under Darlan; Laval had replaced him, too. Much to my astonishment, he told me that he was a Protestant, and a long-established *HSP* one at that. Both had been entirely loyal to the memory of Darlan.

* * *

I taught English to those who had failed to pass the June *bac*, and who were to have a second go at it in September, at a suburban crammer's establishment, the Pensionnat Bigot, at Enghien-les-Bains, near the cream-coloured station: the building, and its name on a large wooden notice-board in bold red letters, could be seen from the main line by passengers heading for Lille or Brussels. I got there, twice a week, in time for the first class at 8 a.m. during two successive Augusts, in 1950 and 51. August was always a difficult month, with no private pupils and no money coming in – *le trou d'août* – so Bigot provided a welcome lifeline. On my two teaching days I had lunch in a very quiet *pension de famille* in a glass-fronted villa, the back of which overlooked the Lake and the Casino, an unimpressive and entirely banal building somehow hard to associate with such dramatic gestures as are usually attributed, in yellow-covered novels (Paul Morand territory), to suddenly ruined, flushed-out gamblers straight from the green-baized tables: *une balle dans la tête* (the correct form of departure), or a jump into the conveniently located, but not very deep, lake.

The elderly couples having lunch at the *pension* spoke in whispers. Those on their own sat at single tables towards the back of the room, and at progressively shadier distance from the glass-fronted veranda, housing a ragged assembly of rather anaemic potted plants and cacti turning brown at their extremities, as if they had been the object of some mild form of disgrace as the result of a previous lunch-time or dinner-time *faux-pas*. When the *patronne*, in her shimmering silk dress, came in during the first course (*radis beurre* or *pommes à l'huile*), she did the rounds of all the couples sitting to the front, shaking their hands and exchanging with them a few conventional low-voiced greetings in the form of questions that did not require an answer, but she did not include in her measured progress the 'singles' – mostly males, but including two females, further back; these read *Le Figaro*, making quite a meal of it, if that were the right word, turning the large pages with slow deliberation, even going over the process backwards, as if there had been something important that they had missed, or had not properly digested – a quite non-physical problem in the circumstances, at least as far as *lunch* was concerned, though I doubt whether *dinner* would have been very much more copious. Having, on my first appearance, been sent to the very back, I, too, would come in with a copy of the paper, bought specifically as a passport to lunch, at Enghien Station, in a timid effort to conform to what I took to be the discreet *bon ton* of the establishment (*Le Monde*, I felt, would have struck a jarring note, as well as affording much less cover); also in recognition of the fact that I had owed my summer job *chez Bigot* to my second appearance in my unassertive capacity – it was all that I had to offer at the age of twenty-nine, and, indeed, for the next nine years, my only flag of convenience – as 'Maître-ès-Arts de l'Université d'Oxford' (in capitals, and no abbreviations resorted to here), followed by 'offr. lec. angl. gram. conv. ind. gr.', in the tiny print of the *petites annonces* of the Parisian daily.

The dining-room (that looked as if, in better times, it had once been the salon: there was still a grand piano covered with a leopard-skin, including paws and tail, and there were hints, too, of a former oriental connection: three Buddhas in different sizes, all in gilt, a couple of black-and-gold lacquer screens) of the *pension* offered a welcome and soothing contrast to the beargarden of the Pensionnat Bigot (*père et fils*, like *les briquets Dupont*), the noise of which could be heard from the station, as a promise, or, rather, a *warning* of what was to come, once under the glass roofs of the corridors. In the *pension de famille*, everyone had his or her own napkin in its bone ring. I had one, too. The napkins were changed once a fortnight. I had lunch there, with the standard *quart de rouge*, Tuesdays and Thursdays. The dessert always consisted of a *baba au rhum*, which seemed appropriate, in a setting in which Babar's protectress, 'la Vieille Dame Distinguée', would have been entirely at home. I have seldom been so grateful for the quiet, for the low voices and the whispers in which, in careful, refined French, one ordered, from a choice of two, diminutive *plats du jour*.

Once I varied my usual *pension de famille* reading material of *Le Figaro* with a copy of my very first book, a hundred of which had just reached me from the printers' in Lyon – Imprimerie Rachais, Éditions de la Guillotière, which I thought sounded rather impressive. The big packet, containing the first 100 copies, had arrived the previous morning and I had picked it up from the *loge* of the red-haired Breton concierge, 12 Rue de Tournon, and dragged it up the five storeys to my room in the big flat. The book had an attractive ochre cover: the colour had been my choice. I looked at it lovingly, and, leaning it against my *carafon* of red wine, flicked through the pages. Several of the other *pensionnaires* were in the habit of bringing books into lunch, to supplement *Le Figaro*. But they had not *written* them. The book with the ochre cover attracted no attention beyond my table, which in any case was right at the back of the dining-room. I carried it around with me the whole of that summer day, reading it on the bus, then on the Métro (Clignancourt–Orléans) from Gare du Nord to Odéon.

Several of the elderly male *pensionnaires* wore cream-coloured alpaca jackets; one of the elderly female *pensionnaires* had a beige-and-white *camée* representing a feminine figure with piled-up hair seen in profile – the *camée* was attached to a thick black velvet band that went round her neck. I was only a lunch guest, not even a *demi-pensionnaire*. I wondered if all the full *pensionnaires*, who presumably had rooms upstairs, changed for dinner: I rather thought that they would have done. Lunch at the *pension* would conclude my teaching day, and, after the *baba au rhum*, I could take the bus, via Saint-Denis, back to Paris.

The two successive Augusts went off all right. Two of the whispering couples in the *pension* were replaced by two others; the lady with the *camée* disappeared. My pupils, with the repeat of the *baccalaureat* in September hanging ominously over them, gave me no trouble from a disciplinary point of view. Most of them were very stupid, their translations were sloppy and full of howlers, their *compositions* (for I had been further engaged to teach these sub-urban dolts at least a smattering of what was supposed to be their own written language) revealed to me a range of spelling mistakes in French that went quite beyond the more inspired approximations attempted by the innumerable writers of anonymous letters to Fouquier-Tinville during the Terror, who provided much of my reading material when away from Bigot. Most of the *recalés* (and the rather more numerous *recalées*: scholastic lack of achievement among the *bougeoisie commerçante* of this northern suburb seemed very much to be declined *au féminin*) were the no doubt rather overindulged sons and daughters of local shopkeepers, tradesmen, and minor *fonctionnaires* (including *la police munici-pale*); some of my pupils held out to me the prospect, as if in some way I should *share* in it, that, in the event of their passing the second *bac*, they had been promised, as a reward for their labours, an autumn exposure to the *sports d'hiver*.

But, having been unexpectedly successful as an August crammer, in the second year, M. Bigot *père* took me aside at the end of the summer session and offered me a more permanent post as a late-September crammer. With the fear of a no longer impending *bac* now months and months away, my pupils soon proved beyond any control on my part; the telegraphese of 'to get', 'to keep', 'to put', 'to pull', 'to look', and so on, combined with a full range of preposi-tions, that I had previously used with such apparent success, first in the Army with the Poles and the Czechs, and later with my indi-vidual French pupils, as a short cut to rough-and-ready spoken English, completely failed to attract their at best flickering atten-tion, and the noise of each one of my English (so-called) classes could, I was told, by a visibly impressed regular fellow-passenger, an electrician, who read *Libération* on the 7 a.m. train from the Gare du Nord, be heard from the *far* platform of the station of Enghien-les-Bains. I suppose it was *fame*, both suburban, and even – momentarily, as the big expresses heading for Northern Europe rushed through – international, *of a kind*, regular passengers at least identifying the soon familiar source of the continuous hubbub; 'C'est la classe d'anglais de Monsieur Cobb.' I just managed to last out as a bi-weekly October crammer; but I did not make it into November, not even to the Jour des Morts, a suitable occasion, so one would have thought, for final departures – I would not reach *le temps des chrysanthèmes* in Enghien-les-Bains. For my special benefit the calendar was put forward a couple of days. On October 31, I was summoned to the glass-roofed office of M. Bigot *père*, and told that I was dismissed and that I could call there and then at the *caisse* for my October salary: a *pity*, he added, with apparent feeling, for I had done such a fine job in the two summers; the Pensionnat had never had such a success rate in the two second *bacs* in all his time in the establishment (which he had taken over sometime in the 1920s from *his* father); but then, there it was: I had no sense of discipline. I am sure he was right about that; I was not cut out to be a crammer, but this was the sort of thing that you had to find out for yourself the hard way.

I was quite relieved to see (and hear) the last of the glass-roofed beargarden, but I knew that I would miss the Tuesday and Thursday lunches and my fortnightly napkin in its matching *poche* and awaiting its bone ring, in the quiet dining-room of the lakeside *pension de famille*. I had never actually talked to any of my fellow-lunchers, and had only *spoken*, in a very low voice, to the young Portuguese maid, who took the orders for the (minute) *plats du jour*. But in the course of the two Augusts and part of one autumn, I felt that I had achieved some measure of *belonging*. Each time I had come in, generally a little late, the *radis beurre* or the *pommes à l'huile* already laid out on the white table-cloths, holding my folded *Figaro*, before heading for my single table right at the back, next to a black-and-gold lacquer screen, those already seated, alone or in couples facing one another, having unfolded their napkins, had given me a very slight, discreet nod of recognition. My sudden absence would be noted for a week or two, but would not be commented on.

In the December of the year of my summary (but politely put) dismissal from the Pensionnat Bigot, I was standing at 9 p.m. in a queue outside Le Lord-Byron, Le Max-Linder, or one of the other big cinemas on the right side of the Champs-Élysées, in its upward progress, when I was greeted by one of the most merciless and persistent *chahuteuses* of my worst class, a pretty blonde girl with very blue eyes, who insisted on introducing me to her parents: 'C'est Monsieur Cobb, mon prof d'anglais.' The mother smiled, the father shook me warmly by the hand, pumping it up and down, and saying 'Ma femme et moi, nous tenons à vous remercier; grace à vous, Delphine a fait tant de progrès en anglais qu'elle va passer les fêtes chez une copine de Londres.' I looked at my former pupil and regular persecutress, but there was no trace of a wink from either of her forget-me-not blue eyes, *les yeux de myosotis* of the daughter of a *marchand-quincaillier* of the Rue de la Gare, Enghien-les-Bains.

* * *

Discipline was certainly not the problem at the École des Francs-Bourgeois, a school run by the Christian Brothers, Rue Saint-Antoine, in the Marais, next door to Saint-Paul: the 6' 3" bearded Préfet de Discipline, a man in the national colours – light-blue (cobalt) soutane, dazzling white Geneva bands, and very red face (and huge red hands, made redder in the frequent service of Order) – saw to that single-handed, or, to be accurate, with both.

The Préfet, as his title, his height, and his visible (and even audible) strength of arm and hand made clear, was a specialist who was not concerned with the two-way process involved in either teaching or learning. He spent all the teaching periods in perpetual, frenetic, anti-clockwise motion round and round the arcaded ground-floor quadrangle of the gloomy seventeenth-century building, clattering along in his heavy black boots, and stopping, at each circuit, to bang open the doors of the class-rooms, each of which opened on to what had once been a cloister, his long shadow darkening the far end of the one in which I was supposed to be performing and which was on the east side of the building, to bark out brief orders (he was the only man I have ever met who could make French sound like German) addressed to individual surnames. If any of these were not at once complied with, the huge red hands would be brought into play, over the ears, on the cheeks, or over the back of the head of each of those who had been thus addressed as the owner of the commoner French names (the *noms à particules* would not have been in evidence *chez les frères*) – and there were some Polish, Spanish, or Portuguese ones that the Préfet seemed to manage to bark out with equal brevity.

Within the first quarter of an hour of what was supposed to be my teaching period (for which I was paid very little; this was a school for very poor boys and which paid their teachers very poorly) the boys in my class would nearly all have been transformed into a gallery of living statues, frozen into a variety of peculiar positions (the Préfet was an artist of his kind), each one of which had the effect of depriving them of the use of their hands. (For the generally brief period – ten minutes at most – in which they had still been able to write from what was on my blackboard, I had made the interesting minor discovery that, at this level of French society, there was not a single boy who was left-handed.) In between the incursions of the huge and apparently tireless Préfet, I continued without turning round, as if to dissociate myself from the steadily encroaching battle-scene, to fill the blackboard (with my left hand) in my rather desperate attempts to convey to my by now mostly statuefied pupils some basic elements of English grammar and speech. It seemed a pretty futile task, my presence at the blackboard and my efforts to communicate with the terrorized boys in a few simple words of my own language appeared irrelevant to a situation that somehow placed me on the periphery of, or even *behind*, my class; but that is what I was being paid for, so I kept at it, conscious though I was of being a lone performer, and one unseen, and probably unheard by most of those who had been assigned to me to be taught at least a workable English. Many of these had already been placed in corners facing away from the blackboard and from their would-be English teacher. I endeavoured to retain eye contact with the few who could still command a view forward, but their visual attention would be deflected anxiously in the direction of the door that led on to the vaulted, damp-marked cloister; and most of those who had already been punished and who had not been placed in corners (there was only a limited supply of these, and, already, after a few minutes, I would have a couple of boys, like heraldic supporters that had, by some careless oversight, been placed facing the wrong way round, at the level of my blackboard, kneeling with their backs to it, and leaving it abandoned, in its role as a proud shield, floating in mid-air, while hemming me in behind my desk) had been denied the use of their hands, so that, even with the best intentions – and the few of those who could still move seemed willing enough to learn – they would not have been able to write.

It was worse really than *chez Bigot* in the last, dismal, autumnal phase. There at least I had confronted, and been confronted by, the enemy head-on. The paper darts, the pellets, the indiarubbers, the half-chewed rolled-up balls of chewing-gum, the derisive remarks, and the impudent pseudo-questions, to which I had been remorselessly subjected, had at least acknowleged the simple fact of my physical presence, and I had found myself an active, if unwilling, participant in a role that had been chosen for me. Here, Rue Saint-Antoine, I was not even on the *sidelines*, the action, predictable and repetitive, accompanied by the briefly barked script, took place from behind me, leaving me to talk to my blackboard, as to my only listener and, possibly, friend, to write more and more on it with the stump of a squeaky chalk, then to wipe it all off, to make room for some more useful words, verbs, and phrases, as if I had been engaged to teach myself the rudiments of elementary English. It was like playing to a mirror, or talking out loud to oneself (which is exactly what I found myself doing, even with a sort of gabbling diligence and conviction, on each of my bi-weekly, Wednesday and Friday, mid-afternoon sessions addressing the blackboard, in the class-room to the east of the building, École des Francs-Bourgeois).

I was taken on by the Brothers a few months after my dismissal from Bigot. I had been recommended to them by one of their number, a historian, who told me that he was writing the official history of their Order and who was anxious to try out his halting spoken English on me (most of the records relating to the French Brothers were kept, for some reason – no doubt as a result of the Law of Separation of 1905 – in a private house in the Birmingham area) and whom I met every day in the Salle du Public of the Archives Nationales. He told me that there had been a sudden crisis caused by the unexpected departure of the English teacher, an unnamed compatriot of mine who had simply walked out one Wednesday in mid-term, and had not been seen again. Could I, my historian friend asked, step into the breach? He went on to add that it was only a matter of missing just two hours a week of precious archival time, and that the school was at most a five-minute walk from the Palais Soubise. That is what clinched the deal as far as I was concerned; there had been no mention of any precise scale of payment, save a discreet reference by my friend to the fact that the Order was a *charitable* one. I have never been much good at refusing offers or requests made to me by those whom I liked, and the Frère-Historian fell very much into this category.

I had come in in mid-term, sometime in November. I remained at Rue Saint-Antoine for the rest of the teaching year till its end in July. But, though it had been assumed by those in charge that I would, I did not go back there in the following October. It was not so much that I disliked the place and its blackened vaulted corridors, nor that it took up much of my cherished Archives Nationales time (enhancing all the more the value of what still remained of it after my bi-weekly excursions down the Rue Vieille du Temple): I just got fed up talking to the blackboard.

* * *

For most of the nine years that I spent living permanently in Paris from the time of my demobilization in the autumn of 1946, I was to enjoy one complete sinecure that, while taking up hardly any of my research hours – just a visit between 8 and 9 a.m. on the last Friday of each month to the *caisse* at the top end of the Rue Claude-Bernard to draw my salary in crisp Banque de France notes (all my English teaching was remunerated in cash) helped keep me in pocket all the year round, even during desperate, parched August, for my work in the Palais Soubise or in more specialized Parisian or provincial records. Early in 1947, on the chance recommendation of M. Louis Carpentier, at the Lycée Saint-Louis, to one of his regular bridge partners in their early-evening sessions in the upstairs section of the Cluny, I was appointed official *lecteur d'anglais* at the École Nationale Agronomique. My appointment had been confirmed in a letter contained in a franked envelope headed 'République Française', addressed to me personally by the Chef de

Cabinet of the then Minister of Agriculture (I cannot remember his name, but I think he was a Socialist). It could indeed have been a life appointment, at least for as long as I managed to turn up in person on the last Friday of each month (excluding such *jours fériés* as 14 July, 15 August, Christmas, New Year's Day and so on, when those happened to fall on a Friday). The original statutes of the School had laid down that two language teachers *d'origine*, one for English and one for German (so that a New Zealander or a Canadian, or presumably an Austrian, would not have qualified) should be taken on to the permanent strength of the establishment. Perhaps, at some distant time nearer the School's original foundation, the aspiring *agronomes* had given evidence of, if not an eager desire, at least a resigned willingness, to put themselves down for weekly conversation classes in the two uniquely agronomic languages (Danish and Dutch had not made the grade). But, by the time I had appeared (even eagerly) on the scene, carrying my République Française envelope, with the Chef de Cabinet's letter inside, interest, even of the most tepid sort, had clearly evaporated. Using the suitably headed note-paper of an institution that had been afforded National status, I wrote that I would hold myself available for English conversation classes every Wednesday in term, between 2 and 3 p.m., Salle Olivier de Serres. On the first Wednesday, two *Agro* students, one a red-faced Cauchois, the other an Auvergnat with shaggy eyebrows, turned up, looking at me expectantly as if I were suddenly to reveal the secret of the Gift of Tongues. I did in fact do nearly all the talking: indeed, in my nervousness, I was only too aware of talking too fast and too much; but at least I could *see* my pupils, it was not like just talking to the blackboard. The Wednesday following, only the Cauchois turned up. After an awkward start spent silently looking at one another, he broke the spell and boldly took the initiative, though not in the statutory Anglo-Agronomic, suggesting, with feeling: 'Si on allait boire un coup?' – which we did, once we had found a table in a quiet corner near the back; he told me that he came from a small village near Luneray and that he hoped eventually to take on the family dairy farm.

For the rest of that term I looked in on the faithful Olivier, at

2 p.m. on every Wednesday, but his bleak little room was always empty. It was the same the following term and, indeed, throughout my official tenure of the post, the title of which (*lecteur d'anglais*) seemed as empty as the silent Salle, during the next eight years. There were no takers, and if there had been any *reading* or, for that matter, *talking* to be done, it could have only been to myself.

My first German colleague, a rather cynical and very rotund *Sarrois* (in 1946, and up till about 1950, all the *lecteurs d'allemand* I came across in Paris, in Vanves, and in Versailles, were from the Saar) reported, not at all gloomily, a similar lack of enthusiasm. No one had turned up, even at his first session. He had given it *one* more try, and had then decided, as he told me with some relief – I did not feel that he was a dedicated language teacher – to pack it in, save to call at the School on the last Friday of each month. I still felt the need to go through the motions – who knows, there might all at once have been sudden and passionate mid-term converts to spoken English? – just to be on the safe side. My Saarlander friend and I had very soon discovered a powerful mutual bond in our shared delight and wonder at having survived the recently terminated war, though *his* survival had been much more surprising than my own. Much of the war from 1941 onwards, he had piloted ancient *Luftwaffe* transport planes engaged in the perilous business of bringing up urgent supplies to the Eastern Front, and, on one occasion, he had had to make a forced landing in the snow in an area in which Russian partisans had been active. My own survival had contained no such elements of danger and drama; I had served exclusively in Headquarters units, and the providential Atom Bomb dropped on Hiroshima had saved me, in the nick of time, from being posted off to the Far East. Despite such disparities in our wartime experiences, we could readily recognize one another as kindred spirits. He had never been to Paris before, and was determined to make the most ('most' covered a limited number of activities, best provided by the Rue Saint-Denis and the Rue Berger) of his stay. Being from the Saar was quite a bit of luck, he explained; it helped a lot with the French authorities. He took a healthily pragmatic view of our current situation; clearly it did not seem to worry him at all to be paid regularly (in cash) for doing absolutely nothing, though, it is true, he had further to come than I did to reach the monthly hand-out (which it was, quite literally; it was not even contained in the sparse decency of a beige administrative envelope). He lived out in some *Sarrois* establishment in the far-away Cité Universitaire, whereas I had only a gentle uphill walk from the Rue de Tournon, crossing two sets of lights at the level of the Luxembourg station. But it still left me with a nagging sense of unease and of uselessness, and, perhaps, even of loneliness. I never entirely gave up hope of finding someone waiting for me in the little room on a Wednesday afternoon.

My German colleague returned to the Saar after a couple of years of our shared idleness. I think he got himself some sort of important position with a French firm there. He returned to Paris on regular visits (not *monthly*, but six-monthly, or even annual) and he would always make a point of looking me up, generally a little after midnight, in Le Tournon. I think he had a genuine liking for his fellow-survivor; he always seemed overjoyed to see me, in my usual corner beyond the bridge players and the American intellectuals on the Richard Wright Trail. But he brought with him a rather insistent aura of affluence that contrasted with the appearance of most of the regular night clientele, and I noticed (as no doubt I was supposed to) that, on each successive visit, he would be more smartly dressed, and that he had put on even more weight. From the time when I had first met him at *Agro*, in search for pupils (or even of *a pupil*, I would willingly have shared one with him in Anglo-German), his physical appearance had not at all conformed with what had, from prep-school days onwards, always been *my* idea of an airman. A *fat* pilot had seemed to me as someone both unsuitable and improbable. Airmen, of all categories, would have to be thin and very light. It is true that he had flown in the transport section of the German Air Force. He always made a point of calling in at Le Tournon, not merely to see me, but in order to greet other *Luftwaffe* survivors, who, from about 1950 onwards, had started returning to the café that had been their nearest drinking-place, just opposite the Luxembourg Palace, their Paris Headquarters, where, unlike my colleague, they had spent some of the war years in comfort and *not* flying at all. After shaking hands with his compatriots, he would come and sit opposite me, slapping me on the shoulder, and grinning (he had acquired some gold teeth while serving on the Eastern Front) brilliantly. How was *Agro*? *Still* no pupils? What a joke! And what about historical research? Still at it? There was no money to be made in *that*! The last time I saw him, larger than ever, he told me that he had moved out of the Saarland and that he was living in Baden-Baden, where there were plenty of pretty French girls, AFATs and so on. It was evident that my co-survivor from the other side had remained a conventional German Francophile.

The successor to the fat ex-pilot was an earnest young man from somewhere in the Hamburg region. He seemed so full of enthusiasm for what he regarded in advance as a cultural challenge – that of communicating in German with the future *agronomes* – that, without wishing to be unduly discouraging, I thought it best to try and bring him back to reality and to the situation at ground level; and it was now over three years since my brief conversation (in French) at the Mahieu with the son of the Cauchois dairy farmer. I suppose my new colleague thought that I had succumbed to some acute form of Parisian sloth or had become infected with a more general, and no doubt irreversible, Gallic indifference (to be detected in the way I shrugged my shoulders, or turned up my open hands in a feeble gesture of mild disbelief or of tired resignation), for he looked at me pityingly as at one who had given up the struggle almost from the start. There did not seem any point in attempting further to disillusion him. I thought a succession of failed Wednesdays (three or four would suffice) – or whatever other day he chose for his conversation classes – would bring him back down to earth. Even so, I was both surprised, and considerably alarmed, for it seemed to jeopardize my own long-standing and uncomplaining position as a silent sinecurist, by the drastic action to which he told me, with a sort of satisfied gravity, that he had resorted after only his first month in (lonely) office. Thursday had been the day that he had chosen (I could have told him that it could not have been a worse choice, as a number of the students had girl-friends who were *lycéennes*), and four Thursday afternoons had gone by without anyone turning up in his class-room (he steered clear of the patient Olivier, no doubt as likely to bring him bad luck and as being too closely associated with my own impressively long run of failure, and had opted instead for the more dynamic Sully). At first, he had been inclined to put down to the supine passivity, not to say sloth, of his Saarlander predecessor the absence of any pupils, but then he had become convinced of an inner rot that went to the very core of the system: there was no *need* for a *lecteur d'allemand* (nor, by implication, for its English companion; like the Lion and the Unicorn, joint supporters of the original Statute, the two stood or fell together). So he had written to the Directeur, a mysterious figure whom I had never seen, up till then, and would never set eyes on in the remainder of my time in office as an obscure State Placeman, to tell him that, as he had no pupils, he felt it his duty to resign from a post for which there was clearly no purpose. The Directeur wrote him a stiff, but polite, letter which formally accepted his resignation, accompanying acceptance with a brief expression of regret for what appeared to be a decision both hasty and unprecedented (all previous *lecteurs* had apparently stayed the no doubt equally lonely course without a murmur). At the beginning of the following term, a new, and more pliant, *lecteur d'allemand* turned up, and everything settled back into its comfortable and unquestioning torpor.

When, in July 1955, I was suddenly appointed a full Lecturer in Modern History at the University College of Wales, Aberystwyth, I was left in some hesitation as to what I should do about my French agronomical sinecure. On the one hand, there was a lot to be said for holding on to it. Judging from the experience of the previous eight years, it seemed highly unlikely that, in the next decade (that is, up to 1965), a Wednesday pupil would all at once turn up, eager for English conversation, Salle Olivier de Serres. Even if he did, it would be a one-off situation; he would not come back on the Wednesday following. It might even be worth pushing my luck to a twenty-year period, which would bring me to 1975 (and to the age of fifty-eight, still much too early for retirement, especially from an agricultural occupation). In thus holding on, I would only be conforming to a well-established French tradition of academic absenteeism among State employees. And, by not making a fuss and

by keeping quiet, I would not be causing any offence to the authorities of *Agro*. Turning up early in the morning of the last Friday of
every month at the top end of the Rue Claude-Bernard would not
offer any insuperable difficulties; my lecture and tutorial timetable
could be adjusted to that, and, in any case, I was keeping my room
in the Rue de Tournon all the year round and would actually be in
it for a total of about six months of each year. And it would be nice
to retain this regular *pécule* from Marianne for going on doing
nothing. It was not just a matter of money; it was my own personal
link with the French Republic.

On the other hand, as a historian, I was well aware of the volatil-
ity of French political life. There might be sudden, even violent,
changes at the top, and that could even affect *Agro*, though that
seemed highly unlikely. (I think even *ces événements*, May 1968,
merely lapped round the fringes of the School.) And the monthly
trip could have been burdensome in the long run: I might fall ill, and
miss one (and miss the extended hand with the crisp banknotes at
the little raised window of the *caisse*) and a single miss would be
fatal. Thinking it over, in the course of a summer that was agonizing to me from every point of view (especially that of its not being
followed, in my own case, by the joys and excitements of the sense
of *renewal* of *la Rentrée*, of *not* being in Paris at the beginning of
October), I decided to play safe (or almost safe). In September, I
wrote the Directeur a polite, even fulsome letter, saying how much
I had enjoyed the valuable experience of the previous eight years
and had profited from the friendly contacts with my pupils (all two
of them, one seen *twice*), and, in view of my appointment to a university post (I thought that 'l'Université du Pays de Galles', in fact
a mythical institution, sounded especially grand in French; I even
used it, in the form of 'chargé de cours à l'Université du Pays de
Galles' – certainly a step up from my overused and dog-eared
'Maître-des-Arts' accompaniment to my name – in a farewell piece
for the 'Tribune Libre' of *Le Monde*) in my own country (well, not
quite), tendering my resignation as from 30 September, 1956. At the
last moment I had hit on the idea of this slight compromise: to give
my sinecure the run of an extra year. It only involved two Friday-
morning presences in what was left of the current year, and five in

1956, seven trips in all, easy enough to manage. At about the time my resignation became effective, in September 1956, I received, at Rue de Tournon, an official summons from the Mairie du VIme Arrondissement. I reported there on the day and the hour mentioned (in mauve ink) with some trepidation – summonses on administrative blue paper 'pour affaire vous concernant' (its very vagueness carrying a wide variety of threats) were not to be dismissed lightly – and, after a short wait, a *huissier à chaine* called my name and, asking me to follow him, opened the double doors marked 'Cabinet du Maire' to a room with a huge chandelier. Once inside, I was greeted by a man wearing a *tricolore* sash, who, standing up and coming, smiling, from behind an elaborate Louis XVI table, introduced himself as the *maire adjoint* and, shaking my hand vigorously, informed me that I had been appointed, by a decree issued by the Minister of Education, Chevalier des Palmes Académiques, 'pour services rendus à la culture française'. *Les Palmes* had a mauve ribbon. I bought a length of it in the Palais Royal the same day. A *green* one, that of *le Mérite Agricole* (nicknamed 'le poireau'), would have been more appropriate.

* * *

I gave a regular Monday-morning English-conversation class at the Centre National de Télécommunications in the Avenue de Breteuil. The Centre and *Agro* shared, in different genders, the same adjective, but, in all other respects, it might have applied to two quite distinctive nations that had absolutely nothing else in common. For the Centre was a hive of eager activity. My class started on the dot of 8 a.m. in a sixth-floor conference room furnished in green leather, and was regularly attended by fifteen to twenty – the numbers actually increased in the course of the year – highly motivated electronic engineers anxious to keep up with the steady flow of the latest American and English technical publications in their own specialized and fast-moving field. They were charming, enthusiastic, intelligent, and very demanding. Each session lasted an hour and a half, so that I had plenty of time to reach the Palais Soubise by 10 when the Salle du Public opened.

I worked intermittently, mostly during the desperate summer months, at a very different level from that provided by the Avenue de Breteuil, as a stand-in English teacher, on instant call, in three other Parisian institutions: the Cours Pigier (there were a number of these scattered across the city, but all in the *arrondissements* of the Right Bank: Ier, IIme, IIIme, IXme, Xme), the Berlitz School, and the British Institute in Paris. The three had little in common, apart from their purely commercial aims, their low standards, and the way in which they exploited their temporary teachers. The Institute was on the Left Bank, Rue de la Sorbonne, a good address, and one designed to deceive, as indeed it did, the gullible, for, in fact, it had nothing to do with the Sorbonne, apart from proximity. The Cours Pigier did not lay claim to any such academic associations, whether totally spurious, or (as in the case of the Institute) relatively so. They advertised themselves in the second-class carriages of the Métro (they did not bother with the cream-coloured first-class one in the middle of the train), at eye-level for standing passengers and a bit above it for seated ones, alongside the other advertisements for tonic waters, cures for liver complaints, and *voyantes* (the Pigier, too, offered a look into the future, though a less exalted, more mundane, one). The little rectangular boxes, bearing the name Pigier in light-green letters, addressed themselves to the attention of aspiring or fully qualified typists hoping to improve their professional status by the acquisition of a foreign language (only English and Spanish were being proposed to a potential 7–8 a.m. female Métro audience in the second half of the 1940s and throughout the 50s – though no doubt German had been offered, as a language of upward mobility, to those living in the eastern suburbs during the previous four years of the 40s). Pigier had at least the merit of being brutally frank and unashamedly commercial: an improved typing or shorthand speed, plus a foreign language, and the prospects, preferably matrimonial, and with the VIIIme or XVIme beckoning, these might offer. My own assigned Pigier was in the more commercial section of the Rue de Rivoli, among the cheap clothes and shoe shops, just behind La Samaritaine, a location ideally matched to the prevailing seediness of the bare, noisy building (all the staircases were of iron), and to the rather acrid armpit smell (July and

August were my usual, desperate, Pigier months), combined with powerful wafts of Prisunic scent, of feminine sweat emitted by my eagerly upwardly mobile pupils.

Stand-in jobs came up at pretty regular intervals, especially during flu epidemics – there was even one of smallpox, originating from Saint-Nazaire and Nantes, sometime in the 1950s – between 1947 and 55. For one thing, they enabled me to spend the better part of a working day either in Soubise, or in one of the many collections of records scattered throughout the Paris area. Historical research I regarded, perhaps quixotically, as a privilege and a joy; I did not want it to be associated with the sordid details of financial constraints, in fact I did not like the idea of being paid for what I most wanted to do. So the Institute, Pigier, and Berlitz could be cut down to size: mere providers of pin-money, or a bit more than that, which would enable me to get on with the really important job of research. But I did not long remain so singularly motivated. The three stand-in jobs offered an interest of their own, and one that, in the course of time, I came to appreciate. The Institute – to which I was often summoned, urgently, by *pneumatique*, to replace one of its regular staff of teachers, ill or in temporary disgrace with the Director – drew on a largely predictable, mainly female, middle-class clientele drawn from *les beaux quartiers*: the XVIme, the VIIIme, with a sprinkling from the XIVme provided by the academic ghettos existing on the fringes of the Cité Universitaire: Rue Monticelli, Parc Montsouris, already by the 1930s a potential, and expanding, North Oxford-type donland, soon to be checked by *autoroutes*. But Les Cours Pigier and Chez Berlitz introduced me to a much wider range of the varying social components that helped to make up the population of the Paris region in the 1940s and 50s. English teaching brought in a pretty wide net. But there remained also many indicative sectors of *non*-takers: Faubourg-Montmartre (what had been Céline home territory in the 1930s), Pigalle, Barbes-Rochechouart, La Goutte d'Or, Clichy, La Chapelle, Porte Saint-Martin, Porte Saint-Denis, République, Le Sentier, Gare de l'Est, Les Halles, Quartier de la Bastille, Les Batignolles, *les Puces* did not bite. *Le Milieu*, whatever its own inventive and coded language, wisely kept its own counsel in it, though, *chez Berlitz* – they were,

as I shall suggest, in related trades – I did have one or two eager and
intelligent pupils from among the more motivated prostitutes of the
Quartier de Ternes: perhaps it was the *quartier* that attracted the
better class of girl.

The high-heeled girls clattering up the iron fire-escapes of the
Cours Pigier building in the Rue de Rivoli (*not*, I think, in very eager
expectation of Monsieur Cobb on English prepositions, my special-
ity, even on the fifth or sixth floor) and smelling of moist armpits
(also marked visibly, like spreading dark continents), only ineffec-
tually countered by Houbigant (Prisunic or Monoprix), in
July–August, came in by shoals (*par rames de métro*), emerging
from one or two of the many exits of Châtelet, from the east and
the north-east: Villeneuve Saint-Georges, Vincennes and its beyond,
Villiers-le-Sec, Pantin, Fontenay-sous-Bois, Le Perreux, Pantin,
Aubervilliers; a few, too, from Arceuil, Kremlin-Bicêtre, Vanves,
Robinson, Issy, and Montrouge (the home of Mauricette, a stunning Viking blonde of Breton origin, an ex-Pigier girl I had met
when she was working in the *économat* of the Lycée Saint-Louis
and whom I had taken out on two successive Sundays to the woods
of Saint-Nom-la-Bretèche, picking bunches of heather to go with
her pale-blue eyes): fast-learners, easy to teach, and uninterested in
la langue de Shakespeare. The turnover was so rapid, my own
sudden spells on various levels – one was always running up or
down, but it generally seemed up *and up*, in the resounding iron-
clad building, between teaching periods, so that, after three consecutive hours one would still be seeing the roof-tops of the
adjoining big stores – were so short that I never got to know any of
my pupils personally, and saw more of the backs of their legs
pounding in haste just ahead of me, than of their fronts and their
faces, and could only identify them collectively as speaking a French
that, even to my own inexpert ear, was unmistakably confined to the
native-born of *le bassin parisien*, with an emphasis on its eastern
and north-eastern peripheries. Pigier, then, offered no surprises.
Advertising itself in the Métro, it would not have been expected to
do so. So, as I climbed from floor to floor, in the wake of my pupils'
legs, in various shapes, sizes, and colours, and of their agreeably
wiggling bottoms, and of those of others – there was no telling

from behind – more concerned to improve their typing and short-hand speeds than to acquire the rudiments of written and spoken English, the combined potencies of August sweat and Monoprix and Prisunic scent always seemed much the same. Even when seen from the front, between hurried hourly ascents to the urgent ringing of electric bells, they did not run to the minimal luxury of Christian names. But I was glad that it was generally an upward journey, as I panted behind the many-coloured legs and the varied, but always mobile, bottoms. The view on the way down was less inspiring: shoulder-straps coming undone, backs of necks that could have been cleaner, bouffant hair-styles, dandruff. Going up or coming down, I followed the febrile movement of an army of Gabys and Denises and Francines.

* * *

Chez Berlitz, on the other hand, offered a rather surprising combination: one that, in any case, came as a surprise to me. It catered (in one sense, literally) for two specific components of the Paris population: *l'hôtellerie* and the police. The Institute had been out of action for a period of four years; Pigier had no doubt managed to cope with the different priorities of 1940–44. The Métro would have brought in much the same girls from the same localities, though in wooden-soled shoes (*cothurnes*) and stocking-less, with their legs painted in convincingly natural colours: a very light shade of brown, a much darker one suggestive of *la peau mate* of what was further up, or a delicate rose, one favoured by girls from the Nord and from Belgium, depositing them at Châtelet, leaving them to run up the iron stairs, perhaps unscented (but GI-issue scent would soon be available, in massive quantities, so as to add potent chemical sweetness to the deeper moral joys of Liberation), in pursuit of a different, but equally urgent, language.

Berlitz, with its own prominent building (Palais) on the Grands Boulevards, did not need to advertise its existence in the Métro. From 1940 to 1944, it had switched, with commendable agility, to the teaching of German (the 'language of the future') – everything had been laid on for *la rentrée* of October 1940 – and, towards the end of the stifling summer of 1944, and well ahead of *la rentrée* in October 1944, it had managed to make an equally rapid transition back to the urgent new priorities imposed by the sudden and quite dramatic turnover in distinguished uniformed clientele of both the four-star hotels and the more fashionable black-market restaurants (I never met any of my unfortunate German predecessors *de chez Berlitz*, but I am sure that they would have been as ruthlessly exploited as their English successors). As far as the Meurice, the Majestic, the Crillon, the George V, the Saint-James & Albany, and the Scribe were concerned, the switch-over would have had to be completed in the time it took to change the sheets and pillowcases of the beds vacated a few hours earlier by the top brass of the *Wehrmacht*, the *Kriegsmarine*, and the *Luftwaffe*, and remake them, smoothing out the creases, seeing that everything was properly tucked in, plumping up the pillows, and making sure that there were fresh towels and large quantities of black-market soap and lavatory paper, for the still hot and dusty newcomers. *L'hôtellerie*, in the nature of that welcoming (in many languages) profession, had to be able to keep up with the spanking pace of public events. There would have been no time to pause even briefly for regrets at the loss of a familiar clientele, some of whom had enjoyed a four-year stay, often in the same set of rooms, nor for sitting back, for a moment snatched between two calls or two pressing enquiries, in order to take in the full significance of historical change: the uniforms had certainly taken a turn for the worse, the colour had gone a muddy green, and they did not look as if they had ever been starched and ironed; they did not fit well, hanging casually over their slouching owners, whose boots did not shine with polish and had ugly lace-ups. No doubt the older personnel, those who had already been in employment in the top-ranking hotels through most of the inter-war years, would have been able to slip back into a workable English or American without too much effort. It would have been like turning the knob back (or forward). But it must have been much more difficult for the young men who, thanks to the right connections, had managed to avoid work in the Service du Travail Obligatoire by obtaining work in the hotels set aside for their exclusive use by the Occupying authorities. In many cases their English would have been non-existent, and they would have been quite unprepared for the casual, but utterly self-confident, approach evinced by the new lot of customers. Even chamber-maids might find themselves tongue-tied and simply unable to cope.

I was told, two years later, when I first started at Berlitz, that most of the big hotels had sent their junior staff off on special crash courses held at hours that had to be carefully staggered: bedroom staff from 10 to 12 a.m., bar and restaurant staff from 3 to 5 p.m., night staff from 6 to 8, lift boys (*lifters*) – much the brightest of my pupils, receptive and quick to learn, also easy to distinguish, both by age and by their beige, peach, or blue uniforms and brass buttons, so good, in fact, that I sometimes wondered if I should not have gone in for full-time schoolmastering – from 8 to 9, which was when the big concrete building on the corner of the Grands Boulevards finally closed for the night. The schedules were very tight and had to be adjusted to a rigorous time-scale in order to cram everyone in. In my recurrent appearances on the many floors of the hideous multilingual factory, I found it pretty easy to spot those who worked as waiters in the more prestigious restaurants, or who did the inside or the outside of the bigger cafés and brasseries, by the fact that they attended classes between 8 and 10, they had their dark and heavily brilliantined hair parted down the middle, and they sat together, right at the back, in matching rows: parted hair, pale faces, dark jackets and trousers, white shirts. The girls employed on the upper floors of the big hotels were as readily distinguishable, in the rather brutal process of their force-fed anglicization, by the black cotton blouses and skirts and black buckle-shoes (the white starched pinafores and the little frilly caps did not accompany them on their brief enforced trips from floor service in the hotels to floor presence in the ill-named Palais) that they wore while sitting in the middle rows of the class-rooms. I suppose they had no time to change into their more colourful off-duty clothes.

My pupils, male and female, only came from the junior ranks of *l'hôtellerie* and *la restauration*. Head waiters, *maîtres d'hôtel*, *sommeliers*, seasoned and knowing barmen ('Bonjour, Monsieur Bob'), grown grey, or a distinguished and abundant silver, in deferential, or mock-familiar, but always observant, service, had no need of my elementary tuition. It was like being confined to the lower forms and landed for ever with the rapidly succeeding ranks of beginners. It might have been discouraging thus to have been stuck, week by week, month by month, at the same immobile educational level: one at which all life had long since gone out of an escalator originally designed to lead upwards, at easy stages, to the yet to be revealed wonders of a more sophisticated English. But my confinement to an apparently never-ending Stage One, in the course of time, provided unexpected benefits; and, as a long-standing resident in Paris, I soon found myself as having quite unconsciously invested in the future. Every time I went to the Brasserie Lipp, the Flore, or the Deux-Magots (the Balzar eluded me, all its standing personnel being in their fifties or over), I would be greeted, often from the other side of the big room, or from the far end of the *terrasse*, ten tables or so from where I was sitting, by cheerful young men wearing long white aprons, balancing silver trays covered in glasses of many-coloured liquids on their extended left hands, and with long white napkins neatly draped over their free arms, and with their thinning dark hair stuck down with grease and parted in the middle. One or two would also have faintly pencilled-in black moustaches. Such signals of recognition, semaphored from across the whole length of a busy, smoke-filled room, or from the far end of an L-shaped *terrasse*, the gas heaters of which emitted fierce alternating blasts of hot and cold – and, I had to admit to myself, signals fully deserved when following even an only brief spell in the Berlitz concrete grindery – seemed to have the effect of giving me a semi-privileged status with the *whole* of the black-and-white, long-aproned corporation that operated with hieratical gravity and studied unhurriedness in these well-known establishments.

Sometimes my former pupil would come right across the room, carrying his tray of office, and following a zigzag course between tightly packed tables and chairs, to exchange a few words, shake my hand with his free one, before working his way back, in a similar balancing act, to his assigned territory. Such visible marks of personal attention, pleasing in themselves, especially at the cost of such physical dexterity, had the added advantage of distinguishing

me from the anonymous mass of casual *consommateurs* in the eyes
of the senior ranks of the tray-bearers. I would acquire a personal
identity, audible even over the hubbub, 'Bonjour' or 'Bonsoir,
Monsieur Cobb', possibly even accompanied by a rapid handshake,
the hand hastily wiped in advance on the long, draped white
napkin: a sort of papal benediction not lost on the close-packed and
watching seated clientele, who, apart from talking to one another,
or reading, or pretending to read, *Le Monde* (a paper easy to
handle, and still offering a view forward from the sides of its smallish pages), spent much of their time just being *seen* to be where they
were, or, looking around to see who else were where *they* were too.
Puzzled looks would be directed briefly in my direction, heads
would come together across the width of marble-topped tables, and
I could almost *hear* the whispered queries. Had they missed something? Did I form part of the recommended décor? Thus personally
blessed, and raised to the very rare level of an *habitué* (and one who
might be able to count on a favourite corner: an observatory provided by a short length of a single-seater dark-red banquette facing
outwards and commanding a clear view over the rest of the main
room and the revolving door leading from the Place and the
Boulevard), and taken in, grudgingly, as an extra item on the literary tourist circuit, my *drink* might also be awarded the equally
prestigious favour of being named: 'Un frontignan, comme d'habitude?', the dismissive tone of voice clearly indicating that the question mark was purely formal. And so, whatever the season, or
whatever my desire for a change of drink, a *frontignan* it would
have to be, at least the first time round; I could always switch to
what I really felt in the need of (*un vin blanc sec, un ballon de
Brouilly*) on my second order, my special status having been
convincingly established, both visibly and audibly. *Le Monde* could
then come into play in its own right.

At the Palais Berlitz there was absolutely nothing to indicate even
a discreet, muted police presence at my intermittent crash courses
in spoken and written English. There was no visible communal flag
such as that provided by the brilliantined hair and the partings
down the middle of the younger male representatives of *l'hôtellerie*
and *la restauration*, to offer me the slightest hint of another, much

more alarming double presence: that of the Préfecture and the Quai des Orfèvres. I could hardly have expected to find myself confronted with docile rows of blue-uniformed *agents de ville*, their *képis* bearing at the front the nautical arms of the City of Paris, laid out neatly at the proper angle, beside the inkpots. A line-up, further back, of identical Maigrets, wearing heavy black overcoats with velvet or astrakhan collars, despite the central heating, their obligatory black bowlers likewise laid out, this time the right way up, on their brims, would have been equally improbable, if only because Maigret was unique and could not be multiplied. I would, of course, at once have identified even a single pair of matching Duponts and Duponds, with handlebar moustaches, wearing *their* bowlers, and correctly shod in iron-studded black boots. But apart from the rather insistent black-and-white presence (female as well as male), there was nothing in the sharp-eyed rows further to the back, and likewise expectantly facing me, hanging on my every word, to indicate any sort of collective provenance. The black-and-whites sat together, as if to affirm their solidarity and to intimidate me with this display of visible strength. But, further back, there was a confused chaos of contrasting colours: brightly printed flowered dresses, beige-coloured long-belted macs, surmounted by polka-dotted or zigzag-lightning-patterned bow-ties of suspicious neatness that offered the unmistakable appearance of having been made up and then clipped on to the edges of collars – the wings fanned out too widely and displayed a give-away similarity – black leather jackets slung over the backs of hard tubular chairs, thick *canadiennes* in tartan patterns, still zipped up and causing their owners to sweat profusely, short dark skirts that revealed to advantage elegantly booted legs, one swinging nonchalantly over the other, a variety of hats and caps, a solitary pearly-grey Homburg on the desk of a fat man who was totally bald, two or three berets of various dimensions: close-fitting and tight, floppy and pulled over to one side, suggestive of ecclesiastical associations, Alpine or Basque, pulled over to the other side, and all of such variety as not to indicate any collectively held extreme political convictions on the part of their owners.

The *faces*, too, apart from the shared intensity of their expressions, indicating that they had all paid up in advance for a full course, including trimmings such as pronunciation and basic verbs used with adverbs, and that they were jolly well going to make sure that they were getting their full money's worth (it was made quite clear to me, when thus exposed to that barrage of attentive, and possibly accusatory, eyes, that the Berlitz ethos had rubbed off on the consumers), did not reveal any clear indications of shared social or regional origins. There was one face, very wide, that went with a tartan cap that had a furry bobble on the top, and with a broken nose in the middle, that I thought should rightly have belonged to a *fort de la halle*: I had seen scores of its almost identical partners, similarly capped with woolly bobbles at the top and displaying flattened noses in the middle, round there, in the early hours just before daybreak, having drinks and eating huge sandwiches in the warm, steamy, crowded Au Chien Qui Fume (they would be, too, the place would be covered in a pungent blue haze), opposite Saint-Eustache. But it did not make sense. What *would* a market-porter from *le quartier des Halles*, or a nurseryman from Fontenay-sous-Bois, or an asparagus-grower from Montreuil, be doing with English? Most of the faces were youthful, those belonging to *l'hôtellerie* and its twin were pallid; but others, more weathered, seemed to indicate a very wide range of activities that would have taken their attentively staring owners as much out of doors, in all seasons, as in overheated, glass-walled, and glass-roofed premises.

Already by the late 1940s I had taken to flattering myself on what I regarded as my steadily increasing ability to put an immediate professional or occupational designation, and a reasonably accurate regional origin, on what was on offer, among the tightly packed rows, confronting me *chez Berlitz*, provided by the *masculine* faces. I felt much less confident of my ability to decipher the *female* ones, due to the fact that the coloration was so often boldly artificial, and even deliberately designed to put such cheekily inquisitive observers as myself completely off the track. A further difficulty arose from the fact that, in an age-group that seemed to range principally from eighteen to the early forties – the bright eagerness of the rows of eyes facing me brought it home to me most convincingly that the acquisition of a foreign language represented a reasonable claim on a fairly immediate future, and that it would probably have much less appeal to the over-fifties (though even *then* there was really no telling, it might appear as a last chance, a final throw of the dice, to be seized upon without hesitation, or, better still, as a new departure, this time no longer alone, but in young feminine company), for which English, or any of the other languages on the abundant Berlitz programme (I thought Romanian would have been a pretty dark horse), might provide the most convincing passport – the varied coloured flags of regular alcoholic intake (the colours ranging from those of the habitual Ricard drinker to those, a purply mauve, of the eight-litre-a-day man of *le gros rouge*) did not offer an equally straightforward topographical guide to the much more enigmatic, and even deliberately misleading, *feminine* countenance. I felt sure that I was on quite safe ground in supposing that most of the partings-in-the-middle originated from Menilmontant, Belleville, and the Buttes-Chaumont, or from somewhere a bit further out to the north-east. Their halting English, such as it was, revealed a powerful and rather engaging back-wash of long Parisian 'a's, rich and glutinous. One of the flattened noses had a Belgian accent that was so strong that he might have been in the part of a stage-Bruxellois as rendered by a French actor, from the repertoire of the Duc de Brabant or from some other mocking take-off of the inhabitants of the small kingdom adjoining the Nord and the Ardennes. People from certain specific regions really did speak in the way that they were imitated professionally, as though they had actually been playing themselves in an effort to raise an easy laugh. I had often been surprised at this, when hearing for the first time the genuine natives of this or that town or rural area speaking either in English or in French. Two of the heavier moustaches gave strong hints, just below them, of the Haute-Saône, one of the few areas of the East that, thanks to my old friend Maurice Chauvirey (first met, Boulevard Bonne-Nouvelle, in 1935), I knew about. But that was about as far as my cursory reading of the faces, and my not very attentive ear, casually attuned to garbled and hideously emasculated English, would have taken me. Thinking back, I suppose I should have listened out for more Southern renderings: Sud-Est, Sud-Ouest, or the slow, lazy, hesitant *accent lyonnais*; and indeed I expect that there they were, too, and that I may have missed them.

It was only a couple of years after I had been doing stand-in, mostly desperate summer (July–August) jobs for Berlitz that I spotted the owner of one of the more obviously clipped-on and garish – it seemed to be sending out signals in brightly coloured Z-waves – bow-ties; or, rather, that *he* spotted *me*. I had been working for some months in the Archives de la Préfecture de Police, on the seventh floor, just below the roof and the gently cooing pigeons, of the Police Judiciaire, 36 Quai des Orfèvres. I had just reached the first floor (children, lost or found, or in trouble, were at ground level), an easy walk up, in fact the first adult stop in the tiered grey house of crime, the floor which was assigned to *les moeurs* (a vague, but extensive area of uncertain frontiers, and that could have covered a multitude of ingenious and highly specialized exercises in over-elaborate vice), and their more elegant-sounding (carrying a hint of a Longchamp Sunday) and much more straightforward sister, *la mondaine*, and the almost exclusively feminine clientele of the latter. It was early on a Monday morning, a time when the high-heeled, raucous, and chain-smoking ladies of the Quartier des Halles and adjoining areas – the Rue Saint-Denis, the Rue Berger, the Rue de la Lune, the Rue du Faubourg-Montmartre, the Rue Quincampoix, the Boulevard de Sébastopol and its intersection with that of Bonne-Nouvelle – would always be especially numerous. I had noticed many times before that Monday always seemed to be their big day, whereas, on floors further up, as I ascended slowly through successive layers of misdemeanour, fraud, and crime – *coups et blessures, homicide, agression à main armée, vol avec effraction, attentats, assassinats, faux en écriture* and its first cousin *faux et usage de faux, brigade financière, contrefaçon*, and the rather uninspiring, at least in such exalted company, *grivèlerie*; all of them spelt out in black letters, some of the letters missing, as if they had given up, on glass doors – the crowds would not be so thick, and Monday would be like any other day of the week.

I was just heading for the next lot of bare and well-trodden stairs (*faux en écriture, faux et usage de faux, contrefaçon*, giving the second storey at least the hint of skilled specialization), when, cutting his way through the closely packed groups of high-perched prostitutes, using his elbows to shove them aside, the very tall, sandy-haired owner of the most dramatic zigzag bow-ties came up just behind me, when I already had a tentative foot on the first stairs leading up to Fraud, and gave me a massive slap on the back, causing me, especially in this locality, a panic feeling compounded of alarm and instant guilt, so that I dropped my dispatch-case, as if it had contained unmistakable evidence of my criminal intentions. He then grabbed my hand in his, which had long reddish bristles on its back, while asking me if I remembered him as one of my former pupils at the other Palais (perhaps I am imagining this, it would have been rather an elaborate sort of joke, and I expect that what he actually said to me was 'Chez Berlitz' or, more familiarly, 'la boîte Berlitz'). Picking up my case, I said at once that I did, indeed; and I did, though I did not mention that it had been as the wearer of the Z-ray bow-tie (the one that he had clipped on on this Monday morning seemed to be giving out S-rays, in shining gold and brilliantly verdant green). He seemed to be highly amused and, at the same time, slightly flattered at my presence in the busy, smoke-filled building, rather as if I had been making him a personal call; and, on Floor One, it was at once apparent to me that I was indeed *chez lui*, that this was *his floor*, and that he had caught me, with one of his big pale hands still on my shoulder in order to emphasize the fact, just as I had been heading up to one that was beyond his powerful reach. I needed no further convincing, I had already heard him addressing his Monday clientele in familiar *tutoiement* – and there was perhaps a slightly mocking, yet semi-affectionate, familiarity in the use of Christian names: Gaby (they ran into double figures), Denise, Mireille, Francine, Francette, Lucienne, Bernardette, Pierrette, Thérèse, Irma, Élise, Colette, Gisèle, Adèle, Léa, Fernande, Pauline, Michèle, Micheline, Lucette, Françoise, Catherine, and even an incongruous Adélaïde who seemed as if she had stepped out of the previous century – giving each of their bottoms a gentle tap, and asking them what they had been up to since the last time that they had met on Floor One (as if he had not known).

But I thought that I could detect, beneath the sheer cordiality of his greeting, a very slight element of disquiet. I could almost *hear* the unspoken question marks that had been hurriedly aborted before trying to get out. Or they may not have been there at all, I was probably imagining too much, I was even taking in the greyish-green wash in which the walls of No 36 had been painted many years before. My appearance must have spoken in my favour, too; I was shaved and was wearing a tie (though not a bow one). Anyhow, how was I? Was I still teaching at Berlitz? And what had brought me *here* of all places? The first two were purely formal, and I went on to tell him that, every weekday, Saturday mornings included, I worked up on the seventh floor. Floor Seven evoked no visible interest in him. It was clear that he had never been up that far. I told him that the Police Archives were kept up there. He did not seem at all convinced by what he must have regarded as some sort of effort to put him off the track as to the *true* cause of my presence, on a Monday morning, too, in the dusty, noisy, overheated building. But whatever doubts he may have had were soon dispelled, at least outwardly; for he went on to explain that he was a Chief-Detective-Inspector of *la mondaine*, and backed this up by handing me a visiting-card that spelt out this impressive trinity in elaborate italic and that gave him a surname beginning with a 'W', a letter that I found much more welcoming than those previously emitted by the bow-tie, as it left me in little doubt that he must have been from the Nord or the Pas-de-Calais, or, possibly, the Ardennes. (I learnt much later, when I had got to know him a good deal better, that he was from Mons-en-Barœul, on the fringes of Lille, familiar territory as far as I was concerned, and so one that spoke strongly in his favour.)

He must have felt the need to do a bit of explaining on his part. He had enrolled with Chez Berlitz, he told me, in order to pick up the bare rudiments of spoken and written English, so as to keep up with so many of his regular customers who were themselves in the process of learning it by the Direct Method from their black GI instructors. I retrieved my dispatch-case from the floor, and was about to go up the next lot of stairs, when, taking me by the right arm (despite his huge hands, he had a very gentle touch), he gave me a broad grin: pointing towards his 'regulars', he said that, if ever

I felt *that* way inclined (I certainly did, especially on the last Friday of the month), he would tell me a thing or two about each one individually (and I am sure he *would* have, he was a living Archive and one dealing with living subjects, unlike my informants six storeys up – *commissaires de police* of the forty-eight Paris *Divisions* and of the twelve Paris *arrondissements*, and *their* habitual clienteles: no Gabys, no Mireilles, plenty of Adélaïdes, Charlottes, Sabines, Carolines, Justines, Lucilles, and Sophies, of the second half of the 1790s and the first decade of the 1800s). And then, much to my astonishment, he said, 'Tu es un copain, on se reverra.' I was *in*, and we *did*. He was a great friend of my massive (eighteen–twenty-stone) publisher, Raymond Clavreuil, and, from that time, we used to meet, three or four times a week, between 6 and 7.30 p.m., in the little bar, three doors down from Raymond's bookshop; and, sometimes, on Saturday, before he closed his shop, Raymond would invite the two of us to a (massive) lunch *chez* Allard, two doors up from the shop. (Raymond's itineraries were strictly circumscribed, I don't think he ever got as far as the Place Saint-André-des-Arts, and he certainly never took the Métro, neither at Saint-Michel nor at Odéon.)

My Chief-Inspector friend was called Maxence. He seemed to be quite well known in the Quartier de Buci, especially among the noisy market women standing behind their barrows in the narrow streets there, who addressed him as 'Monsieur Max'. Like the huge bookseller, whom I had first met in a much smaller version (eleven–twelve-stone), in 1936, when I had first taken a room in a *meublé, chez le père Moïse*, 63 Rue Saint-André-des-Arts, Max was a man of habit who, once down from the level of Floor One, in the black building just over the river, liked to follow an itinerary that must have been fixed years back, perhaps in the inter-war period, and had persisted, or been revived, in the second half of the 1940s and throughout the 50s and 60s: *un petit blanc sec*, followed by several *tournées*, in the little bar, then a Ricard, followed by several more, in the *tabac* on the corner of Raymond's street (he was certainly the best known, most visible, and largest figure in it, as well as the most popular) and the Rue des Grands Augustins. The invariable early-evening itinerary had probably been dictated at some stage further back by Raymond's sheer volume; but Max (like myself, just topping eight stone) seemed quite happy with it, following it, along with Monsieur Clavreuil's three or four assistants (they did not employ *le tutoiement* in either stopping-place), without question. In any case, questioning would have been difficult; Raymond, walking slowly and with deliberation, at our head, visibly took the impressive form of a steadily moving and irresistible ship's prow, clearing the narrow pavement leading from the bar to the *tabac* of any effective resistance on the part of tourists or students, and leaving it free for the rest of us to follow, unimpeded, in its wash.

I don't think the Chief-Inspector ever married. He never wore a wedding-ring, and I thought he was the sort of person who would have done if he had been. He never seemed to be in any hurry to get back home, wherever that was: it was not the sort of question that you would have asked him. Removed from the official stage provided by Floor One, he was no longer a public person, though the bow-tie remained as a reminder, to myself at least, of his professional status. Sometime in the 1950s, the rather loud, clip-on version was replaced by a more discreet, tie-it-yourself one in polka-dot pattern. I don't know *what* that indicated: probably nothing at all. He had by then lost any lingering interest he may have once had in English, most of the GIs having long since departed, with or without their Direct Method-instructed French GI Brides or Brides To Be. I may have had other pupils at Berlitz from No 36, or from other police establishments, but, if I did, they never identified themselves to me. I should not have been too critical of the Palais Berlitz: it paid its temporary staff very badly, but it had provided me with one of my most discreet and predictable French friends.

6

Bar-sur-Seine

SOMETIME IN the early 1950s, late April or early May, I am with my friend Maurice, in his three-wheel car that runs on a two-stroke motor-cycle engine, and which he had acquired, by some devious means, from the *Wehrmacht* – it still had *Wehrmacht* camouflage on it. Maurice had used it, rather unwisely I would have thought, in 1943 and 44, to transport rustic wardrobes and massive Franc-Comtois dressers from his native Vellexon, in the Haute-Saône, to Paris, where he sold them on the flea market of Saint-Ouen. The dressers were the origin of the prosperity of my friend in the last two years of Occupation, when furniture would fetch enormous prices. The Resistance people had had a go at 'requisitioning' my friend's van and had threatened to shoot him, but he had got by somehow. I liked the van, its little engine made an agreeable sound, '*tuff-tuff,*' and one sat rather high up in the nose of the thing; the single wheel was in the front, it did not need very much petrol and chugged along at a steady, soothing 40 or 50 km an hour. We had gone out of Paris for the day, with no particular purpose in view, there was nothing in the back, we had not brought anything with us, we both had a free day and had thought it would be nice to get out of the city in the spring sunshine. I remember we were chug-chugging along – '*teuf teuf*' – a very straight avenue cutting through a double bank of trees in the Forest of Fontainebleau, the road heading more or less south-east. We seem to have had the same thought at much the same time, and the silvery road, the shadows of the trees heavily marked at both sides and moving gently to a light breeze, stretched out ahead of us, dead straight, as if to invite us to go on and on, just to keep going, with no particular destination in view. Why not? Maurice said he could do with a visit to his parents, he might pick up one or two bits of furniture in Vellexon, let's make a leisurely trip, stop off for lunch, then dinner, and sleep in or under the van at whatever point we had reached by 10 p.m. or so. It really did seem quite a little adventure, all the better for having been totally unrehearsed. I had a bit of cash and my French PO book, no problem there; Maurice always travelled with quite a bit of cash, he never used cheques or banks. The silver road was almost empty, it was a Tuesday, outside any holiday period, and the traffic in these early 1950s was still very light. We had a very good lunch, I think at a Routier – it was before these had become fashionable and self-conscious – at Maison-Rouge. By evening we had reached Romilly, rather a seedy, semi-industrial town, very dusty, and with long grey walls of factories spelling out DÉFENSE D'AFFICHER. We had supper in Romilly, then found a quiet spot by the river; Maurice settled down to sleep in the van on some sacking, I decided to sleep underneath it, had a bad night and got bitten by masses of mosquitoes.

The van seemed to speed along as the road started climbing in rolling country, the green, gentle hills, heavily treed, separating the valleys of the Seine and the Aube. We stopped off for lunch at Bar-sur-Seine. It was another good lunch, the people in the restaurant were friendly, and I decided that I would leave Maurice at this point, and spend a night in Bar, to explore the place, and walk in the hills the other side of the river. The Seine at this point is quite a small stream, only about five feet deep in the middle, between banks covered in willows. It was very clear and one could see the big silver or greyish fish. First, I went to look for a hotel, and found one actually *on* the river, by a weir, at a place called Bourguignons – maybe that was where we had lunch, I cannot remember – anyhow I booked in for the night, the room was very cheap. As I had no luggage, I went into Bar, bought a sailor's sausage-shaped bag, pyjamas, a razor, soap, at a Prisunic. I had nothing to read, so went to a *tabac* and bought a cheap edition of Maupassant's *Une Vie*, his longest novel, and a very sad, hopeless one at that (I still have the copy, which is my reminder of Bar). I also bought the local paper, *Le Bien Public*, published in Dijon, but with a special Bar edition. I like local papers, they seem to help one to belong: news of sporting events, schools, weddings, *faits-divers* (nothing very alarming, poaching offences, illegal fishing, etc). I spent the rest of the day by the river bank or walking up through the woods. I had dinner at the hotel in Bourguignons, with a bottle of red *vin du patron*, a light burgundy, then a marc with my coffee, and went happily to bed about 10, I was very tired after the night under the van. The bedroom was white, walls and curtains, and I had a huge double bed, very high up and with a massive white bolster, an inviting *polochon*. I left the windows open and could hear the steady sound of the weir. I thought that I had been very lucky to have ended up in this spot. Furthermore no one knew where I was, and I had absolutely no reason to *be* where I was. I woke up to the crowing of the cocks. I had breakfast downstairs, brought to me by the son of the owners, a boy of about eleven, who was very polite. After breakfast I told the people I would be staying that night as well, it seemed a special luxury to have one whole day ahead of me, to explore further, and I had checked that there was a station and that I could get back to Paris by train. I wandered about all the morning, bought a towel, and had a swim, wearing my pants, it was very hot for May, and they were soon dry. Then I had an aperitif in the *tabac*, walked back to Bourguignons for lunch. I was the only person staying at the hotel, but there were several farm workers having lunch. In the afternoon I dozed by the tiny river. In the evening I had more than one marc and went to bed quite late. I had *Une Vie* out on the bedside table, but was too sleepy to read any of it. In fact it remained unread, though I had anchored it firmly in its place of purchase: 'R.C.C. ***mai, 1951 – Bar-sur-Seine'.

I stayed there three more nights: the Thursday, the Friday, and the Saturday, having all my meals at the hotel. I felt as if I were playing truant, though in fact I wasn't missing anything, save my working days in the Archives Nationales. The unplanned holiday gave me a wonderful sense of freedom. No one knew where I was, I think I sent my mother a postcard of the parish church of Bar, that is all. I was completely on my own, in an unfamiliar place that I had all the time in the world to explore. I had established a regular daily and evening routine and begun to recognize the people who had aperitifs in the *tabac*, and those who had lunch in the dining-room of the hotel; they even greeted me and I did not have to be asked what drinks I would want, just 'Comme d'habitude, Monsieur?' – the question mark a pure formality. There were rather more people at lunch on Saturday, a couple of families who had come by car, giving the place a weekend feeling, and this was not *quite* so nice as the quiet and the semi-isolation of the week. I could not afford to stay on into another week; I would take the train back on the Sunday afternoon. I could feel the Sunday difference: church bells in the morning, the *tabac* was closed, the men were in suits. I had been living outside time – no, that was not quite it, I had been *inside* time all right, each day: Wednesday, the first delight of exploration and discovery, Thursday, going over the same ground, Friday, striking out eastwards through the horse drives cutting through the thick woods as the yellow track climbed up to the top of the valley, with a view on to that *other* river, the Aube, and, if I could have seen it, the twin of Bar-sur-Seine: Bar-sur-Aube. Saturday a slight change of itinerary, to take in the station and look up train times. Every afternoon I had a swim, at much the same spot, beyond a bridge, where there was a deep hole in the river and the long green plants swirled around. On the Thursday I bought a pair of blue-and-red swimming trunks from Prisunic: another bid, too, to store up a claim to the location of my unplanned out-of-season holiday. Out of season, and all the better for that, the two local schools were noisy with children, giving Bar a feeling of everything as usual. Out of season, but the weather remained very warm, with a slight breeze; I had come without an overcoat or a mac, and their absence even added to my sense of freedom and truancy. I have done the same sort of thing in winter, but that curtails the time for exploration and out-of-doors habituation. When I paid my bill at the hotel on the Sunday morning, the family seemed really sorry to see me leave. They told me that, in the summer, quite a lot of English people came through on their way to Dijon and the Midi or the Alps. They knew I was English, because I had to fill in the thing for the Préfecture (no one knew where I was, but the police in Troyes, or maybe Dijon, would, in due course, and on the Thursday, at the *tabac*, the *capitaine de gendarmerie* had given me a wave when I went past his table, on the Friday he had shaken my hand).

I returned to Paris refreshed. It had been a bit like an Italian film I had seen that year: *Quatre pas dans les nuages* was the French title; it was about a rather harassed commercial traveller from Rome who had taken a bus out into the remote countryside. On the bus he had met a girl, there had followed a week of semi-fantasy. I suppose I was a bit romantic myself, I had seen the film several times. But Bar-sur-Seine had produced no girl. I had just wanted to be completely on my own, unattached, in an unexpected place in which I had no business to be present. I met Maurice on the Wednesday of the following week. I had called round in the evening at his ground-floor single room in the Rue d'Obligado; he had cooked a meal on his tiny stove, which we ate at a small round table, while he put on the Can-Can Bal Tabarin record in his gramophone – also a product of *les Puces*. His trip had been profitable, he had brought back two more heavy wooden wardrobes and had sold them at Saint-Ouen. He too was looking very well, refreshed, and even redder than usual. He asked me how I had spent my time in Bar; quite a nice little place, he had always thought, but had I not been a bit lonely? I did not really try to explain that I had not. Perhaps too I was being a bit coy, or a bit selfish: those few days in Bar had been my private treasure, another sort of pink cloud (as Mauricette had described our weekend encounters in 1947 – she *would* have used the expression 'petits nuages roses'), my exclusive possession. Still, as always, it was nice seeing Maurice again, things were looking up for him and he had discovered a source of unrationed petrol for the *Wehrmacht* (or ex-*Wehrmacht*) van.

Fifteen years later, on the way to Ferney Voltaire, with my wife and two children, we came down through the Bars and I had decided that we should spend the night at the hotel in Bourguignons. It was a mistake. Maybe one should never go back. The hotel had been spruced up, there were window-boxes with red geraniums, a *terrasse* with large sunshades, the dining-room had been provided with what looked like a ceiling of false beams, there were lights with pink lampshades at each table, and red-and-white table-cloths and napkins *en éventail* on each table. There was even a pseudo-rustic bar in the dining-room and the hotel now had a sign marked Auberge des Bourguignons outside – there had also been one to the right of the main road, a little before the left turn to the village. I knew what *Auberge* meant, and it did. The hotel was now in a guide. The people who ran the place were new, they told me that they had recently come in from Troyes and had taken it on. They seemed very house-proud. 'You should have seen the state we found it in when we succeeded the other people.' Still, no one could take away my five days of freedom, the glimpse of complete happiness.

* * *

I have been quite absurdly pleased with the little piece on Bar-sur-Seine that I wrote. It has a sort of springlike innocence about it, and not that of a public spring, but a private spring chosen at random, on the spur of the moment, more or less mid-week and right outside any holiday season: a secret in fact shared by Maurice and myself, and enjoyed, after he had dropped me off, exclusively by myself. I think another reason is that the Bar piece illustrates a theme always very dear to me, as an individualist: that of public catastrophe being put to good private use, a theme that I have tried to develop in all my historical writings – hence the concern with 'marginals' – how there were things that ordinary, but ingenious people could get out of anything even as awful as the French Revolution.

That is one of the themes, the other is the wonderful feeling of *escape*, simply for its own sake: not escape *from* anywhere or anything in particular, or *to* any precise destination, but just the enjoyment of the thing itself, of the open road, perhaps preferably heading south, or, as in this case, south-east. It is something that is wonderfully well expressed by one of the fairly early, and innocent, H. G. Wells novels, in that same luminous category as *Kipps* or *Mr Polly*; the one about the young shop assistant who takes to the very uncertain saddle of his wobbly bicycle – it is his first time on – in Bromley High Street, and then we follow him, with his own mounting sense of excitement and joy, as he heads south towards the Sussex Coast. There are a whole series of episodes, most of them involving some beauteous, not too well-spoken, didactic young lady (womens' movement *circa* 1910) and some vile pursuer. There is a chase, a meeting in a pub, a railway station, I cannot remember; but it is a sunny, optimistic little story in which Wells mocks his own rather gawky, socially insecure self. The old old theme in fact of the open road. So much for escape, a theme used by all the 1900 advertisements of the bicycle manufacturers both sides of the Channel.

First of all, there is Maurice's ex-*Wehrmacht* vehicle, something made on the cheap and mass-produced, for the specific needs of a highly motorized war, on the part of a country that was likely to be very short of fuel and that would have to think of every possible economy in petrol. Hence all those motor-cycle-and-side-car combinations that one sees in the war photos of the triumphant May–June 1940 lightning advance into the very heart of France; as if the British family engine of escape – husband on the bike, wife and baby in side-car – had all at once been transformed from the innocent instrument of getting away to Brighton or Hastings it had been, to a weapon of war: the side-car even carried a machine-gun. Hence, too, the two-stroke three-wheeler, little more than a covered-in motor bike – such as figures innocently and clumsily enough (it succumbs, in a clatter of dismemberment, to a single artillery shell) in Gracq's marvellous novel *Un Balcon en forêt*: a poor fragile thing – converted by Maurice, while the war was *still on*, as a vehicle of his private enterprise, his individual and inspired opening-out into the economy of the Black Market: the regular provision to the Paris flea market of furniture of an enormous scarcity value. A double triumph, or, possibly, a *triple* one, for some ingenious German soldier, possibly in supply or transport, or in repairs and mainte-nance, what we would have called REME, must have seen the advan-tage of flogging the little van – a very risky business, with an ever-vigilant *Feldgendarmerie* – or it may have passed through several German hands before ending up with a red-faced, now, since the Occupation, quite corpulent, apolitical Maurice, a man who, throughout the war years, had managed to live quite outside official public quarrels. He had absolutely nothing against the Germans – Maurice thought in terms of individuals, not of countries, nationalities (he would have made a good historian) – they were *around*, some of them must have found their way to *les Puces*, they were potential customers, people to do business with (Maurice, by 1942, had acquired a workable smattering of spoken German), all due precautions having of course been taken, by both parties, or by several of them; Maurice had also secured *Wehrmacht* petrol, not at the source, but no doubt at several removes. There is something admirable about Maurice's attitude to the war: he had not wanted it, had managed pretty well to avoid it, had demobilized himself in the favourable circumstances of June, 1940; for him, total defeat and national humiliation had meant individual escape – I think he took one or two Parisians with him at the same time, though he had been the only one to have headed, in a German furniture van, straight back to an empty Paris (and an *empty* capital is the *individual's* opportunity) – and a welcome return to civilian life. Maurice seemed to me a sort of French Švejk, he even *looked* a bit like Švejk, with his pudgy features, his high colour – a drinking man – his jaunty hat, and his catskin waistcoats; I had been drawn to him just for these reasons at the time that I had first met him, early in 1935. He was a natural rebel, but also a very prudent one. He took precautions. He was not, had never been, a violent person.

And here we were, using the little camouflaged van, demobilized, now civilianized, its black-on-white 'W' number plate replaced by a French Departmental one, white on black, like a negative of its former adherence – I think it had an Haute-Saône number-plate; Maurice favoured that, so many of the Paris traffic police came from his native Department, they would not have asked too many questions of a driver of a vehicle with that number-plate, whereas a '75' would have cried out for attention – here we were, using the van, in its leopard stripes of grey, red, and green, with black blobs, for a private excursion of the most private kind. I think it chugged on for a year or more on the Vellexon–Paris run, bringing in the big peasant wardrobes and rustic dressers, a panting apostle of peace, reconstruction, private enterprise, even climbing up steep Franc-Comtois inclines. Then, I think, that little two-stroke engine gave out, and Maurice could not find a replacement for it. I rather believe that it was succeeded by a small green van with a white star on its sides that had somehow found its roundabout way out of the US Army. There is something *symbolic* about the little *Wehrmacht* van.

Bar-sur-Seine would have been quite different had Maurice decided to stay on there with me, he would have got bored and grumpy, would have referred to the place as 'un trou', he was very much a neo-Parisian, he did not warm to the countryside although he came from a village, and he did not like walking, nor swimming. We spent quite a lot of time together, both before the war and after it, but it was nearly always in Paris, either in *his* territory, Les Ternes, or in *mine*, the VIme. And Maurice, in some respects, was a pretty coarse, vulgar fellow, he pinched girls' bottoms and was good at chatting up prostitutes, but I don't think he had much of an eye for topography, the beauty of a sky, the quality of light and that sort of thing. Maurice in fact suited admirably my baser, cruder Saturday-night needs; I am not a madly sophisticated person myself, and Maurice had a certain rough *joie de vivre* that I found infectious. And he *loved* food and drink, and could be very funny, in a bantering, cheeky sort of way. He would engage the first comer in conversation, addressing him suddenly from one table to the next, often sending him into fits. And he liked shocking people. But he could also be tedious, his political ideas were of the crudest, pre-Poujade stuff; there was an anti-Semitic streak that I found both puerile and ugly: he believed in Jewish 'plots' and attributed any set-backs he had suffered in his Black Market transactions to the malevolence of individual Jewish hucksters who had undercut him. But we generally kept off political topics, confining our mutual observations to the appearance of any girls to be seen in the cheaper restaurants that we used to frequent – often the Ternes branch of La Bière, a long, deep room where we could sit against the wall, enjoying a general view of all the tables. Occasionally we would indulge ourselves in a gastronomic splash: La Potée Champenoise, on the corner of the Rue de l'Odéon, was a regular monthly treat, if either of us had had a bit of luck; mercifully, after the war, Maurice had given up going to Vincennes – horses had been his undoing when I had first met him; he believed in *la martingale*, a system that, with constant repetition, would enable him to beat the bank and score over the PMU, and the strength of his conviction showed in his appearance and bearing: he had only one jacket, blue and very worn, and big holes in his socks, which he would reverse, his shoes let in water, he was bald and bare-headed, and had been unemployed since the slump of the early 1930s, when he had lost his job as a skilled make-up man with the film studios of Épinay. What we had in common was a fairly anarchical approach to life and total disrespect for authority. Later, he introduced me to a *petit bourgeois* world that extended from *les Puces* to the local *crèmerie*; he got on well with small shopkeepers, barmen, *tabagistes*, and, as I have said, prostitutes. To me, he was as much a guide as a fellow-observer. He was certainly a very welcome change from any of the sane intellectuals that I knew. Anyhow, Maurice and I did in fact do an awful lot together, especially in the second half of the 1940s and the early 50s. We were natural survivors, Maurice more experienced than myself – quite a veteran, in fact – and he enjoyed watching things from the sidelines. I never knew him get seriously involved with a woman, or indeed with anyone at all; though he was quite fond of his parents. I think he was very afraid of involvement, it might have interfered with his freedom of movement, something enormously important to him. He was a very free person, totally averse to any sort of work discipline; I think he found children boring. I was very surprised when I heard that, in his mid-sixties or early seventies – I think he must have been between thirty and thirty-three when I first met him in his hatless, shoe-leaking period in 1935 – he had set up with a lady of no doubt similar age in the small town of Genlis: at least a place in an *easterly* direction. I suppose Paris had become too tough for him and that he wanted to put on slippers. In 1970, I had dedicated a book to him, *The Police and the People*. I had sent the book to the Rue d' Obligado address and had got a very formal reply from the lady: 'M. Chauvirey me charge de vous remercier du livre et de vous assurer de nos bons sentiments', and an address, Rue de la Frane. Perhaps he might even have opened a bank account! (Crédit Agricole de la Côte d'Or?) *Enfin, sans la voiture.* I remember him still with great affection. He was the Frenchman I knew best, and he was the perfect companion for a Saturday night, whether in the Ternes or at the other end of

Paris. In a different age he would have gone for Dranem or the old music-halls of the Grands Boulevards. I suppose it was symbolic that I should have met him for the first time opposite Le Rex, that huge monument, in ice-cream blocks, to the optimism of the late 1920s, the largest cinema in Paris, Boulevard Bonne-Nouvelle.

7

'Comme un Titi parisien'

I ONCE heard myself described, much to my surprise, as 'typiquement oxfordien' – as if I had acquired a *double* – at a 'Thursday evening', sometime in November 1951, in the Cinéma Bonaparte, next to the Mairie du VIème, by a group of *normaliens* (judging from their semi-coded vocabulary and their references to some of the personalities of the Rue d'Ulm whom I knew at the time) three rows ahead of me, during the entr'acte of some old favourite, perhaps *The Magnificent Ambersons*, not dubbed but with subtitles. The descriptive adjective and adverb had come in response to a question put by another member of the group 'Qui est ce Côbb?' with all the *contempt* contained in the purity of the open French 'ô' in my one-syllable surname. The dimly lit screen was displaying advertisements for the local *bondieuseries* of the Quartier Saint-Sulpice: religious publications from Desclée et Brouwer (Tournai & Paris) and from Chez Mame of La Bonne Presse (Tours), medallions (to go round pious necks – like the unburnable British Army identification discs) of Bernadette, Jéhanne, and Thérèse, rosaries, leather-bound missals, white *première communion* ribbons, silver-framed pictures of *le père* Foucauld, and so on, while, between the seats, the attendants with trays went up and down the aisles: 'Chocolat glacé, Esquimau Gervais.'

Fame of a *sort*, I suppose, to have been thus described: 'typiquement oxfordien', three rows ahead, in the semi-darkness of a much-frequented cinema. But of what sort? I had hardly been in Oxford at all for the previous eleven years; still, there was a recognizable

French adjective for the apparently inescapable condition; try and apply that to Cambridge: 'typiquement' what? 'Tu sais que je suis typiquement oxfordien?' I said quite loudly, enough to cover the litanic 'Esquimau Gervais', to Hélène, the White Russian girl I was sitting with, before the lights went out, and some of the *normaliens* had had time to turn round, take a further look at 'Ce Cobb', and giggle. Then back to more important matters: the second half of the *Ambersons,* or whatever other classic we had all come there for.

Still, *visually* I belonged to an easily recognizable group: not *ethnic,* but still *typical,* a pretty good specimen, it seemed, almost a collector's piece. I suppose I could have given a hand to my collective identity by wearing a striped blazer in Merton College colours (maroon and white, a particularly dreadful combination) and a crest of red, blue, and gold chevrons over the pocket. Perhaps my recognition could have been pushed further if I had been wearing a boater with a maroon-and-white ribbon around it. But it would have drawn justifiable protests ('chapeau' . . . etc) from the rows behind, unimpressed by my obvious typological provenance; and it was November. My sticking-out ears, as viewed either from behind, or from the front, might have been a give-away of nationality, but not of an *Oxonian* species. (In profile I looked like a bird of prey, and one of a maritime habitat.) Were flippancy and frivolity visibly marked as physical attributes of those who had a penchant for both? Big questions, indeed, to which, no doubt in *my* innate frivolity, I had completely failed to address myself.

On the Sunday before the Bonaparte Recognition, the first Sunday of November, I had given a paper (*communication*) to the Société d'Histoire Moderne, which held a meeting in the Amphithéâtre Michelet (where Mathiez had died: there was a plaque on the front of the rostrum) the first Sunday of every month (July and August excepted). It was a very important occasion for me. In the previous two years I had given a number of papers to local gatherings of *sociétés savantes* in Saint-Germain-en-Laye, Mantes, Rouen and Le Havre, all in the valley of the Lower Seine (a river which I had described in my talk in Mantes, as a 'ruban argenté'; pollution, it is true, had not yet set in, and Mantes itself could still parade as Mantes-la-Jolie); and, at some stage, I had addressed a *séminaire* in Toulouse. But this was the first time that I had faced a Parisian audience, composed mostly of *professeurs d'histoire* at *lycée* level – many of them as rowdy as their pupils, talking loudly throughout a *communication*, moving about from row to row, and ignoring the pleas of 'Silence, svp' from the rostrum – but with a sprinkling of (equally ill-behaved) *universitaires*. I had prepared my paper with considerable care, both as to contents and as to the French; and I had timed my talk to exactly fifty minutes, so as to leave about three-quarters of an hour for questions, discussion, announcements, and so on, before adjournment of most of the *auditoire* (something of a misnomer for a group not always given to listening), the chairman, the Secretary and the speaker of the day to the Balzar for aperitifs and academic gossip.

The chairman of that session, M. Gadrat, a massive Béarnais, was a retired Inspecteur Général, a post of enormous prestige in such a gathering. After the Secretary had dealt with the Business of the Day, M. Gadrat, in his gravelly accent ('rocailleux' would have been the word, a French unmistakably from the South-West, that seemed to echo that of President Vincent Auriol), opened the proceedings: 'Je donne la parole à notre ami' (I could not be 'notre collègue', for I had no formal job) 'Monsieur Cobb' – and, in this case, the 'ô' was warm and friendly, even inviting – 'pour sa communication sur l'armée révolutionnaire parisienne.' I must have been nervous and gone a bit too fast in the first twenty minutes or so, then slowing up as my self-confidence increased, for when I had finished I found that I was five minutes ahead of my own much-rehearsed timing, and that my *communication* had in fact taken only three-quarters of an hour. There may have been the usual (and quite vain) appeals, 'Messieurs, je vous en prie, un peu de *silence*', but, in my nervousness, and speaking louder as if I had got into a second wind (dating from my few years as a long-distance runner), I had not heard them. The paper seemed to have been a success – possibly helped along by the prospect of the collective transfer to the Balzar coming five minutes early. There was plenty of applause, and in his formal expression of thanks, in the name of the rather mixed company of listeners, regular *non*-listeners, noisy late-comers, movers from row to row, and chain-smokers, to 'notre ami que l'on vient d'entendre avec tant d'intérêt', M. Gadrat had congratulated me on my mastery of French: 'Comme nous pouvons tous constater, Monsieur Cobb manipule notre langue avec l'aisance d'un *titi parisien*' (loud applause, habitual non-listeners included), or something to that effect. I did not know, and still don't, just *what* accent I had and have in French; it is something very difficult for even the most regular *usager* to establish – I could not hear myself, but I would have been only too happy with almost any snap judgments, so long as it wasn't one that could detect the slightest trace of an *English* one (my 'r's, for instance, were not quite sure of themselves, but nor were those of Martiniquais and other French citizens from *les Antilles*). I might well have had unmistakable traces of a Parisian one.

'Titi parisien' would *do*; I think it was meant to be both friendly and humorous and hardly to be taken literally. It was a tunic I was only too pleased to put on, once it had been offered to me. It was at a very far remove from my disguise of the following Thursday as 'typiquement oxfordien'. Two or three of Thursday's *normaliens* had been sitting in the – always noisy – back row of Michelet, of my Sunday exposure. 'Titi parisien', however it might be taken, was still several notches up on the question often put to me, on public transport or in cafés and *restaurants d'habitués*: 'Vous êtes Belge?' Or 'Vous êtes du Nord?' – though any of these would have been perfectly acceptable. Sometimes I even tried them out as a borrowed identity: 'Oui, je suis bruxellois' (the 'x' duly pronounced as an 's'), if in Paris, Rouen, or even Amiens. In Lyon, I would respond to an origin a bit further down: 'Oui, je suis roubaisien', or 'Je suis originaire de Hem.' It was enormously pleasing to get away with such assumed linguistic origins, though I always avoided them when crossing a frontier by train: the blue passport with the royal arms would give the show away.

It is also true that I had first stumbled into the spontaneity of that ultra-subtle language, with its enormous range of delicate half-tones and minute, almost imperceptible nuances, even to the extent of *thinking* in it, Boulevard Bonne-Nouvelle, next to La Piscine Neptuna, opposite Le Rex, and above the street bands on the broad pavement playing 'Madame la Marquise' and selling it by the sheet

– certainly the terrain of the weekend arrival of *les titis parisiens* from Bagnolet, Pantin, and Aubervilliers as they passed round the two Portes, Saint-Denis and Saint-Martin.

Quite recently, in the late 1980s, after giving a talk (on Louis XVIII) to the Royal Stuart Society, in an annexe to the big Jesuit church in Farm Street, London, I was approached by much the most conspicuous figure among those present at the meeting. He was a very tall man who had a curious tic: that of rubbing his left hand up and down his left cheek, and holding it lightly in his right hand, as if to prevent it from going off on its own. He had curly dark hair and a most engaging smile and he was dressed in a long, old-fashioned soutane, with buttons, either black or, I think, *red*, all the way down, from his neck to his black silver-buckled shoes covering a hint of purple or mauve socks. 'Monsieur Côbb,' he said, smiling, 'vous êtes bilingue.' I was puzzled by this remark, for I had used *no* French in my talk. I made this point. 'But', he grinned, 'you mentioned Collot d'Herbois, and that was enough'; 'Votre façon de prononcer ces deux mots m'a amplement suffit. Vous êtes bilingue.' Another member of my recent audience, as people moved off towards the table for drinks and *amuse-gueules*, whispered to me, on my enquiry, that the smiling priest was *le père* François Charles-Roux, whose father had been Ambassador in Prague and a very influential figure in the Quai. His sister, Edmonde, had written a novel, *Oublier Palerme*. If the son of an Ambassadeur de France, on the evidence offered by the double name of an ultra-terrorist, said that I was 'bilingue', then I must be, must *be bilingue*. Collot had done at least *one* good deed, however unwittingly, before perishing from yellow fever, somewhere in Guiana, in 1795 or 1796. *Le père* François had made my evening – though it ended in acrimony over dinner, in a noisy dispute between two leading female members of the Royal Stuart Society, each of whom claimed to be my hostess and, therefore, in charge of proceedings at the dinner-table, the seating plan, and so on. This branch of the Royal Stuarts appeared riven with internal divisions: *tiraillements* would have been the right word for what had clearly been an in-house split. It was also made clear to me, during a hurried dinner in an excellent Italian restaurant, that Louis XVIII was *not* a figure that a substantial section of the Royal Stuarts warmed to: he was too fat and too sensible. I wished *le père* François had been there; but his ecclesiastical duties had kept him in Farm Street. In the taxi (hastily summoned by my two rival hostesses) back to Paddington, I repeated out loud, 'Collot d'Herbois'. Perhaps it had been the two 'o's?

8

Rouen from the Sotteville Tracks

MOST OF the time that I spent working, in the Rue de Crosne, on the criminal archives of the courts of the then still Seine-Inférieure (and yet unaware of its degraded designation) and of the État-Civil of Rouen and its satellite communes, I was put up in an SNCF hut, wooden with concrete floors, erected by the French Army in 1938, amidst the marshalling yards of Sotteville-lès-Rouen, and offering quite acceptable accommodation to twenty lodgers, ten a side, with ten wash-basins facing each row of ten beds. The beds were not bunks, but real beds, with pillow-cases and sheets, and covered with thick dark-grey blankets marked in red with the letters 'SNCF'. Each bed had an accompanying small wardrobe and drawer. At the far end of the long wooden hut, there were two showers and five lavatories with seats. For the time I was put up there, the weather was warm, and the big coke stove remained unlit. The other nineteen lodgers were young trainee *cheminots*, mostly future signalmen. They were friendly, but not very communicative. On Friday and Saturday nights, I was left in sole possession of the hut, my fellow-lodgers gradually trickling back in the course of Sunday evening. They all had families in the Rouen area, mostly in the Left Bank suburbs of Grand and Petit Quevilly.

Over the far side of about twenty tracks and trip-wires, and the long slow-moving lines of six to eight coupled trucks – long silver containers: Vins Gévéor, Vins du Postillon (a huntsman with a twisted horn), Bières du Lion, Dumesnil (both with lions, the former, red and with curly braided tails; the latter, a yellow, shaggy head), petrol, a liquid gas, toxic fuel – there were about thirty red Michelines, each opened at the end, like a raised snout, showing a mass of pipes and all their innards, in front of the rather precarious-looking driver's stool: cross-country via Serqueux to Amiens, or, via Bernay, Lisieux, to Caen; some also, via Maromme and Clères, to Dieppe. But nearly all the strings consisted of the huge containers, pushed indolently by shunting engines with zebra stripes, and some all at once taking off, clanking, apparently moving on their own, then stopping for a rest. The gasping Michelines, like open-mouthed pikes, were over by the main lines from Paris to Rouen-RD (Rive Droite), before the first tunnel. There were no passenger carriages in sight, and the big Also-Thom Fives, diesels, also no doubt opened up to display their complicated insides, must have found a resting place further down in the direction of Paris, between Sotteville and Oissel.

There were no waiting trolley-buses on Sundays, so one had to walk over the wires and sleepers to near the dark entrance of the first tunnel, taking care to avoid the sudden burst of air-pressure from the fast-moving Paris train, then cutting down the steep slopes of Bonsecours, through a maize of little brick houses, to reach the level near Eau-de-Robec and Saint-Ouen.

The red trolley-buses waiting at their weekdays terminus the far side of the tracks carried on their sides the city's crest, a white Holy Lamb, trussed up by its legs, beneath a fleur-de-lis on a blue shield, far into the Communist-dominated industrial suburbs of the Left Bank, the two Quevillys, and so on, and the big Centrale: the main prison for the whole of Lower Normandy. The city's escutcheon carried a timid message that was perhaps not even noticed, or just taken for granted, by the early-morning passengers. What would the Holy Lamb be doing in one of the Quevillys or in Saint-Sever? My own route to the Rue de Crosne would take me to the rather impersonal Rue Jeanne-d'Arc, at the stop by the big Café de la Poste.

From the black wooden SNCF hut one could see, at some distance, and beyond all those obstacles, wires and suddenly moving strings of trucks, the waiting trolley-bus, its cable unhitched, as if resting. Then a *wattman* (or driver) in peaked cap and smart blue uniform pulled the drooping cable into place on to the overhead electric wire, indicating an early, but leisurely, unhurried, but silent, departure, the red bus soon filling up two or three stops beyond Sotteville: a muted progress suited to a muted city (only in the markets would one hear a raised voice), the passengers mostly silent, whether seated or holding on to the rail at roof level. There would be a lot of wet umbrellas, making the red floor of the bus very slippery, and the smell of wet rubber and damp clothes. The dank smell would be partly overlaid by cigarette smoke from rolled-up Rizla paper. The windows would be misted over by the third or fourth stop. But the passengers knew their stops, pushing their way through the puddled wetness, to reach the opened swing-door, and trying to avoid the torrential flow of the paved gutter.

On Sundays, there was *no* waiting bus, Sotteville seemed sleepy in the still silence; but there was still the intermittent clanking and coupling of the small strings of ten or so containers; coal trucks spewing over, or long low-slung chassis bearing tree-trunks, all at once deciding to make a move down a slight incline, then stopping and going into reverse. You had to keep your eyes about you, in every direction. The little strings seemed to be tracking one by stealth. Apart from the discreet clanking and the low rumble of wheels, a Sunday silence (almost palpable) was all at once broken, in unison, by church bells coming from the deep bowl of the city: the grave, clanging ones of the Cathedral; less insistent, but recognizable, those of Saint-Ouen, Saint-Nicolas, and Saint-Maclou; the tinkle from many small shrines on the slopes to the east and to the north. And a Sunday *rain*, even more implacable than a weekday one. It was time to break my own rules, as I slithered down the steep muddy banks, and put on a blue beret, with a coloured silk lining (Basque, probably), that had been tucked in the pocket of my mac, along with the two heavy keys that would open the green *porte cochère* of the Rue de Crosne, giving me Sunday access to the huge minute-books of the État-Civil of Rouen and of some of its communes: Sotteville itself, Darnétal, Bonsecours, Déville, Oissel, maybe others.

Early on Sunday, I had swept thoroughly right through the long hut, cleaned the wash-basins and the lavatories with Javel, and shaken out the yellow SNCF mats. My weekday companions were very neat and tidy; perhaps they had PCF mothers back in the two Quevillys, and I wanted to impress them. I enjoyed the lonely activity of the quiet, wet Sunday morning, as if I possessed the hut. I even had a go with bucket and mop, opening the main door to look out on the gentle warm rain. First thing Sunday was to wash out my socks in my basin and put them to dry on the bar at the end of my bed. The rest of my clothes would go to a *blanchisserie*, open on Sunday morning, over the bridge beyond the far platform of Rouen-RD. The young trainees would turn up in the early evening with big Monoprix bags containing their washing, to last them out till the Saturday morning. They would also bring large black containers divided into compartments, which contained their food for the same period. There were no heating-rings in the hut, and they took the containers to the *cheminots*' canteen beyond the tracks, in a brick building near the Mairie, in the main street of Sotteville itself, which also contained a Decorated church with delicate fan vaulting. Sotteville had a pre-railway past.

The rest of Sunday I would be alone with my dead *fileuses*, later just numbers to figure in my only graph, drawn up with the expert help of Jean Meuvret and appearing, both dramatically and rather unfeelingly, in an article republished in my book *Terreur et subsistances* (Clavreuil, 1965). La Moulière was shut; I had to make do with a restaurant of only four tables run by two almost identical red-haired ladies – in fact, mother and daughter – who took it in turns to cook. There was only one *plat du jour*, *petit-salé aux lentilles*, which marked out Sunday like the steady warm rain; almost invariable *radis beurre* (salted) and Camembert. The occupants of the three other tables ate there all through the week; they had credit, written on a slate. None was from Rouen, they were elderly couples from the Centre of France, two men had lived in Senegal and spoke nostalgically about restaurants and cafés in Dakar. The tiny restaurant was in the Rue des Mauvais Garçons. Whichever of the redheads was doing the cooking would talk through the hatch, with her sleeves rolled up, addressing herself to the couple from Moulins. The other lady sat on a lonely chair, smoking Gitanes. The single table had been left for my use: 'le jeune homme au petit-salé'. But they had paid me no further attention. Each place had before it a full litre bottle of Gévéor, which seemed appropriate. Whether you drank it all or left a bit would not make any difference, you still paid for the whole litre (not at all expensive), and there would be another bottle laid before one's place in the evening, with the second round of *petit-salé*. Sometimes the two ladies changed places in the evening.

One Thursday, La Moulière was closed for some reason. The little table was occupied and I was told to come back in an hour. All the litre bottles were empty and the six 'regulars' had moved on to *café-calvados*. I was assigned the tail-end of Thursday's *plat unique*: *boeuf au gros sel* (and waiting litre of Gévéor). Dakar was on the menu again. One of the redheads had rolled herself some Dutch tobacco in Rizla paper. It would have been interesting to identify the other five days and their accompanying *plat*, the faithful Gévéor as a sentinel (and a reminder of the long silver bullet that rumbled through the night); but I was frozen as 'le jeune homme au petit salé'. Was Friday *raie au beurre noir*? Did *tripes à la mode* have a day? Was *la potée champenoise* a Monday or a Tuesday? I never found out. I had to stick to La Moulière in the week: I had my place there, at a single table, right at the back; a *pichet de cidre* laid out, but one which the waitress, in a flowered plastic smock, would at once replace by a *demi-Côte, vin du patron*.

In Sotteville, as in Rouen, Rue Fontenelle, or Rue de Crosne, I was a prisoner of habit; I *liked* my prison, especially getting back at night by the trolley-bus to the terminus, then crossing the trip-wires and the rails, under the arc lights and the winking yellows, greens, and reds, the strings creeping up in shadow, and the *berceuses* of the night's rumbles and clinkings and the gentle breathing and occasional exclamations of my nineteen companions. I had six weeks in the hut and my regular Sunday routine. I even worked in the *archives communales* of Sotteville in the Mairie. The *secrétaire* told me I was the first person ever to have consulted the minutes of the *conseil général* for 1793 to 1795. There had been a royalist riot there in the spring of 1795, the Sottevillois (and Sottevilloises) had reopened the handsome church, sawn down the Tree of Liberty, burnt the wooden Déclaration des Droits de l'Homme, and then marched on Rouen down the steep slope of Bonsecours, and besieged the Hôtel de Ville, demanding both bread and a King. I wrote a short article about the riot for *Annales de Normandie* and sent an off-print to *la secrétaire*.

I had been happy in the hut as well as in the Sunday freedom of the Rue de Crosne. I had found the trainee *cheminots* much less demanding (and much cleaner, they all slept in pyjamas) than the occupants of bunks in a Nissen hut provided by the British Army in 1942. They did not ask me questions or confront me with *L'Huma-Dimanche* or 'la vie soviétique'; but I was very grateful to the PCF deputy of one of the two Quevillys – or maybe of both – who had fixed me up with this long stay, free of charge. Much later, I acted as interpreter for him at the time of *ces événements*, when he confronted a group of Balliol Maoists, whom he infuriated when he described the Billancourt activities of their Parisian counterparts, mostly from the XVIme, as 'ces enfantillages'. He was a Rouennais born and bred and knew his way about the industrial Left Bank, and the *other* termini of the trolley-buses bearing the Holy Lamb. I think he got on very well with the eminently sensible and pragmatic Waldeck-Rochet.

I liked living on the fringes of places and organizations, and 'lès' always seemed a good sign, something to go for, in its tricky relationship to the larger unit: Sotteville-lès-Rouen, the scene of a major anti-mobilization riot in August 1914, led by the *cheminots* and their wives. Sotteville reminds me of past happiness, the excitement of local archival research, the rumble of wheels and buffers, and being alone throughout warm, wet Sundays, Rue de Crosne, with the huge green-bound *registres* marked, in pale, browning ink, 'Rouen' or 'Darnétal', or my subsidiary identity as 'le jeune homme' (I was thirty-five or so) 'du petit-salé aux lentilles' or 'le jeune homme du dimanche' – especially those last, despite the absence of the trolley-bus.

The SNCF had done me proud.

9

A Balkan Experience

It HAD all started in the form of a letter: a surprise invitation, quite out of the blue, to give twenty lectures in English on nineteenth-century European diplomatic history to a summer school composed of adult Americans and Canadians at the impressively named Istituto di Studi Europei di Torino (financed, as I was later to discover, by Olivetti; there was a statutory visit each summer to Ivrea, to the factory, the forecourt of which was presided over by a large stone statue of 'Il Fondatore', a stern bearded figure sitting bolt upright in a tall-backed chair. I think that Institute also had some close connection with *La Stampa*). The notepaper was as impressive as the title, the building itself was rather less so (I felt an Institute should at least have marble columns): a two-storeyed, squat building, in grey cement, the two lecture rooms and the office on the ground floor, the open windows – it was very hot in July – letting in the constant blare of the traffic and the ringing bells of the trams. The summer school went off all right, the Americans were almost painfully grateful. There was a banquet in a big hotel, followed by speeches. I suppose it had been an important occasion, for this was the first time the organizers had tried out a Summer School. After that there would be a regular July one.

After the first Summer School in Turin, I was asked to return for a three-week lecture course each Easter. This time the lectures were all to be in French and were to range over the diplomatic history of Europe in the nineteenth and twentieth centuries. My Easter visits began in 1956 or 1957, and continued for two or three successive years. I don't know how the students who attended these courses were selected, but, as far as I could make out, almost anyone who applied would be accepted, provided that they were enrolled in a university in their country of origin. I think the Institute was anxious to keep up numbers, no doubt in order to impress Olivetti, *La Stampa*, and the Prefecture of Turin (which also contributed to the funding, as a modest contribution to Piedmontese Euro-imperialism). There were always more men than girls. On completing the Easter course, each student would obtain a diploma of European Studies: the diploma was seen, rightly or wrongly, as a help to eventual employment in one or other of the various European institutions. In the course there was a strong emphasis on International Law and on economics.

Most of the students were in their twenties, a few of them were older. Apart from myself, the other lecturers were French, Belgian (including my friend Jan Dhondt, a historian from the University of Ghent), or Italian. Among the students, the West Germans always formed the largest contingent; they were also the most professionally and solemnly 'European' – they did not make it seem an easy state, it sounded uphill work all the way. There was a scattering of Austrians, Dutch, and Belgians, the rare Frenchman or Frenchwoman, a few Yugoslavs, and, each year, one or two selected Spaniards, always male, let out by Franco Spain. The students were a cheerful bunch, and I often used to spend the evening with them in an underground wine bar full of huge wooden barrels, a cool and welcoming place called La Casa Paluch, which served Bardolino, Barolo, and other excellent Piedmontese wines.

Either on this particular course, or on the previous one, there had been a surprise newcomer: *one* Bulgar – female, dark, almost luminous hair with a blueish tinge, very pale skin, well-formed features, eyelashes that came half-way down her cheeks, eyes that she could cause to roll most alluringly, a trick I have always associated for some reason with lovely Turkish girls straight out of Pierre Loti's oriental novels. I did once imprudently make the association, later in Sofia; it could not have been worse received: I had commented in admiration, after a spectacular eye-roll from the other side of the table over lunch: 'Maria, tu es belle comme une turque' (I might have used the form, more intimate, 'turquesse'). No, it had not been appreciated, I had counted without Bulgar national susceptibilities; though it could have been even worse if I had said 'une roumaine', or 'une serbe'. I was to learn the hard way about the intricacies of Balkan nationalism.

At my very first lecture that year, I had spotted the Balkanic presence. I had gone to the office, and had looked up her card. Her name was given as Maria Peneva, her age as twenty-nine, and she was described as a graduate student in the Law School of Sofia University, working on a thesis on the International Law of Contract. Her eminently desirable presence certainly represented an important change of policy on someone's part, for, up till then, there had been no students from beyond the Iron Curtain, with the exception of Yugoslavs. Much to my delight, Maria became a regular attender at our evening sessions at La Casa Paluch. As if by accident, she generally seemed to be sitting directly opposite myself. I noticed that she could handle considerable quantities of Bardolino and Barolo. Her French was very good, with an unfamiliar, exotic accent. She told me, on the first evening that we had been there together, that she had noticed that I had taken a strongly pro-Russian line in both my nineteenth- and twentieth-century lectures. She was glad that I had made a fuss of the Tsar Liberator, it sounded almost as if I had paid her a personal compliment. I was sorry when the course came to an end that year.

Five or six months after my return to England, I began to get a flood of letters – one or two a week – with pretty stamps marked 'BULGARIJA', with a 'SOFIYA' postmark on them. There were long descriptions of the autumn tints in the northern part of her country, beech, elms, poplars, birch turning, as she was driven back from the Romanian frontier, to convoy to Sofia some high-up African Marxist ladies: Mme Veuve Lumumba, and suchlike, the honoured guests of the Bulgarian Womens' Committee. (Maria explained, in one of her letters, that she worked as an interpreter and general introducer and guide for the female section of the Central Committee of the Bulgarian Communist Party, or something of the kind.) Her letters were affectionate and delicately descriptive. Why did I not come and see for myself? She would be my guide, show me around, there would be no language difficulties as she could act as my interpreter, she thought that she could free herself of most of her work engagements over the period of the New Year, and, anyhow, she would very much like to see me again, she had so much enjoyed our evenings together at La Casa Paluch, and it would be so much easier for me to come and see her, than for her to come and see me. She would introduce me to her mother and to some of her friends, and would show me her home (by then, after more than a dozen letters sent in both directions – for I sent prompt and affectionate replies to all of hers – I felt that I already knew 19 Ulica Luben Karavelov, having written it, not without tremor, on so many Basildon Bond envelopes).

I had no need to be asked twice (in fact, she had asked me six or seven times; that was the general drift of all her letters sent to me in October and November 1961, and that had brought the autumnal hues and the brightly coloured BULGARIJA stamps to the thick yellow fogs that hung over the playing-fields of Leeds Grammar School as seen from the dining-room of my flat). I was quite un-attached at the time, and such an insistent series of appeals had been pretty irresistible; it all seemed so *difficult* (and was), and was all the more romantic for that. I had a colleague in the French Department, who lived down the road and who had a Bulgarian wife, Helene, whom I consulted. I joined, as a Life Member, the Anglo-Bulgarian Friendship League for £1 (the Friends seemed a pretty undis-tinguished lot), set about the long-drawn-out task of obtaining an entry and an exit visa – these eventually came, in Cyrillic lettering, two sprawling signatures in violet, with more brightly coloured stamps, a transit visa both ways through Yugoslavia (in roman script), hotel bookings in Sofia (Hotel Bulharija), a banker's order on the National Bank of Bulgaria for the sum of £150, the corre-sponding sum in lewas to be delivered on arrival, and various other operations carried out through the auspices of Balkantourist, an agency of remarkable dilatoriness and inefficiency. Before my departure from Leeds, I bought a first-class return from Paris to Sofia, on the Orient Express travelling from Paris to Istanbul. I was told the train left the Gare de Lyon at 7.30 in the evening.

* * *

The date is approximately 29 December, 1961, sevenish in the evening. Gare de Lyon; I am about to take the Orient Express, as it still was, though with no uniform carriages – mostly SNCF, Italian wagons-lits – from Paris to Istanbul; I have a first-class return from Paris to Sofia, a couchette as far as Venice. The last carriage of the train, its end almost level with the ticket barrier, is a *wagon-restaurant* of the best sort, the menu displayed in the window, a seat ticket obtained from the head waiter in white jacket with gold epaulettes, who tells me they will start serving, there is only one service, at 7.15, a quarter of an hour before the train's departure. I check my bags – several of them, for I am carrying a lot of stuff to Helene's sister, a doctor in a Sofia Polyclinic – in my first-class couchette compartment; the couchettes have not yet been made up. I leave everything in my reserved seat, hand in my numbered ticket, am directed to a small table for two, at the far end of the *wagon-restaurant*, on the right. One or two other tables are occupied; I am alone, facing the direction of the train. I can watch the late arrivals, the waiter comes round with his tray of aperitifs, I select a Campari-Soda, taking a long time over it, as more and more people rush ahead past the barrier, burdened with luggage. This is the way to travel, already sitting at the beautifully laid table, immobile under the huge glass dome of the station, sitting up high above the flustered travellers, sipping my Campari. Sheer luxury, such a very good start on a long and (to me) mysterious journey (I have never before been beyond the Iron Curtain), on a prestigious train. And, indeed, it looks prestigious, there are three or four blue-and-gold wagons-lits, green carriages of Yugoslav origin, SNCF, red carriages of Italian FS – they won't all be going to Istanbul, some will terminate at Trieste, some at Belgrade.

As I have the night ahead of me, and it is still early, I decide on a second Campari. Whistles, the train starts with a very gentle jolt, making the glasses rattle. The lights of Villeneuve Saint-Georges, the headlights of cars picking out the dark rain puddles, a wet, windy night, the train gathering speed. I have just been served from the hors-d'oeuvre tray, a wide selection; I order a half-bottle of Saint-Émilion, pop, it is open, I hold it straight as the train takes a curve, propping up *Le Monde* against it.

Enter a very well-dressed, youngish man, a fawn-coloured suit, buttoned-down shirt collar, elegant hands, good-looking, very well cared-for short fair hair, mid-thirties. 'Vous permettez?' Of course I do, putting away my paper. He takes his place opposite me, orders a whisky. We start to talk, rather formally, in French. His French is very good, but he is not French (my French is very good, but I am not French). We seem to be matches for one another. We start talking about this and that, how agreeable it is to start the journey in this way, a second serving of hors-d'oeuvres as the Banlieue Sud-Est slips by on a wet, greasy night, the lights of the *wagon-restaurant* reflected in the puddles of the black road that runs parallel to the line. My *vis-à-vis* eats like a Frenchman, using only a fork, leaving the knife beside his plate (I do the same: we are not giving anything away as yet). He asks me where I live, I say in Paris, for the moment; he tells me he lives near Chartres, in a château that belongs to his mother. They had thought of living in England, but *maman* and he had decided against it – since Attlee you cannot get decent servants there – they have a Portuguese staff, very reliable and hard-working. And so on, in our careful, cautious, polite French, through the entrée, beef, *pommes lyonnaises* very well done. We had each finished our half-bottles; I offer two more, he accepts. Cheese (Pont-L'Évêque in my case). He puts the question: let me guess your nationality. I take it up. He opts for my being 'Belge'. No. I opt for his being 'Danois'. No. More tries. No good. *Cartes sur table*. I say I am English, he says he's American. We both laugh, and start talking English. He has only a slight American accent. Oh yes, before that, while still talking French, he asks me where I am going, I tell him, 'Sofia', he expresses alarm, you are going among barbarians, it will be dangerous and uncomfortable, I put on a brave face. He tells me he is changing at Milan for Florence, or perhaps he says that he is in a wagon-lit that is merely detached at Milan from the main part of the train. What is the purpose of my journey? Sentimental. And his? The same, a choice between two loves, a French one, and an Italian one. What is my opinion? I opt for Italian, *Italiennes* are more loving than *Françaises*. A look of distress on his handsome, slightly sunburnt face. Not *girls*, he exclaims, as if I had said something vaguely obscene: a French boy of seventeen, a Florentine boy of sixteen, a crisis, the boy's mother, a Contessa, has sent him a telegram. I own up to the fact that I am travelling to meet 'une bulgare', he looks even more shocked. Then comes the guessing game, then both of us in English. His mamma cannot live in the United States, he looks after the château for her, keeps her entertained; they have many friends among the French nobility, local chatelains and chatelaines, royalists from the Noble Faubourg, parishioners from Sainte-Clothilde, and so on. I cannot compete in that league. Are they not a little boring? Well, yes, some are, but mamma enjoys that sort of company.

Digestifs: I have an Armagnac, he a marc. Then each another. We share the wine, and each pays his own bill. It is now about nine, we must be about the level of Dijon. He suggests that we go to his wagon-lit, he has a single one, for a night-cap. He certainly knows the drill: he rings, an Italian attendant in brown uniform comes promptly, my friend addresses him as 'Gustavo', and orders a whole bottle of Italian white; his Italian seems very good. I sit down on the bed, it is rather hot, I take off my thick red pullover, bought two days before at the *marché de Buci*, to protect me from the Bulgarian winter. Burton – he had given me his card: Burton something something Jr (there had been no mention, in the course of our conversation over dinner, of something something Sr), Chateau de . . . , Eure-et-Loir; I had had to own up to the fact that I did not possess a visiting-card, adding, rather perfidiously, that in England people did not use them – becomes rather pressing, I try and convince him that it is a very long time since I have had any approaches of this sort, not in fact since Shrewsbury, almost a quarter of a century ago, I am sorry, I really cannot oblige, he even starts crying. Do I not love him? No, I don't. The bottle is finished, it seems late, I say it is time for my couchette, or I'll be waking up the other three. I leave hurriedly, walk the length of four carriages, climb in on top, amidst muffled protests in Italian. I wake up a bit before Venice, realize that I have left my new pullover in the wagon-lit, go and look for it, am told that it had been detached at Milan. No pullover, and Sofia is quite close to Witocha or some such mountain; I have been told, before leaving Paris, that people go skiing there by tram. A bad start. And much the worst of the journey yet to come. I wonder whether Burton will opt for the Italian boy. I thought it a bit inconsiderate of him to have made such a direct approach – *and* to have been responding to a crisis, the sixteen-year-old Florentine boy had been threatening suicide . . . ! I suppose both Burton and I were romantics, in our differing ways.

After Trieste, the journey became vastly uncomfortable. It was just before the New Year, and the whole of Tito's army seemed to be going home on leave. At Ljubljana, the train was more or less taken by assault, soldiers, in evil-smelling khaki or poor-quality serge, climbed in through the windows, first-class was no protection; still more clambered in at Zagreb, and from there to Belgrade I was blocked in my seat by the window, soldiers standing up landing on top of me every time the train swerved. There was no possibility of fighting my way to the restaurant car, and, in any case, the man with a bell said that he would only take dinars he would not accept francs. At Belgrade, a station that drew attention to itself in two huge electric signs, the one in Cyrillic script, the other in roman, 'BEOGRAD', all hell was let loose: as one lot of soldiers climbed *out* of the windows, another lot climbed *in*. I had nothing to eat throughout the length of Yugoslavia. But after Niš, there was a strange quiet, and I went to sleep.

I was woken up by the silence, the utter stillness, and the complete lack of movement, as if the train had given up the ghost. It had stopped in gently rolling, thickly wooded country, a bit like Central Wales, save that it seemed completely uninhabited; there was not a farm, nor a cottage in sight. There was a big, burly man with dark curly hair, and wearing a black suit in my compartment; he must either have got in at Niš or only just got on the train while I was still sleeping. He told me, in halting English, that this was the Bulgarian frontier. Was I going to stay in his country? I told me that I was going to Sofia. He said that he was sure that I would have a most pleasant stay; he seemed to mean it, it was something more than a polite formula of welcome. Then there were faint sounds, in the still, clear, morning air. Then they got louder, a sort of chant: 'Hurrah, hurrah', accompanied by accordion music and slightly doleful, repetitive singing; then, suddenly, from nowhere, four soldiers, arm in arm, led by an accordionist and a soldier with a fiddle. The soldiers were dressed in long, greenish winter overcoats, with big brass buttons in double rows down the front, and peaked caps. Soon about twenty of them, in rows of four, clinging on to one another in an apparent effort to remain standing, began weaving around on the far platform of the little yellow station; some of the soldiers were holding earthenware bottles. A blanket was produced from somewhere, four soldiers took each corner of it, the others gathered round, shouting, clapping, and singing. Suddenly a huge man with a thick black moustache, also in a long overcoat, but with a thick gold stripe on his sleeve, was thrown high into the air, his vast mass showing up in black shadow against the bright, clear morning sun. Down he came, then up again, five, six, seven times, his cap had fallen off, and one of the soldiers had picked it up. 'They are happy, you see', the big man in my compartment explained to me, as if the whole scene had been laid on for my exclusive benefit (I think I was the only passenger from Paris still left on the train, so perhaps I was indeed a privileged spectator of this outburst of exuberant joy). 'They have just finished their period of military service', my informant went on, 'and they have been celebrating all night with their drill sergeant.' I could not imagine this sort of thing happening in our Army to an RSM or a CSM. The noise gradually diminished as the uncertain crocodile moved away from the station, disappearing into the trees.

More men in long overcoats, peaked caps with green-and-white favours, climbed into the train and opened the sliding doors of the compartment. One of them, after examining my visas, gave me my passport back, saluted, and said something to me in Bulgarian. My ever attentive fellow traveller told me that the official had wished me a pleasant stay in peace-loving Bulgaria. I wished that I could have reciprocated. Then a severe-looking lady, also in a long winter overcoat and uniform, went through all my bags, in search of food, fruit, and vegetables to confiscate. After she had gone, the train started with a sudden jolt, pulled by a magnificent steam loco-motive – I had seen it earlier, waiting, with its steam up and hissing, on the opposite line – decorated with a glass Bulgarian lion and a red star. My black-suited, peace-loving mentor went to sleep, rather to my relief, for I had feared that I might be treated to a further, more intensive session on the subject of Bulgaria's pacific aspirations, all the way to Sofia. I remained awake, looking out for the first suburbs of the capital city. But there was nothing to be seen other than brownish, waterlogged fields partly covered in thin snow.

The train came to a sudden halt in what appeared to be *rase campagne*. There was nothing to be seen that might have suggested a station, no glass roof, no waiting-rooms, no great portico, indeed, no platforms, no bustle; there was complete silence, apart from the panting of the huge engine: just an anonymous stop on the main line to Istanbul. It seemed something of a let-down to the former reader of *Le Journal de Bulgarie*. Surely the Tsar Boris would have insisted on something more impressive at the start or the conclusion of his engine-driving outings? There was not even a notice in Cyrillic characters to say: 'SOFIA'. I would not have known that I had actually got there, had it not been for the presence, standing in the fresh snow (the whiteness of which accentuated the blueish blackness of her hair and the high colour of her cheeks) of a dark-haired person who was the object of my long journey from Paris, via Trieste and Belgrade (two nights in the train, one supper, no other meal). Maria, who was standing on the sleepers between the lines (there were only two lines), was dressed in an old beige duffel coat, a product of the West that she acquired during her spell in East Berlin a few years before, of which she was extremely proud. She claimed that it was the only genuine British duffel coat in the whole of Bulgaria. The coat was to be very much in evidence throughout my stay.

In fact, I was rather touched by the modesty of the place in thus coyly not advertising itself: Maria, in her hooded coat, standing there between the lines, sufficed to give a firm identity to the locality. I threw down my bags and cases, then climbed down from the steep SNCF carriage, and walked across the other line. I could not see any other passengers, and Maria appeared to be the only person waiting for the Paris train. The train itself had got much shorter: only five carriages and a postal van. Perhaps few people travelled to Sofia around the New Year, even though there was only a train twice a week. There was no one to collect my ticket. It was a suitably romantic arrival, and I was grateful for the informality of an occasion to which I had been looking forward so intensely for the previous two months. As we left the non-station, Maria told me that the train had only been half an hour late, quite good going really, it could be anything up to three hours overdue. Clearly, she had spent quite a lot of time hanging about at the non-station, or waiting at the fog-bound airport, for her African female delegations. Waiting was very much part of her job with the women's section of the Central Committee. Indeed, as I was very soon to discover, waiting was something of a Bulgarian national occupation. Maria was not only patient, she certainly knew her way around. She had even secured a taxi, an untidy Mercedes that had seen better days; it was waiting dejectedly, like its driver, in a gloomy square. The taxi was to take us to my hotel, the Hotel Bulgaria, Boulevard Russki, in the centre of the town, opposite the old Russian Embassy church. There were no other taxis to be seen. The streets seemed quite empty. There was a twenty-minute ride along wide, foggy avenues, on which a few muffled family groups were walking. At the hotel, we had a very welcome lunch in the smaller dining-room. Maria was keen that I should try what she described as a typically Bulgarian dish, which seemed to be like any other shish kebab. We had a bottle of rough red wine. I liked the coarse rye bread. I was ravenous. Maria told me that we would be having dinner at her mother's, 19 Ulica Luben Karavelov; she would call for me at the reception desk at six that evening.

* * *

Who was Luben Karavelov? I have no idea; I expect some hero, heavily moustached, either of the 1923 uprising, or of the so-called Liberation, after the fall of the Regents. The entrance to the block was next to a red-fronted bookshop. Maria told me, as we approached the place, that there was a neighbourhood watch, the man on the ground floor. Maria's flat was on the third floor. It was a big flat: five rooms. She lived there with her mother; they should have had only two rooms, but there had been some sort of a fiddle, these things could be arranged: Mme Peneva's health was not

good, there had been a medical certificate, so they had been able
to keep most of the flat. There was a student in the fifth room; he
must have been very well-behaved, for I never heard a sound
coming from it. Maria's father had been a leading Agrarian, a
friend I think of Kostov. In the first Government after the
overthrow of the Regents, he had been appointed Bulgarian
Ambassador to Ankara. He had been lucky, for he had died there
after a heart attack sometime before the Kostov Trial. Maria had
studied Law and was doing her Law thesis on Contract; but she
had been mobilized into Party work owing to her knowledge of
French, German, and a bit of English – though I never heard her
speak that. For some time she had worked in East Berlin in some
women's international front organization. She had not enjoyed her
time among the East Germans. She must have had protection in
high places, for she was the only Bulgarian ever to have been sent
to the Turin Institute. She wanted to get a teaching post in the Law
School, but she had made herself too useful dealing with all the
Mme Lumumbas of African Marxist regimes, as a sort of guide-
cum-interpreter. There was certainly nothing vaguely proletarian
about the family background.

The main room in the flat, with windows on to the cherished
Luben and on to the back, which offered a close-up view of the
Television Tower, combined as sitting-room and dining-room. It
was overcrowded and a bit musty, a peppery smell. It looked as if it
had been furnished in one go in the early 1920s: a lot of German or
Viennese kitsch – stuffed dolls, black-and-white pierrots, elabo-
rately embroidered cushions (not for use), Egyptian motifs, lots of
little tables covered in mother-of-pearl designs, in fact quite an
abundance of Central European *petit bourgeois* bad taste. There
was even a terracotta sphinx in light beige, with black vertical
stripes which gave it a baleful Red Indian look, that stared from the
top of a covered piano. The sofa was draped in what I took to be a
Turkish silk cloth. The whole décor seemed to have stuck firmly
somewhere in the mid-Twenties. It was very much the sort of furniture I would have expected in one of Eric Ambler's Balkan stories:
the run-down villa of an elderly Professor, or a former Minister, in
peeling yellow stucco, among the fruit trees, behind a tall, grey wall.

I can remember little about Maria's mother – we had no common language – she seemed friendly, and, for my first evening, she cooked a pleasant, rather spicy meal. There was a young couple, a sculptor and his wife, friends of Maria's. After supper, I went to sleep for a couple of hours on the sofa. This was the only time I ever went to the flat. Maria explained to me that I had better not call there, but always wait for her in the hotel, she would ring me and let me know when to expect her. When we were walking together, we were always followed. Every morning, throughout my stay, she received an eight o'clock visit from two men from the People's Militia to tell her everything that the two of us had done on the previous day. It seemed a bit pointless, as she knew already.

Over meals, especially in the Klub Russki (still frequented by some elderly White Russians), we talked over our plans for the future. How could she get out of Bulgaria? – it was clear she wanted to, had given it a lot of thought – the problem was her mother, they would never let *her* out. And so on and so on.

There were one or two very bad days, when Maria rang up in the morning to say she would not be able to come, some old trouts, etc. Then I would be confined to the hotel, though I did once walk to see some Roman baths, visit the Tomb, and a sixteenth-century Turkish mosque. I would on these occasions have to have all my meals in the hotel. I would drink rather a lot. I was reading Lampedusa; he made me very nostalgic for the Other Europe. My bedroom looked out on to the huge clock tower of Boris's former palace, now the Museum of the Revolution (I am not sure *which* one), that looked like the casino of Enghien-les-Bains or Divonne-les-Bains – I think the German princeling who took on the job in the first place must have been pretty pushed to be willing to reside in such a place – and of course there was the hideous nineteenth-century cathedral of St Alexander Nevsky, the gift of the Russian People to the Liberated Bulgars. There was also an equestrian statue of the Tsar Liberator, Alexander II, outside the Party building; it had a fresh wreath in the Bulgarian colours – the same as the Magyar ones, but in a different order – of green, white, and red. And there were twenty statues in various parts of the city of St Cyril and St Methodius. Nationalism really stronger than Communism.

The suppurating grey Central Committee Building, the clock lit up red at night. It was a depressing outlook. The building had long black windows and dirty yellowish blinds. I should have brought more books to read, there was no question of getting any here. I wrote a lot of letters, the hotel sold stamps.

There was a Fraternal Banquet laid on at the hotel for the visiting Cuban delegation: all the speeches and toasts in English; my little table with my back to all the long-winded jollity. My table for one marked me out as one excluded from the Fraternal community with a sad little paper Union Jack on a bit of toothpick. For once, I felt quite attached to this symbol of a disgraced national identity, as the speeches at my back went on and on in equally bad English – but a badness that *differed*. After getting grimly through my embattled and lonely meal, I ordered four or five *digestifs* of the local *alcool de roses* as a manifestation of national defiance. At the usual early-morning phone call from Maria, my palms were sweating a powerful and rather sickening distillation of roses.

Still, the next night, she took me to a dance and cellar-restaurant dive; some Cubans were dancing with Bulgarian girls, enter students in their long blue overcoats and peaked caps, a terrific fight, enter the People's Militia, they weigh in to the Cubans. Peace restored, no Cubans. I make no comment; Maria says they shouldn't have danced with Bulgarian girls. I had seen the sad little groups of Ghanaians, looking cold and lost, standing in the snow, from the Peace University.

We were in January. In March there was to be a Women's Peace do, a Conference, a Front affair, in Vienna; Maria might be accompanying the Bulgarian delegation, we worked out a simple code by which she could let me know if she were coming, a reference to a law book, *chez Sirey*, I'd buy her in Paris. 'Will you pay me back in March?', that would mean Vienna. And of course she would go on writing regularly, as before my trip. Klub Russki and the Klub Cechoslovenski, the Ulica Luben Karavelov, the green trams, the sad, empty, dusty shop-windows – some of them just displaying a faded piece of red serge, discoloured with damp, on which was placed a cheap terracotta bust of a man with his eyes shut, it was about the only article that seemed to be in abundance, Dimitrov at a cut rate; at least it did help to fill the dreary shop-fronts. He had a *tomb* too, opposite the statue of the Tsar Liberator.

There was a seven-hour bus journey in an ancient Berliet, 1933 or so vintage, *packed* with Bulgar peasants, male and female, *and* in the regional costume – but not assertive, like my first encounter with the Tyrolese. Goatskin coats, white leggings tied together with criss-cross black thongs, the very powerful smell of unwashed bodies and goat cheeses and spirits. I did not feel that they were dressed up; they were wearing clothes that they had made themselves from goat and sheep. The men sang in a rather mournful choir, an endless song about a girl called Maria who had eyes like cherries. They were cheerful, a huge glass container, covered in wicker, kept on being passed around, a very powerful alcohol, *slivova*; 'the gentleman' (me) had to drink some (every foreigner was 'a French gentleman'), they clapped their hands as I raised the thing higher and higher. We went through tatty villages with scraggy camels in the main square, dilapidated mosques and dis-integrating Party slogans, black letters on rotting red. I enjoyed the journey, and the good spirits; there was an old lady with two geese in a bag, they got out. I came to the conclusion that I rather *liked* the Bulgars – though they really did smell very very strong; I suppose it would have been like that in medieval England. But, with every gulp of *slivova*, I became more indifferent to the smell from feet wrapped up in white sacking held together by the criss-cross thongs, a bit like ancient Greeks on the side of vases in the British Museum. They were not being consciously rustic, they were merely clothed in the skin of beasts. Later, in a cellar-bar-restaurant, Boulevard Russki, a very large, very drunk man came and sat oppo-site us, saying something to me, Maria explained that I was a 'French gentleman', the man seized my hand in his own huge grip. *Slivova* again. And, at Monastir, a man in his forties, covered in sheepskin, dead drunk outside a painted wooden monastery, zigzagging in the snow and singing a long-drawn-out mournful dirge, New Year's Day, 1962. He kept on falling into the snow, clasp-ing a dark-brown glass bottle which he managed to hold upright. No sign of folklore. But, the night before in the Balkantourist wooden hotel-restaurant, the New Year's Eve dinner, we sat at a table for four; all round us, fat men in rumpled blue or black suits, little red metal badges in their lapels, their amazingly vulgar wives, too much make-up, furs, clanking jewellery, noisy, spoilt children trying out their presents. In the courtyard, a score of black Mercedes with Sofia number-plates (recognizable above all from the 'Φ' in the middle). The New Class, very much in evidence in all its arrogance, high-ranking Party officials. Their chauffeurs were having *their* dinner in the kitchen. Queues. Queues, even to get bus tickets, people running beside the bus as it moves off, with imploring gestures with their hands, like some Ancient Greek choir. At the reception desk in the Hotel Bulgaria (a relic from better times, much of it pre-1914), the dark girls with big eyes, to whom one handed in the enormous keys, holding their arms up as if to protect their faces, to stem the flow of German fury, enraged East German business men going on and on about the lift not working, and when the storm had abated, the girls as it were appealing to *me* with their liquid Turkish eyes, saying, by way of explanation – no explanation was needed – 'Nemsow' (pronounced 'Niemsoov'). At least they did not take me for a German, I was a Gaul.

I'll try and get this into some sort of coherent narrative, right up to the time, lateish, after supper, that Maria accompanied me to the station; she got up into my empty SNCF compartment, all at once, with a violent jerk, the train started up, she had just time to jump down from the high step, shedding a shoe which I had to throw down to her. No whistle just the sudden lurch.

She did not seem as upset as I was at our last meal at the hotel. We had gone into it all again and again. We agreed we must play it by the book, do everything on the level, through the Embassy. We discussed possibilities of marriage at most of our meals together. Of course, it may have been fantasy, a form of escapism, though the sheer difficulty of the whole enterprise appealed to me; silly, really, but it seemed to be a bond between, not just there and then, but a bid on the future, the guarantee that we would be meeting again somewhere. Of course, it is just possible that she may have been stringing me along from the start; she had taken the initiative with the letters to me in Leeds. But what would have been the point? I was not important: just a lecturer in a big civic university. She was very cool and collected over supper, but, when I threw the shoe down to her, as the train gathered speed, I am pretty sure I saw big tears coming down her very white cheeks. Then, once back in Leeds, the line went dead. *Nothing*, for weeks. I became frantic, time and again I was tempted to ring her number, my friend Sandy said, 'No, *wait*, be patient.' Then, in late February, there was that very brief, quite impersonal postcard; she had had the Law book I had bought in Paris, and would pay me back in schilling in March. Ah yes, I have it now, the code word was not 'March' but '*schilling*'. (I was going to need a lot of those!)

Now I would go ahead with planning. What were the dates of the Conference? I wrote to a friend in the Parti Communiste; he provided them. I asked him how I could find out where the Bulgarian women would be staying; he said write to Georg Eisler, I did. Got, almost by return, a postcard neatly typed. Two hotels in Taborstrasse, Hotel Tabor and another one, ordinary two-star hotels, just beyond the Canal. Where should I stay? Goldenes Lamm, an old-fashioned posting-house. When I got to Vienna, I asked Georg about the two hotels: did they have any connection with the Security people? No, he did not think so, they were frequented by commercial travellers. I decided to get to Vienna two days before the Conference opened, to scout out the terrain, have a look at the two hotels, fix up daily and hourly locations, a café, a restaurant, establish a regular timetable; I enjoyed doing all this, there was the feeling of anticipation. I tipped the head porter of both hotels; would they deliver, in person, to Fräulein Peneva the two messages I had prepared and was leaving? Would they do it discreetly? Not put it in a pigeon-hole with the key to her room. I tipped them well. They were knowing men, they *winked*, they would look after it all for me. Luckily, they both spoke French of a sort.

In my notes, I gave Maria the name, address, and phone number of my hotel. From 10 a.m. to 12 each day, from 3 p.m. to 6, I would be at the Café Museum; I would have lunch each day Restaurant Lügeck, Lügeckstrasse, would have dinner there at 8 each evening. That would be my timetable, I would stick to it rigorously.

The Goldenes Lamm had been a good choice, it was an old-fashioned hotel with very long corridors, my room was at the end of one of them; it was fairly central, but still retained a provincial calm about it. There did not seem to be many obvious tourists, rather people carrying nondescript document cases in simili-leather. But I should have given more time to my daily locations: they were not elastic enough – on the other hand, I had been in a hurry, I had to be able to offer a fixed programme throughout the day before the Conference had opened. (I gathered from Frau Eisler that it would take place in some large and ugly stadium, decorated, I suppose with all the flags of the sororial participant States; anyhow, it was an area to be avoided.) I had chosen the Café Museum because it was reasonably central and easy to identify. As it turned out, the choice had been a mistake. I had imagined that Maria would have been eager to snatch any little break in the dreary routine of a Conference to rush off and meet me at one of the locations I had assigned, so I sat facing outwards, with my eyes on the main door, a revolving one that opened on to the apex of a wide boulevard and a side-street. The café was very long, and was divided into booths with partitions half-way up. From my booth, I had a clear view of a line of mostly pink bald heads, all of them, like my own, facing outwards. The door was revolving continuously, from the moment I took up my position in the booth half-way down on the right, which gave the best view of the fork of the two approach roads. By 10.30, all the other booths were occupied, and opposite each bald head was an abundant female one, in varied hair-styles and varied sheens and colours. On my very first morning, it became clear to me that the Café Museum, far from having any staid academic distinctions, was a pick-up place at which elderly men – elderly then to me, I was in my mid-forties – encountered younger and obliging ladies. I noticed that there was a steady, constant turnover of heads, as spied just below the top level of each booth: a renewal that took place approximately every twenty minutes. This was not a place to linger, yet this was just what I was doing. I felt I must be very conspicuous and that the waiters (were they still 'Herr Ober'?) must have been amused at my being literally the odd man out, all alone in my desolate booth. All the baldpates had had their eyes, like mine, fixed on the revolving doors, but none had long to wait: the expected redhead, raven locks,

blonde were soon through the door and making fast for a given
booth. What made the Museum even more distracting was the fact
that the walls were lined with mirrors, and these doubled, trebled,
quadrupled the lines of baldheads, seen from a variety of angles,
while, at the same time, I could catch glimpses of my own, raised,
rather birdlike profile – a heron, a sea-bird – in neat ranks of ten,
fifteen, caught between the two facing mirrors. Every time I lifted
my head from my glass, the other ten would do the same. The
mirrors seemed to multiply my visible oddity, my isolation, as if to
emphasize that I had no right to be in there all on my own, that I
was breaking the rules. All the heads were uncovered, which made
it worse, accentuating the intimacy, as well as the formality, of this
well-lit Hall of Mirrors. Normally I would have enjoyed being on
my own in some such public place, observing and listening, but here
I could not listen, and all I could observe was the constantly revolving door, the obstinately hopeless door. I felt like getting up and
taking a short walk; but I could not risk it, suppose she turned up
and looked in vain for me? So I stuck to my fenced-in observatory.
. . . After two hours at this game, I got cramp in the neck; I was also
beginning to get a bit drunk, having switched from lager to red
wine. Still, I had to remain vigilant, Maria might turn up at any
minute, I imagined that even in these solemn Conferences there
must be a few breaks, and I did not like to settle down to read *Le
Monde*, on its hook, in case I missed the door at the crucial
moment. After the first session, it was a relief to make for the
Lügeck, at least it was a walk and a change of scene. The afternoon
and early-evening sessions in the Café Museum were even worse,
though I slept through some of them. The sociability became both
accelerated and more animated: still a hard core of baldheads, but
now some young couples, too, the booths filling and emptying at
increasing speed; tea, coffee, then aperitifs. I started my vigil on a
Monday, by Thursday I was deeply depressed and feeling hopeless.
Something terrible must have happened. The waiters started to look
at me as if there was something peculiar about me, as indeed there
was: I was alone. Perhaps even worse, on the Tuesday afternoon, an
attractive girl, dark with very blue eyes, asked if she could sit down
in my booth, well, I could not allow that, had to explain that I was

waiting for someone (had been for a day and a half), she did not insist, but soon found a seat in a nearby booth. I saw her leave, accompanied and talking volubly, fifteen minutes later. I lasted out Wednesday. Wednesday evening, I went to see the Eislers; Frau Eisler took pity on me. She was someone who had at one time been very high up in the Austrian Communist Party, I think she had lodged Josip Broz (Tito) when he had been on the run. I told her about my relentless vigil. She volunteered to look in on the Conference, saying she was sure that she would be able to spot Maria – there would be a table, covered in green or red baize, marked 'BULGARIAN' – she would go on from there, deliver her a verbal message. She assured me that this would not get the girl in trouble; on the contrary, she, Frau Eisler, was something of a heroic figure in the Communist international community. In fact, the next day, she did call in at the stadium and went over to the table during a pause in the debates.

The Restaurant Lügeck likewise turned out to have been a mistake, though for different reasons. It specialized in Magyar cooking; on the menu there were twenty-six varieties of goulash. I tried, on my twice-daily visits, to vary the topography – Debrecen goulash, Esztergom goulash, eating steadily around the country, a hard-going gastronomic *Tour de la Hongrie* – all the goulashes were heavy, strongly spiced, and seemed to be made up of much the same ingredients. To make matters worse, my progress through the heavy-going cuisine was often accompanied by gypsy orchestras. The restaurant was popular, at lunch-time it was very crowded; but in the evening, apart from myself, there would only be one or two couples and a few men on their own, reading newspapers with titles ending in '-hirlap'. Of course, I should have set up a more varied itinerary: two or three cafés, a choice of five or six restaurants; but time had been pressing.

On the Friday, I think it was then, I saw Frau Eisler. Yes, she had spotted Maria, a very pretty girl, all the prettier because she was sitting at a table with a group of enormous women with melon faces. She had talked to her in German, had told her how desperate the poor Englishman was to meet her, if only for a few minutes, he had come all the way from England to do so. The girl had not been very responsive, had explained that she deeply loved her country

and did not want to leave it. Frau Eisler was, however, quite optimistic; she thought that the girl was probably frightened or nervous
and that she was afraid some of the melon-faced ladies might have
understood German.

Anyhow, on returning to my hotel from the Café Museum at 6
p.m., there was a telephone message with my key: 'Fräulein Peneva
would meet me that evening at 9.00 in the lounge of the Hotel
Tabor, Taborstrasse.'

So, for once, patience and prudence had paid off and the longed-
for word had come at last. It had been worth all that waiting, I had
been right after all not to have phoned Maria from Leeds, not to
have bombarded her with anxious letters and endless question
marks over those agonizing two and a half months. Worth all those
hours stuck in the Café Museum watching the door, or watching the
rows of bald pates, multiplied to battalion strength, and moving
with a single *élan*, perfectly drilled, in the long gilt-edged mirrors.
Worth the ten or a dozen goulashes of various provenance I had
ploughed through, to the sound of gypsy fiddles, in the Restaurant
Lügeck. Worth enlisting the kindly help of Frau Eisler. Now everything would be made clear, and, above all, I would have an answer.
The period of endless questioning would be over.

I got myself to the Hotel Tabor at about 8.30, so as to give myself
plenty of time. I took a seat on an ugly sofa in light beige simili-
leather, near the foot of the wrought-iron staircase leading up to the
bedrooms. To pass the time, I ordered a lager from the bar at the far
end of the lounge, and spread out the latest number of *Le Monde*.
After about five minutes, I heard some steps coming down the staircase. Looking up, I saw Maria and a voluminous melon-faced
woman; they were both holding cardboard boxes full of cards.
They came right past me without giving me a glance and disappeared through the main entrance on to the Taborstrasse, returning a few minutes later empty-handed and heading straight for the
stairs. A little later, two youngish men, one of them wearing a
belted mackintosh – I at once attached some hidden significance to
the belt – came in from the street and went up to the receptionist.
Belted-mac (who was evidently the senior man, his companion was
wearing a nondescript brown overcoat) could be heard quite dis-

tinctly from where I was sitting asking for 'Fräulein Peneva' in a
questioning way, in what, from that distance, sounded like fluent
German. I felt myself going into a cold sweat, I was all at once quite
terrified, my hand was trembling, and some of my lager spilled on
to the low glass-topped table by my seat. I should have known: this
was Graham Greene territory, or Amblerland, or a bit of both. The
two young men did not *look* like Bulgarians, but of course, it stood
to reason, they wouldn't – that would have been too obvious. But it
was clear that they knew all about Fräulein Peneva. Furthermore,
they did not so much as glance in my direction, sitting at the far end
and whispering to one another. I wondered for whom they were
working, thinking grimly that I would soon find out. I was tempted
to get up and check, as casually as possible, whether there was a
back entrance to the hotel. But I resisted the temptation. 9.00, then
9.15. The two young men seemed unhurried and I found this sinister. At 9.20, Maria came briskly down the staircase, alone. She went
straight across to the two young men, who stood up and shook
hands with her. Then she came across to me, the two accompanying her. She said in French that I would surely remember them, Alois
and Erich, they had been on the course at the Institute in her year,
they were both students at the University of Vienna, Erich was
doing French, Alois was studying for diplomacy. And, indeed, with
the benefit of Maria's introduction, I did recognize them, though
my face cannot have been very welcoming. So this is what she had
thought out so as to avoid having to meet me alone! I was filled with
rage. Maria went on to say that she could only spare an hour, she
had to be back at the hotel at 10.30, the Conference was over, and
the Bulgarian delegation was returning to Sofia early the next
morning, there was packing to be done. Why did we not the four of
us go somewhere near by to have a drink and a talk? The two
Austrian students eagerly agreed. They were very polite to me,
asking if I had been enjoying myself in Vienna. I was so consumed
with impotent rage that I did not even attempt to reply. They must
have thought me very rude.

We went just round the corner to a small bar that faced on to the
quay of the Canal. The place was empty. Erich insisted that it was
his round, we were in his country. What would we have to drink?

Maria said she would like a Coke, I asked for a *carafon* of red wine, the students ordered lager. I was sitting next to Alois and managed to explain to him why I had come to Vienna. He was most apologetic; if only he had known, Erich and he would not have thought of coming, but, he went on, Maria had been most insistent. It looked as if she had planned the whole thing. I tried to contain my rage and ordered another round of drinks, including a large *carafon* for myself. Whatever happened, I was going to get drunk. We accompanied Maria back to the Tabor and took our leave. I tried to persuade Erich and Alois to spend a bit more time with me, the evening was still quite young, but they insisted that they had to get home early, they both had exams the next morning. I crossed the bridge to the *Innerer Stadt*. Whatever the evening still had in reserve for me, I was going to find a girl. There were bound to be plenty in the neighbourhood of the Cathedral; I knew from my experience of French provincial towns that that was always the most promising area to look for them, at least in a Catholic country. I would try and get one for the night, or, maybe, I would start with one and then move on to several more, making a real night of it. By this time, I was not feeling in the least bit sad; as far as I was concerned, Maria was finished, that was an end to it, I was outraged. I was much too angry to have reflected that, from her point of view, it might have been dangerous for her to have been observed alone, even for an hour, with 'the foreign Professor' (as the Sofia Security people had described me), and of course the Tabor would have been closely watched. But there would have been security in numbers. I was far too furious to attempt at that stage to put myself in her position.

There was a maze of narrow streets in the neighbourhood of Stefanskirche, each of them dotted with bars with neon lights. I went into the first one, it was full of youngish men, there was not a girl in sight. One of them came up to my table, I ordered a bottle of white wine; in the end I was paying the rounds for half a dozen people. I moved on to three more all-night bars, still not a girl in sight; it looked as if I had chanced upon a quarter monopolized by gays. By about 3 in the morning I was past caring, denouncing Maria and women generally; my companions – they may have been the same ones moving with me from bar to bar, or I may have picked up different sets at each new place; anyhow, I was speaking some sort of rudimentary German in which 'die Frauen' were being given a pretty rough verbal knock-about – seemed to find me very amusing, there was a great deal of laughing and of clinking of glasses, the waiter in each successive place hastening to fill them. I think there must have been six or seven stops in all. We were never very far from the Cathedral – it kept on looming up, different bits of it, as we turned from one narrow street into another. Not a girl in sight anywhere, either in the street, or indoors. Perhaps Vienna was the exception to the rule; perhaps the Cathedral quarter was *not* the place to look for girls. A bit after dawn I started to feel tired and walked home, quite steadily, all the way to the Goldenes Lamm.

I woke up about 3 in the afternoon, stretching out my hand to feel in the pocket of my jacket, which was hanging over the back of a chair. Just as I thought: my passport and all my money had gone. I had some traveller's cheques, but could not cash them as I could not prove my identity. I got dressed and went round to the Eislers to explain my predicament. They very kindly lent me a few hundred schillings to tide me over. At the Consulate I was told briskly that passports never got lost in Vienna, that mine had no doubt been retained in some night-spot because I had not paid a round. All I had to do was to retrace my steps over my itinerary of the night before, and, sooner or later, a barman or a waiter would produce my passport.

For the next five days, I spent most of my time going round and round the Cathedral Quarter. I visited scores of bars; all of them were full of attractive-looking and visibly available girls. I took time off to eat, avoiding the Lügeck, and discovering the pleasure of those trays of cold meat known as *Wienertafelspitz*. Early on the fifth day, I was having a coffee in an espresso bar that I had passed several times during my previous days' search (I had mentally eliminated coffee bars, having convinced myself that I had been drinking wine throughout the night of disaster). The waiter came over to me with a welcoming smile, as if he had been expecting my visit. Was I looking for something? Could it be my passport? Yes, he had it. He would give it to me, he had been holding it for me, I owed him

350 schilling on rounds of brandy that I had not been able to pay for. I paid up, cashed some traveller's cheques, paid the Eislers, thanking them for their kindness throughout my stay. The next morning I checked out of the Goldenes Lamm, went to the Westbahnhof, and bought a ticket to Lausanne. I had lunch in the restaurant car; it was not very good, a bit greasy, with dumplings, the menu was covered in stains, but two half-bottles of an Austrian red wine put me into a more cheerful frame of mind as the train headed west. I changed trains at Zurich, and, on my arrival in Lausanne, looked up my friend Sylvain Goujon, who had a flat not far from the Lake, on the road to Geneva. He was much entertained by the account of my misadventures, and it did me good to have someone to tell about them. A Lausannoise, he said, would put all that right: for Sylvain, a Lausannoise offered the cure to pretty well every imaginable hurt. He certainly practised his own line of medicine. That evening we went to Chez Godiot, at the steep top end of the town, and drank a lot of Dole. What a relief to hear French again, even the up-and-down, 'ouin-ouin' French of the Canton de Vaud! The accent was at least friendly and familiar. It was like going home.

The next morning, sitting in Sylvain's chaotic flat, after Sylvain had gone off to teach, I wrote Maria a long and reproachful letter, rather than angry. I knew it would not do any good, but I wanted to get the whole thing out of my system, and I felt I could not do that till I had the last word. I reminded myself that Maria had rather bad teeth, two of which had gold fillings, and that, while staying in the hotel at Monastir for the New Year, I had noticed that her breath had not been too good either. Later, I had taken her to see Helene's sister, the doctor, who lived in a crowded little wooden house down a cul-de-sac that led off one of the dreary empty boulevards of Sofia, the far side of a scraggy, snow-bound park. She had not enjoyed the visit, and, on the way back to the hotel, she had complained, accusingly, I thought, that the doctor, a White Russian, had talked down to her, as if she had been a peasant, in the way that many Russians (both Red and White) did to Bulgars. She had not liked the doctor's Bulgarian husband, an engineer; she did not think he was a proper Bulgar, he had an accent, she thought he was half-

Greek. The flat had been untidy, and she had noticed that the three children had spoken Russian in preference to Bulgarian. I had been too infatuated to pay much attention to her complaints at the time, thinking only that it had been a pity that she had not hit it off with a family that had seemed to me, on my two visits, so warmly welcoming. But now I began to wonder whether Maria was perhaps a bit provincial and rather humourless. I also recalled what she had said to Frau Eisler about not wanting to leave her country. The cure was beginning to work. Still, I could not help going on speculating as to what, if anything, had happened to her between the January of that year and our brief meeting in March. Had pressure been put on her? Or had she merely thought better of it? I am prepared to accept almost anything provided I have a clear answer. Well, I was not going to get one. And, after all, I did not know her at all well. It was easy to see now, in the cheerful light off the Lake, and in the city of the delightfully local *La Feuille d'Avis de Lausanne*, that the whole thing had been a most terrible mistake. No more Balkantourist for me. I did not think I would ever return to Sofia, though, whether I liked it or not, I would remain a Friend of Bulgaria for the rest of my life. Nothing would induce me to return to Vienna, not even to see Franz-Ferdinand's bloodstained sky-blue tunic and Sophie Chotek's bloodstained silk dress and her hat with the feathers of a white bird, and the open car that had taken the wrong turn at the bridge over the narrow river.

10

Rouen and Dieppe

Twice Rouen (mostly Rive Droite) had given me the taste of freedom and being on my own, in the spring of 1935 and again in that of 1952 or thereabouts. Both were pretty wet, though in 1935 there had been enough dry days for me to use my W & N sketching pad.

By 1977, the *voie piétonne* had killed off both those streets – the long one north to south, the very short one leading off it east to west – as means of getting from one place to another, in a vehicle. La Moulière had survived, but not as a cheap *restaurant d'habitués*, most of them alone, with *Paris-Normandie* propped up against the reglementary brown *pichets de cidre*, in a *quart* or a *demi*. *Cidre*, even *bouché*, had gone, to be replaced by a long, white, wine list enclosed in a mica protective folder. The menu in blue and red hand-writing, reproduced by some simple process, had been abandoned in favour of a long printed, menacing affair, with a picture of La Moulière on top. But the picture did not make up for the easy familiarity of the service of the red, blue, and mauve menus of cyclostyled days. Now you sat where you were told, and to be alone and wanting a table for a single (rather apprehensive – once placed, there would be no escape; too late to flee) customer were not what was wanted; family parties of six or eight might cause the bullying waiters even to smile and to deal out the long menus like a power-ful pack of cards, while a wine waiter hovered above a responsible-looking, self-assured occupant of the middle chair.

The chairs had also been changed; no longer the rather rickety wooden round-backs, with their slippery perforated yellow wooden seats, but padded chairs with rather threatening arm-rests. The paper table-cloths, so easily whipped away and replaced in a single swish, had given way to real cloths in red-and-white checks, to match the fanlike napkins. All the warning signals were on display. The fish was still very good: best to forgo the opening item, but the waiter would frown and the entrée would be a very long time in coming, necessitating a second *demi-bouteille* of Côtes. At the end of it all, a coffee without a large very dark calvados (3 Palmiers) would cause the waiters to smirk knowingly. *Not* the sort of customer one wants in a neo-La Moulière: it would have to be just one evening in the week. One would have to fall back on *chinois* or *vietnamien*; they too had prospered, Rue Beauvoisine. And they were generally quiet, without intruding mummers and guitarists. 1977: *l'ère pompidoulienne*, a very bad time for the solitary evening eater, with *Ouest-France* to read (in Chinese or Indo-Chinese semi-darkness).

Still, La Moulière had survived, and the Rue de Fontenelle and the Rue de Crosne still had uneven paving stones, were open to traffic and the gutters running merrily. And there *were* cheap *lunch-time* restaurants near the market, Rue Paul-Louis Courier: the market people, the police from a *commissariat*, and even some middle-aged female owners of clothes shops (not '*boutiques*') ate there off paper table-cloths. Lunch *had* survived for the *habitués*; it was a matter of *looking*: Martainville, La Rougemare, or even beyond the Boulevard des Belges, near the *abattoirs* – large men with large appetites, not Gévéor, but a litre of *vin du patron* (always good) and very abundant helpings.

So a prospect not wholly bleak, indeed, a sort of adventure in patient research: markets, slaughter-houses, *commissariats* (to be recommended), *mairies*, *dispensaires*, laboratories, and *not* anywhere near the Cathedral or the Grosse Horloge. And there was always Rouen-RD itself, with its two classes of buffet, both well-lit and even offering *petit salé*, *choucroute*, or *saucisse*. One could linger and watch the passengers through the Exit and try to guess where they had come from, particularly those from the red Michelines: Amiens perhaps? Or Barentin? Undistinguished luggage, a lot of baskets, children in tow.

In 1977, I had taken the non-stop St Lazare–Rouen-RD train (*avec supplément*). The Quai d'Orsay Relations Culturelles was paying for my trip, and I had the first part in cash; notes for huge sums in hundreds, bearing the portraits of literary figures (Hugo, rightly, scored *very* low, Flaubert topped at a prestigious 1,000; I had never seen the note before and it frightened me). The marshalling yards were still as extensive as ever; trains like bullets were open at their sides, half-way along their right flank, displaying their twisted guts, as if they had just undergone some elaborate surgery and had not yet been sewn up again – and the surgeons had gone off for lunch. Gévéor, Les Vins du Postillon, and Bières du Lion were still moving gently, survivors in a Coca-Cola age. I did not have time to make out the black hut: the non-stop train was still going too fast before it entered the first tunnel – but then provided a startling second appearance of Bonsecours, the iron spire of the huge Cathedral and the Île Lacroix, the cluster of barges and the long bridge across the wide river. Then it was engulfed by the second tunnel, stopping gently, with a very slight jerk, at the steep left-side platform, the one nearest the exit, very briefly lit from above. The passengers for Le Havre were waiting, well-dressed and with cases in real leather. Maybe the hut *had* survived from my time over twenty years before.

Now the Quai had booked me in at the Hôtel de la Cathédrale; an enormous wooden double bed with two armchairs in chintz covers and a little fridge containing mini-bottles, *quarts de vin*, gin, Armagnac, a dark, rich calvados – I decided to start my three-star stay with that and my latest Boileau-Narcejac, this one set, suitably, I thought, in La Roche-Guyon.

Then I walked down to the far end of Martainville, where the white globes and the round stone obstacles ran out and the street became normal and open to traffic. The market people were beginning to pack up, stands folded and their contents – dresses, pinafores and shirts, boots, shoes, caps, berets, crates of apples, plums, pears, bottles of wine and *cidre bouché* – were being stacked into trailers, and the shouts and encouragements had died away. From the *terrasse* – it was sunny for once – I looked inside the big *café-tabac*; the waitresses were laying out the paper table-cloths on most of the tables. Now was the time to move and stake a claim to a round-backed chair with a perforated seat at a table set for two. I wanted to face outwards; the street was being cleared of cauliflower stalks and skins of plums by a man in green with a long-handled brush. Men wearing caps in tartan with pompons sprouting from their tops, women still in their flowered smocks, stood at the long *zinc* for an aperitif, the men a Ricard, the women a Banyuls, all shaking hands with the blue-smocked *patron* and smoking. An oldish man in a corduroy jacket took the seat at the little table, with his back to the street, its gutters runing.

'Vous permettez?' It was a formal question. I asked the waitress what was on: *pommes à l'huile*, a choice of *assiette froide* or *lapin chasseur aux carottes*, Camembert or Pont-L'Évêque. There was no menu, but it was an inviting choice. I went for the rabbit (despite the bones), the sauce was delicious. My *vis-à-vis* got through his meal – *assiette froide* as the main dish – in a quarter of an hour and got up to pay at the bar. He was not a talkative man. I ordered a bottle of *vin du patron*, lingered over cheese, offered myself a pale calvados with my very strong coffee, paid and went back to the *terrasse*, where I fell asleep. I was told there was a market Wednesday and Friday, so that looked after lunch for those two days. They didn't serve food the other days. Friday was always fish: sometimes *sole dieppoise*, poached. In the evening the *tabac* was almost deserted. It would have to be *chinois*, I had spotted two beyond La Rougemare. Over my first lunch I had paid with the Flaubert note, I was keen to break it up. The *patron* took it without comment, he must have been used to large denominations, especially on market days. I went off with a wad of notes depicting other literary figures.

I avoided the Hôtel de la Cathédrale as much as possible; it was just a place to sleep and to read my Boileau-Narcejac. I had my croissant etc in the *tabac*, then walked across the bridge to La Tour, heavily guarded by CRS, on the Left Bank. The Archives Départementales had been moved there, and the friendly Rue de Crosne had been taken over by a tax office. La Tour was very efficient, but quite impersonal.

Rue de Crosne, I had made two close friends, both Rouennais (I loved that sonorous open 'e', brought out to its full value by the two 'n's that followed it, giving the name an expression of asserted pride, though those who responded to it were no boasters, but rather taciturn). There was the *sous-archiviste*, slightly dotty, the Giver of the Keys. His brother had been keen on Pétain. My friend's wife had a children's clothes shop, Le Petit Bateau, opposite the redheads' restaurant – which had, by 1977, been turned into a bar: Le Trou, or something like that. My other Rouennais friend, André Dubuc, was a retired schoolmaster, an *érudit local*, wearing the mauve ribbon of *les palmes*, who contributed numerous *glanes*, with commentary, to *Annales de Normandie*. He never missed the annual October meeting of the Normandy *sociétés savantes*, which, throughout the 1960s, I also liked to attend, always managing to stay somewhere in Rouen, either in a hotel the far side of the station, near my little *blanchisserie* (and starcher) or in what appeared to be a private house, in a quiet street beyond the Boulevard des Belges, where, sleeping beneath a palm cross, I would be woken up at 8 a.m. by the noise coming from a children's playground that my room faced on to and that added to the illusion that I was sleeping in the big bed of what had been a married couple. I think that, along with the palm cross, there was a dried *couronne de mariée*. There was a framed picture of St Christopher carrying a child across a tiny stream – not at all like the broad frontier between RD and RG. In the morning, I left my heavy bedroom key at: 'Sonnez pour l'office svp.' There was a bell, but there was never anyone at the hatch. I hung up the key on its numbered hook; there were four other keys in place. I let myself out of the heavy door and went into the quiet street. There were three nuns on mopeds, their skirts rolled up to reveal long white woollen stockings, the avant-garde perhaps of a more extensive ecclesiastical presence further up in one of the big grey buildings to the west. The nuns were going fast, as if trying to race each other. Each had ten or so baguettes protruding from their two black saddle-bags; but the nuns were in brown with white-edged head-dresses. Although it was early – 8.30 or so, on a weekday there was a Sunday feeling about the long cobbled avenue, with a *boulangerie-pâtisserie-confiserie* at an intersection half-way down. Women in black dresses and thick black stockings, and coloured slippers with pink pompons, hurried along westwards, baguettes and *ficelles* sprouting from the voracious mouths of their shiny, waterproof black *cabas*. There was a green dust-cart in the distance, its hygienic brightness accentuating the universal greyness. A tall, nonchalant Sénégalais, loose-limbed and ebony black, zipped up in green – to match his cart – was sweeping out the gutter with a long-handled broom. Unlike the nuns, he was not in a hurry, taking his time and pushing the water ahead, almost caressingly. He was puffing at a cigarette in crackly yellow paper and seemed quite alone. A yellow postal van – a brighter yellow than the browning cigarette – went by very fast, without stopping at a line of six post-boxes on concrete stumps; it seemed anxious to get away eastwards. Les Belges marked out some sort of unstated frontier; to their west, an anonymous diminishing grey perspective, tall houses with closed rolling-steel shutters at ground-floor level, and that gave nothing away save a hint of desolation and a more positive mistrust, a discreet and unwelcoming stillness, closed, steel-covered front doors surmounted by Second Empire Gothic fantasies: corbels designed to catch the rain, and to proclaim a seedy, suspicious piety somewhere in the dark *entrées* on the far side of the embattled entrances. Anaemic green plants, yellowing at the ends, and waxed polished floors up a few dark steps. No trolley-bus came this way, one was safe at last from *voies piétonnes*, an area *beyond*, best employed as place of sleep. I think now that the noisy children may have been those of a *patronage*. On Sunday, the long avenue would no doubt come alive: the insistent tinkle of small bells, lines of well-dressed families emerging, this time, not with baguettes, but with pastries or *tartes* done up in little cardboard boxes held with gold string, after a service in a Gothic church. For that matter, the street – nameless, as far as I was concerned – was sad enough to have accommodated an undecorated, bleak-looking *Temple*, with a glass-framed notice-board outside, and more family groups carrying little boxes tied up in gold string.

Rouen in 1977 seemed an *early* city, with most places, including couscous restaurants and wine bars closed by 11 p.m. and the chiming of the Grosse Horloge the only sound. So, beyond Saint-Ouen and at the far end of La Rougemare, I was surprised to see ahead of me, lighting up the shiny black blocks of *pavé* with a yellow light, the blazing windows of a huge corner café, neon-lit. Apparently crowded with dimly seen moving figures, in black silhouette, like animated cut-outs. I went into the brilliant yellow light, a challenge to the long night still outside, another three or four hours of inky darkness. The triangular place, like a wedge shoved into the surrounding black, was thick with cigarette and cheroot smoke, and there was a powerful sharp smell of brandy, calvados, strong coffee and stale Kronenbourg.

Behind the constantly wiped semi-circular bar there were four large men, dressed alike in long blue tunics and wearing light-brown corduroy caps. It looked as if they formed a team, they moved together with unhurried ease. All four had drooping sandy moustaches and very pale-blue eyes. They pulled the pumps of Bières du Lion with the casual skill of seasoned drivers. Two had anchor tattoos on their long, hairless arms.

Men stood four deep at the counter, some breaking hard-boiled eggs on its edge and salting them generously. Most likewise wore caps. Trays, and fresh croissants in their wicker baskets, from a neighbouring bakery that lit up a moon-shaped bit of wet *pavé*, were being handed along. Many of the standing men and seated women were waiting for the *chasse-marée*, the refrigerator lorries from Dieppe, due in the early hours between 2.30 and 4. Most of the women wore long plastic overalls in blue-and-white stripes. But there was also a sprinkling of merchant seamen and *mariniers* from the long petrol-container barges, the latter due to head upstream at first light. The ships, docked below Maromme, would have to wait for the tugs to take them out midstream – there was a dangerous current at the level of the two Quevillys. Outside, one could hear the wooden shelves being put up ready for the array of silver fish, pale-pink *crustacés*, pale oysters, and black *moules* that would come a few hours later.

I sat at a table occupied by three Finnish seamen, in peaked caps bearing in front identical flags and capital letters (SKR); they had brought up a full cargo of wood pulp and were waiting to take on a load of vintage wines (*not* Gévéor, nor Postillon) and spirits. They had already been drinking a generous selection from their future cargo, putting down *fines à l'eau* with a rather sullen persistence, indicated by gesture, as the waitress, her hair running into her eyes with sweat, as fast as she could, brought them fresh glasses. They had laid out thick wads of notes – some of them green US dollars – on the watery plastic table, causing them to stick to the damp surface. The waitress disengaged them one by one, slowly working downwards. None of the three could speak a word of French, and they did not have much to say in *English*, nor, for that matter, to each other. They were not there for conversation. The wad looked as if it would last them out to first light.

There was also a small group of women in identical long aprons in blue-and-white stripes that looked, in their exact repetition in triplicate, a bit like a uniform, which indeed it was. The shared purpose of *their* waiting presence was further emphasized by their drinks: three large pale-brown *bols* of *café au lait*, with small brimming glasses of calvados to the right of the insipid-looking liquid, in the role of collective supporters, not assertive, but present all the same, ready on the touch-line. All three must have been right-handed, judging from the thrice shared position of the glasses, reflecting, in the crude neon lighting, an almost golden yellow. The supporters could wait too. One of the three was studying a big black notebook, like a large schoolgirl doing her sums, occasionally putting her Biro into her mouth, then sucking it reflectively, taking it out, adding a figure, and closing the notebook with a snap that could be heard at the curved bar. Their common appearance and the triply shared identity of their drinks – even drunk down, so far as I could see, to exactly the same level – left no doubt that the three of them were waiting for the Dieppe lorries. If the *chasse-marée* arrived early, the market would open early. The stands were already set up, the fish market was just beyond the blazing lights of the triangular café. All three women had powerful arms, with their sleeves already rolled up, and their thick legs harnessed in shining black rubber. The three sat in a row on the red banquette at the far end of the smoky café. The banquette had large rents from which unhealthy-looking wisps of whiteish stuffing protruded. The three women, now engaged in animated conversation, and shaking with vigorous laughter, their notebooks stuffed away in the immense pouches of their striped tunics, seemed unaware of the dubious stuffing. Perhaps, being all three well-covered behind, they did not even notice it. They had an authoritative way of sitting down, and it was clear that the red (or *reddish* – it had dark stains) banquette was their well-established waiting location. There was still an unclaimed area of banquette to the right of no 3: perhaps one of the small squad had taken the night off. I did notice, from my own distant, standing position at the bar, that the sweating waitress did not take any orders from the red-faced trio, simply putting down the three steaming bowls and the first lot of the brimming right-handed golden sentinels.

It was a place for *waiting*. But some of the older men standing at the bar, three or four deep, were merely lonely and eager to talk, so as to see out the night. One, in a shiny, stained blue suit, had a red rosette in his lapel. He had a well-brushed head of white hair and had begun offering people rounds. I chose a *ballon* of alleged Côtes, but I think it was a Postillon or Nicolas product. At dawn, he would go to bed somewhere. The bed would be uninviting, certainly unmade, and the sheets greying. He told me he came every night, generally after 11, 'when things warmed up'. He knew the four blue-smocked men behind the bar, shaking the hand of each in turn. They referred to him familiarly, but with a nuance of affection, as 'le père François'; so he *did* run to the luxury of a Christian name. I don't know what he did on Sunday nights, when the big café was closed. But he could see out the night the rest of the week. Sunday, like Christmas Eve or the *réveillon*, was always a difficult, bleak time for the lonely. In Paris, I would make for a vast, deep establishment, with marble-topped tables and, in an inner recess, a desolate, unheated billiard-room, the green baize lining torn its full length and hanging in sad strands, at Strasbourg-Saint Denis. Two years in succession, I had met there, standing at the crowded bar (among the hurried prostitutes taking a brief break, some of them in tears), and drinking Ricard, an oldish man wearing a green tie and the ribbon, in green-and-red diagonals, of the Croix de Guerre. He always stayed till 7 or 8, I was told by one of the waitresses as she hurriedly washed out glasses and wiped the long counter. I would take the first Métro, which, on Christmas or New Year's Day, would be almost empty when it opened a bit after 5 a.m., the sliding iron bars pushed aside and the sudden breath of hot air welcoming in the bitter cold, the wind from the north-east funnelled through the two black arches and across the wide Boulevard. Only after midday would it fill up with people dangling little boxes on gold string, accompanied by tired, whining children.

In the Rouen café I met two men in smart blue uniforms and wearing peaked caps marked SNCF in red on the front. They were to take out a very long goods train of gas canisters and oil through the two tunnels and the main platform of Rouen-RD at 3 a.m. Perhaps they had been in the black hut in my time. It seemed unlikely. They were cheerful and gobbled three hot croissants each, chased down with the almost inevitable *pousse-café*, one of them wiping his sandy moustache on the sleeve of his blue jacket. They were in a hurry, they had to walk back along the tracks to the Sotteville yards, then form up the convoy; the first passenger train was due in at 5, so the goods train would have to end up at a siding above Maromme. I had become quite familiar with the daytime and first-light logistics of a busy station that had only five platforms and that served six or seven different destinations in addition to the Paris-to-Le Havre main line. Thanks to the daily section in *Paris-Normandie* devoted to 'Mouvement du Port', I could learn the times of the arrival and departure of the ships, mostly Scandinavian or Soviet, to be taken downstream or to be docked in the post-war port, visible from the train, far below Maromme. The knowledge seemed to include *me* in the unrestrained fraternity offered by the long night; much handshaking across the constantly wiped bar, Christian names: Robert, Dédé, Jo, Charles, Bob, Alphonse, Lise, Louise, Mado, Danielle, Rose, Gaby, followed by questions that required no answers, and a general cross-café *tutoiement* and phrases exchanged the full length of the wedge-shaped room, like fast-delivered tennis-balls. Everyone seemed to know everyone else's business, and to rejoice in that shared bond.

But it would not include *me* even in my temporary night status. That might have come later, after a week or a fortnight. But I could not have formed myself (as I had once in HQ L of C) into a *permanent* night worker. My identity, either as a *rosbif* or as a

Scandinavian, had been easily spotted by the waitress when dealing with the three Finns. Could I help out as they did not seem able to speak any French? Twenty pairs of (not unfriendly) pale-blue eyes were momentarily directed at me and my blue overcoat as I shouted, across the hubbub, in what I took to be my *français de Lille* accent, that I *would*, leaving my drink at the counter and going over to their table to sort out their (ongoing) order for the rest of the night till sailing time.

But this was in 1977. I did not get the *ruban rouge* till the last day of 1984. *That* would have done the trick, admitted me, *à part entière*, in my attempted identity. All there would have recognized the brilliant red on a blue lapel, it was like a sort of passport, albeit a false one, of course. But it generally did the trick, especially in *restaurants d'habitués*, when my *ruban rouge* confronted another *ruban rouge* across the narrow frontier of the freshly laid paper table-cloth. No questions would be asked, that would have been rude; but the red ribbon would put me on my mettle. My *vis-à-vis* would score though: he had a yellow ring, a napkin, and a numbered box. He was also in a hurry.

The Rouen yellow lighthouse was a startling discovery in a city that seemed muted at any time of the *day*. The noise was deafening: shouted orders through the hatch; boisterous laughter; a sandwich or a huge plate of *moules* (once the Dieppe lorries had arrived), hot soup served after 4 a.m. In fact, unlike Paris, Rouen had managed to preserve a night heart, or maybe *more* than one. This time, in the spring of 1977, I decided to see it out till 6, cracking large prawns. I did not have a train to catch till an afternoon express to Dieppe-Maritime on the next day and it didn't seem worth going to bed for the morning.

From inside the brightly lit café, I had been able to see (and hear) the actual arrival of the eagerly awaited *chasse-marée* from Dieppe. It took the form of a whiteish and silver-grey long lorry that displayed on both its sides a blue-and-black fish, bent in a wide arc, as if struggling to break clear from an invisible line or net. It could have been a salmon, or a common plebeian cod. It was certainly not a skate – with its unprepossessing, spiky profile, and in no way emblematic. This one was just a *fish*, as proclaimed the capital letters, in a chilly marine blue, 'POISSONNERIES DIEPPOISES'; the firm was housed in a vast building in silver-grey metal at the edge of the inner harbour of that port. The lorry was driven by a man in white overalls and a white cap with a long peak, with his fellow similarly clothed in hygienic purity and chilliness. Down came the big doors at the back marked with the same lettering, but without a fish, followed by a cascade of baskets containing a variety of fish of different contours, some ugly and rather threatening, others elegant, and all that seemed to shine back, reflecting, in various colours, the powerful arc lights and the brilliant, sizzling kerosene lamps. The baskets did not conform to any uniform size or shape or colour: fish quite flat, alongside fleshy-looking monsters of the deep, finned with sharp and scaly protuberances; maybe sea bass, and even swordfish. Not a moment was lost, the Dieppois driver and the man sitting next to him, and the figures, male and female, in blue-and-white aprons and long black rubber tunics and boots, moved with the precision of a well-trained *corps de ballet*. There was a crash of released chains hitting the yellow-shining wet *pavé*, as the contents of the baskets were stacked, at last, like to like, flat to flat, assertive to assertive, sword to sword, and, thus regimented, found their allotted places on the waiting trestles, to claim their price.

The long lorry was only five minutes late: not quite a record, but good timing that must have suited everyone's book. It was all over in about ninety minutes, leaving the inside of the deep lorry sopping with ice-cold water that ran out to form yellow-shining pools running in channels between the uneven *pavé* and the empty baskets neatly stacked inside. Then the tall man with long brushes moved in to clear away the scaly debris: heads with mournful eyes (in a Simenon novel they would have been described as 'glauques', a compulsive adjective that, perhaps in an hour's time, or a little more, could equally be applied to a reluctant, murky Rouen dawn. But Simenon did not have much *time* for Rouen, other than as a terribly dull place to get away *from*; you would not go there voluntarily, but you might have to go *back* there.

The *chasse-marée* had been and gone, the clearing-up had been concluded. But some of the regular participants lingered on. The three striped figures returned to the reddish banquette to look through their black notebooks, have their *bols* replenished and their right-hand yellowish sentinels refilled by the attentive waitress. Then, without a word being spoken, they shook hands with the men at the counter and moved off, in a squadron of three, into the still inky black night. Perhaps they lived together. Maybe they had a vehicle parked somewhere a little further out. They would be back for the next market, perhaps in fuller strength; four or five occupants of the reddish-brown outer fringe, for there had been loud enquiries hurtling across the smoky room, for Lulu and for Zoë.

I decided to see it out till a bit after first light. There was no particular hurry, I had avoided the three-star Hôtel de la Cathédrale, so as not to break into the larger notes still surviving from *la caisse noire*. I had booked in for the coming night at the Hôtel Saint Nicolas in the street of that name. It had only one star. Then I walked down towards Martainville and, already pretty tired, sat down on a wicker chair at the *terrasse* of the big *café-tabac*, Rue Paul-Louis Courier, ordering a strong coffee and a small calvados. After perhaps an hour, I woke up with a start; my coffee was quite cold, but the glass of calvados was shining a brownish gold in the pale sunlight. Its sharp taste revived me and I prolonged the taste by sucking on the sugar lump that I scooped up from the bottom of the curved-lipped glass. But there was not much to watch, I was the only occupant of the *terrasse*, and the street was almost empty, save for a few women in flowered aprons carrying black shopping-bags. There was a *boulangerie* open a little further down the street. The women must have lived near by, for they were all wearing slippers, one with pink pompons, the others in check patterns. The *pavé* had been given an early morning hosing, but it was now quite dry. The big *tabac* was open, two men in corduroy caps were buying cigarettes and *loto* tickets. A postman in a smart blue uniform brought in a pile of letters in bright yellow envelopes and trade magazines tied together in elastic, pushing the packet through the little window reserved for cigarettes and cheroots, hastily shaking hands with the female *tabagiste*, and then hastening on his rounds all the way down the street; some of the shops were still shut: he pushed the packets under the closed doors or wedged them in the space between the glass front and the wooden lintel. One packet, con-

taining a thick wad of blue envelopes, he handed over to an oldish
man in a crumpled blue suit who was walking a black-and-white
dog on a lead, the dog stopping every now and then to raise its leg.
The dog was wearing a tight-fitting tartan jacket; it seemed much
smarter than its owner, who stuffed the blue packet in the pocket of
his suit and shook hands with the *facteur*. I could see the little blue
postal van parked at the first intersection. The postman must have
made a habit of doing this section of his round on foot, at least on
mornings when there was no market. I banged on the window
behind me and eventually drew the attention of the *patron*, still in
shirt-sleeves and wearing a tartan waistcoat – tartan seemed to be
taking over men's caps, women's slippers, and dogs' jackets: it
would be shopping-bags next, then the covers of school exercise-
books, then, in triumph, the intimacy of men's trousers and girls'
skirts; and it all seemed to be Royal Stuart, though I could not be
too sure. But the tartan take-over did not have it all its own way. I
ordered a Kanterbrau, which came in a long glass and had a frothy
top. While I was paying for it, a lady with her hair still in curlers
came by, hobbling unsteadily, she was wearing high-heeled black
shoes, and the heels kept catching in the declivities between the
pavé. But she managed to pursue a tottering course in the same
direction taken by the blue-suited pensioner. She was accompanied
by a white poodle held on a thin lead. The poodle, which had a pink
bow in its curly and no doubt freshly rinsed hair, was wearing a
tight little black jacket with white buttons.

Further down the road, the owner of a small haberdasher's shop
had put on the handle of the glass door, and picked up her pile of
letters and brightly coloured circulars tied in elastic. She was
shaking a mat, which gave out small clouds of dust, and was
banging away with a broom. The bangs offered a peaceful
accompaniment to the stillness of the scene. They were not impa-
tient or threatening. I could not see the *mercière*; I imagine that she
was wearing a pinafore over her severe black dress.

It was that uncertain time suggestive both of leisure and waiting:
les heures creuses, somewhere between 9 or 9.30 and 11.30, after the
early-morning torrent of 7 to 8.30 had receded, and before the
sudden, almost universal, tidal wave of midday, announced in

booming tones by the Cathedral clock, released the hordes of all conditions heading for lunch. The quiet street, almost empty, save for the odd handcart as it bumped noisily over the *pavé*, a reminder that life had not completely stopped, was like a film run slowly and in muted colours: a film that would have a gently soporific and rather agreeable effect on its rare audience, enjoying the respite offered by unexpected inactivity and absence from what should have been hours devoted to work – a holiday feeling that would make you lazily aware of small details, a cat darting across the *pavé*, a shaft of sunlight accentuating the contrasting black and white of Norman wooden eaves, a large rat disappearing down an arched culvert.

This would be Maigret time, as, fresh from the station, and having selected a wicker chair, on the empty *terrasse* of a smallish café offering a view of both the main street and an intersection, he sniffs out (*flairer*) the air, and drinks a local white wine: a pleasant combination of work and self-indulgence. The Commissaire, between sips of his *ballon* of local *Anjou blanc*, will idly question the blue-aproned *patron* (who also wears a cap) about this or that. Slowly drinking my Kanterbrau, my eyelids drooping, I have no such excuse. Just a holiday feeling while most work, a quietness soon to be shattered by the midday rush. No market, so no lunch in the café to my rear; but it soon fills up with hurried people who make do with long sandwiches: ham, *rillettes*, salami, cheese, followed by a rapid *pousse-café*.

I follow one of the tides, uphill, along the pedestrianized Rue Beauvoisine, to Rouen-RD, to book for the fast train, *avec supplément*, for Dieppe-Maritime, which gets in at 3 p.m., giving me an hour before the arrival of the *Villandry*, the SNCF boat from Newhaven, on which Margaret is travelling. I have already checked with M. Vée, the big, red-faced *patron* of the café-hôtel Au Roi de la Bière, Arcades de la Poissonnerie, in Dieppe; there is a big round sign hanging from the vaulted roof of the Arcade depicting Le Père Kantor, in black Tudor cap, putting down a frothing glass of Kanterbrau. M. Vée has told me that we can have our usual room on the second floor.

It is a huge, old-fashioned room that could qualify as a

Dictionnaire Larousse 'Chambre', or better still a Gaston Leroux old favourite: *Le Mystère de la chambre jaune*; but there is *no* mystery, no hint of violence, the *room* is not yellow but has a flowered wallpaper of pink roses and green leaves, picked out with pink borders, a motif running from ceiling to floor. It might have come straight from Oberkanth's factory in Jouy-en-Josas. There is even a key protruding that opens on to a shallow wooden shelf for socks and handkerchiefs. The door of the secret shelf does not interrupt the pink-rose pattern. The top of the window is in the form of two small arches that are above the Arcade and that filter a little light from the quayside street. There is a huge bed, covered in a quilt decorated in red roses. To the right of the bed is an enormous mirrored wardrobe that must be of Cauchois origin and that contains a score of coat-hangers and a number of large keys that seem to have lost their vocation – there is only the *one* little secret drawer. I don't think the pink roses, their green leaves, and the horizontal pink stripes of the *toile de Jouy* cover any more secrets, apart from the little shallow drawer the existence of which is indicated by the tiny, discreet key. I could poke about a bit more, banging the wall in search of a responding hollow echo indicating the existence of another, deeper recess. But I don't poke about. The roses have been in place, to my own knowledge, for at least eighteen years, seem to have guarded their singular innocence, though they are perhaps badly in need of cleaning, a careful sponging down, to restore their freshness. They give the big room a borrowed, early nineteenth-century veracity, 1805 or so, to match the house, a bit older, that rises above the vaulted stone arcades while incorporating them. When the night boat from Newhaven (Harbour) gets in, between 4 and 4.30 a.m., the whole room trembles and vibrates to the deafening sound of the ship's engines. The ship seems to be entering the room itself. It is not entirely an illusion, for its grey sides, rising high above the quayside cafés and restaurants, are only about fifty yards away from the big bed, the wardrobe, and the pink roses. When the boat has docked and has been tied up, the pulsating engines go silent. There is a brief (and deceptive) interlude of total quiet. Then comes the rumble of heavy iron wheels, producing the clanking of couplings. The noise ends with the fierce roar of the snout-nosed train: a snake with two identical heads. The driver has moved from the head facing seawards to the head facing inland. Whoosh! The serpent very slowly gathers speed, the shattering sound diminishing as it skirts the handsome white terminus of Dieppe-Ville. Dieppe-Maritime is an illusion. There is no station: just a couple of railway lines that come to an end on a stretch of *pavé*; no buffers even; the end of the line, without fuss, with nothing to show for it, other than it *is* the end of the line. A few feet beyond, the train would become derailed. The gradual silence is comforting, you turn over and resume a deep sleep, still vaguely registering the fact that the night boat has been tied up and that the train is heading for Rouen-RD and Paris-Saint-Lazare.

A flowered screen, liable to fall over, the flowers blue and red, hides the wash-stand, the lavatory, and the bidet. There are thin strips of unmatching carpet both sides of the bed and opposite the wardrobe mirror, covering the uneven red tiles of the floor that sinks slightly in the direction of the quayside street and the two arched windows. It is a welcoming room – the big key on its hook, at the bottom of the steep stairs – because you know exactly what to expect and that every familiar object will be in place.

It is about 4. The *Villandry* is in, securely tied up. A big green crane has brought up the gangway, and the sailors from the boat have secured it to an exit that opens on the second deck. The trickle of passengers turns to a struggling flood. Soon I can see Margaret, and she can see me, standing just by the first carriage of the train, on the very edge of the quay. She is wearing a stunning new outfit and is smiling. She is the only passenger to go through passport control, in a steel eyrie high above a line of metal steps. We check in at Au Roi de la Bière, she shakes hands with M. and Mme Vée. We have ahead of us the inside of a whole week: time enough to establish a routine and to discover at least a little about how the town breathes, the days of the market held in the long square leading from the lovely late-Gothic Saint-Jacques and dominated by the hatted, prancing figure of Duquesne.

The first morning, when we come down to the big café, the fish market is still in progress: the fish are laid out on wooden trays, with metal words in black on a white background pinned on to each section of the tray. It is Les Arcades de la Poissonnerie, and there is a market there every day save Sunday and Monday. There are many customers, mostly women with big black bags. Their purchases are wrapped up in newspaper, and we can see them carrying them off, as they cross the swing bridge to Le Pollet. The fish market just outside lasts from a bit before 8 to 9.30. Once it has been cleared away and the *pavé* hosed down, it is replaced by an untidy man in a long mac and wearing an old brown felt hat. He lays out three or four wooden troughs containing second-hand books, most of them in yellow covers with a black mark in the top right-hand corner. No one buys his books, but he seems to be a popular joke figure. There are many interchanges between the regulars at the tables within the café and the bookseller. He brings his troughs and books in a wheeled wooden *voiture à bras*, which he trundles off about 11 o'clock, apparently quite happy about the lack of customers.

Coffee or a beer on a big *terrasse* facing away from the quayside, then perhaps the shingle beach between the casino and the château. Margaret chats to a lady from Paris, who has brought her large tabby cat in a basket which she opens up so that the cat can look around at the gulls. On the stroke of midday, a man with a pointed nose comes from the Rue Saint-Nicolas with a bathing-dress wrapped in a towel. He talks to himself quite loudly and distinctly, in a surprised tone, as if he were two people. I can hear him. 'The water will be cold for the season. There is a lot of floating scum on the surface: seaweed mostly.' He swims powerfully for ten minutes, dries, and dresses, still talking.

We have lunch in a restaurant up a flight of stairs, on the first floor, off the narrow Rue Saint-Nicolas. The restaurant has its *habitués*, all with rings in numbered boxes, fifteen to twenty of them. They are from the *commissariat* and the Hôtel de Ville. The *patron* is a former petty officer (*quartier*) in the Free French Navy. He excuses himself for not being able to talk to us in English, but he has never learnt any. This comes as a relief. His wife does the cooking. I choose a half-bottle of *le vin du patron*, which is very good. He asks us if we have seen the glass-fronted Hôtel Windsor; that is where the English go, he states. Most of them are permanent residents. They have to start their lunch at 11.30 sharp, owing to staffing difficulties. The single waiter has to go off at a quarter past twelve. The Windsor behind its glass offers a scene belonging to the mid-1920s that has somehow become frozen in time. There are fifteen single tables and there is only one for a couple; at the singles, old ladies in pink, blue, or emerald dresses, one has a green bandeau like Suzanne Lenglen. The men wear blazers without crests and cavalry-twill trousers. One has on blancoed white tennis shoes. On each table are quarter or full bottles of Évian, Vittel, Vals, Badoit and, scoring highest, Contrexéville (*pour les reins*). The table for two has a timid, almost apologetic *quart de rouge*, dwarfed by a bottle of Vichy-Célestins three-quarters full. We tell the *patron* we have looked through the glass front on our way back from the steeply shelving beach, but had not been tempted to try and eat there. Probably there would have been no table for us, in any case. The petty officer laughs. The next day, we are a little late for lunch: there is a notice on our table near the door from the stairs: 'RÉSERVÉE'. The PO shakes our hands and smiles. He recommends what is on for that day.

In the afternoon, we cross over to Le Pollet and walk along the far quayside to the deep black caverns dug into the greyish cliffs that had housed the enormous German naval guns set on railway chassis. They are empty now, even of squatters. Then we climb up to the little chapel, post-1871, ugly but touching. There is a minutely accurate model of the *Maine*, a troop-carrier of the French Navy that went up on a mine, all hands (mostly Dieppois) lost, in 1916 or 1917. On the walls there are more than thirty memorial plaques bearing the names (in gold) and the photographs of drowned seamen and fishermen, several lost off the Cornish coast. There is also an old sepia photograph of the *Maine*, which looks like a converted destroyer. Some of the plaques have fresh flowers in the little metal baskets placed beneath them. An old woman in a flowered dress and a headscarf is watering one lot; the man in the photograph above it has a big, shaggy moustache.

Two afternoons, we walk as far as Pourville-sur-Mer, another pebbly, shelving beach, with more monuments to officers and soldiers, of Canadian regiments – here, in Pourville, French Canadians; Mont-Royal. Or we walk along the top of the cliffs, beyond the fierce-looking turreted château. The Buvette du Château beneath the black landmark is still closed, its green-stained shutters down: too early in the season, like a lot of things. But the casino and the Société des Bains de Mer are open. I don't think they ever close. Along the top of the cliffs we can walk to the next inlet; not as far as Veules-les-Roses, but I can't remember.

In the evening, a tiny restaurant, served by a girl of fourteen, the cook (her mother?) invisible beyond the hatch; there are only four tables. The restaurant is hidden away from the harbour and the Gare Maritime (*sic*) in L'Enfert, a semi-secret enclave. But at the other tables there are generally English lorry-drivers, some wearing blazers *with* crests and asking loudly for bacon and eggs, sausages and beans, and drinking bottles of Kronenbourg. Most are driving to Northern Spain. They are anxious to talk to us.

Later, a drink, or several, in a tiny bar – two tables, four chairs, a *zinc*, run by a talkative woman whose husband is also a long-distance lorry-driver and does not have any time for Yugoslavs, Bulgars, and Turks. Nor does she. She does not warm to Nord-Afs either. Are *we* invaded too?, she asks. Then she gets into a conversation with a man standing at the bar who works at the abattoirs. Before we leave she gets a phone call, the line is bad, but her husband tells her that he is on time.

I buy a beige corduroy cap at the market by Saint-Jacques. It fits beautifully and has a warm pleated lining in yellow silk. But it doesn't much help young Vée, whom I have known ever since he went to *la maternelle*, and who is now a philosophy student at Rouen university and asks us out to his flat in a modern block, Neuville-lès-Dieppe. He wants me to write a piece about horse markets for *Autrement*. I say I will, but I won't.

The next morning, we take the midday boat, after a drink at the big café that faces away from the quayside and on to the Grande Rue. We have bought some glasses and a bowl in Strasbourg china bearing a chirpy red cock on a leafy green background. The boat is heading the wrong way, the ugly chapel on the hill and the black château are getting smaller and smaller. We can still have a French meal in the Self-Service, the boat is the *Versailles*. I even know the barman, M. Lecarpentier, by name. He has very pale blue eyes and lives in the Rue d' Écosse. In two or three hours, the white Seven Sisters will be rising up, bigger and bigger. Perhaps there is no escape from J. B. Priestley *et al*. But I have tried, and Margaret has helped. I am enormously grateful to her. We have fully shared the memory of that week. I am grateful, too, to Douglas and Madeleine Johnson: he, a *normalien*, she a *Sèvrienne*, the marriage in fact of a semi-coded educational network. Douglas is the last holder of the University College London Chair of French History. He gave the Chair the lustre of expertise. Madeleine is Norman. I want them both to know the affection and admiration which 'Le Cobb' feels for the two of them. Now, as at Dieppe-Maritime, it is the End of the Line. But this one does at least have *buffers*.

Thank you, dear Margaret, for having come across and for having *shared* a fragile happiness, Arcade de la Poissonnerie. And thank you, Douglas and Madeleine, for guiding me through the last nineteen years of the Third Republic and the early years of the Fourth. Dearest Margaret, you have indeed *seen* me to the End of the Line.

11

Endpaper

I THINK I have been ill, often very ill indeed, ever since the late 1980s or so: perhaps 1988 or 1989. I had a major operation on the bowel in the summer of 1994. I was ill again at Christmas 1994. In the spring of 1995, I was, quite literally, saved from death by one of my sons, who held my hand for the whole night, first in Emergency, then once I had been transferred to a bed on Level Seven of the John Radcliffe Hospital in Oxford. He snatched me, I feel, from the Old Enemy. But I was left with an almost total loss of mobility and can still only get upstairs with the help of a double handrail and downstairs by going backwards. I get through the night thanks to very powerful pills that give me a pleasant, but deforming sense of locality: a river that *looks* like the Seine, but then turns into the Yonne, with its line of poplars, and then it is something else, but also inviting – a stretch of water that might be a lake, but then turns out to be the sea, near an estuary.

The pills – it must be their agreeable inventiveness – provide me, in these strange excursions, with always talkative companions who offer me their imaginative and sympathetic company and the prospect of an intelligent foray into some form of educational communication: a public lecture, a talk to a seminar, a discussion on some historical topic, followed by polite applause. I have a companion on a walk – and we are both walking well, I have no stick, my left foot does not drag, I am even striding, in order to meet some important commitment in which my mother (never actually seen) is involved: a train from Waterloo, not Charing Cross, then

Tunbridge Wells Central and a stop for a drink at a pub in the High Street, but a pub that does not exist. I do not see my mother. I know somehow that I can't, she has been dead for years. But the interior of the house, when I get there – somehow I have a front-door key – seems familiar, most objects in place. Then I wake up, oddly reassured.

The End of the Line; and so it must be for myself. There is a series of cities that are awaiting my visit: St Petersburg and Moscow, Warsaw (but not Kraków), Berlin, Hamburg – but not Munich, above all *not* Munich, nor Prague, nor Budapest, nor Athens. But I *longed* for Istanbul and its three seas, and for Buenos Aires, which, I know, is a combination of Paris in the 1930s and Kensington in the 50s. I am proud because a book of mine has had a favourable review in the *Buenos Aires Herald*. I am glad to have been to Calcutta, sorry that I won't get to Tokyo, never want to go to San Francisco, found South Africa sad and a bit second-rate, wish I'd spent more time in Madrid and Salamanca and places in Central Spain. I would like to have seen a volcano, with smoke coming out of it. But, on waking up perhaps at 3 or 5 a.m., I know that I won't. I think that Chicago is beautiful, that Washington is awful, that Halifax in Nova Scotia is walkable, and that Toronto is safe. I don't ever want to go to Australia, or Tasmania. I am not a *belonger*, even in these dream, pill-induced fantasies. I am a leper, not a fit participant in the Rudé cult; there could never be a Cobb cult.

I am not a novelist and could not rise to literary invention. My characters, those who figure in my social observation, are *real*, and not just forms of self-congratulatory indulgence within the context of food or drink or the busy routine of a fish market. I could not have invented the Grand B, nor the Monsieur Jacques I have written about; those had a real existence, in their own right, as extreme cases of different eccentricities. The same would apply to my account of the movements and attitudes of Jean and Colette Meuvret, whether at the top flat, Quai de l'Horloge, or at Sunday lunch, 104 Rue Houdan. Jean was a youthful enthusiast who, late in life, acquired both the love and the reverent respect of his three or four *Japanese* research pupils – one quite famous locally, in the Pays de Bray, as 'le japonais d'Envermeu' – not an invention of my medically induced states of deceptive euphoria, but a real person, marking a real map.

I feel that the Old Enemy – the one with whom François Mitterrand has seemed to come to terms by a sort of private treaty – *trousse-galant*, or whatever alias he adopts with myself in mind, may indeed be spending a bit of time on my own case, busy though he must be with so much calling for his ministrations. Back in the 1950s, there was a melancholy *salutiste* who used to visit the Café-Tabac de l'Odéon, once the chattering actresses had gathered there: 'Jeunesse passe' (the poignancy of those two long-drawn-out 'a's in Salvation Army tones– 'pa-asse'; *la Bible, la vérité*.) It does indeed! In 1996, I am entering a crucial year, having already put a couple of years between my own *personne physique* (in French legal language) and the duration of the Russian Revolution.

I would like to leave to the trusting care of my dear Margaret, and to the combined attention of herself and Christopher Sinclair-Stevenson, the most suitable manner of dealing with my evocations of Sotteville and of Rouen and all the other places I have called to mind, and of an epilogue that endeavours to tie together a narrative drawing on a quantity of observed minutiae that I have thought significant: the End of the Line, *voie de garage*, *plate-forme arrivée*, Rouen-RD, or should it be Paris-Saint-Lazare? Up to them; but with my own grateful and affectionate *thanks*. Not quite *une voix d'outre-tombe* – nor a Proust. But the best I can do for now.

Index

Index